W9-AFC-779

WITHDRAWN

Relocating Agency

SUNY series

EXPLORATIONS

in

POSTCOLONIAL STUDIES

Emmanuel C. Eze, editor

RELOCATING

AGENCY

_____

Modernity and African Letters

OLAKUNLE GEORGE

STATE UNIVERSITY OF NEW YORK PRESS

Published by

STATE UNIVERSITY OF NEW YORK PRESS, ALBANY

© 2003 State University of New York

Portions of this book appeared earlier in the following journal articles and are used here in revised form: "Cultural Criticism in Wole Soyinka's *Death and the King's Horseman,*" *Representations* 67 (Summer 1999), 67–91, by permission of the University of California Press; "Compound of Spells: The Predicament of D. O. Fagunwa (1903–1963)," *Research in African Literatures* 28.1 (Spring 1997), 78–97, by permission of Indiana University Press.

For information, address State University of New York Press,
90 State Street, Suite 700, Albany, NY 12207

Production by Diane Ganeles
Marketing by Jennifer Giovani

Library of Congress Cataloging-in-Publication Data

George, Olakunle.
    Relocating agency : modernity and African letters / Olakunle George.
       p. cm. — (SUNY series, explorations in postcolonial studies)
    Includes bibliographical references and index.
    ISBN 0-7914-5541-6 (acid paper) — ISBN 0-7914-5542-4 (pbk. : acid-free paper)
       1. African literature (English)—History and criticism. 2. Literature and
society—Africa—History—20th century. 3. Achebe, Chinua—Criticism and interpretation.
4. Fagunwa, D. O.—Criticism and interpretation. 5. Soyinka, Wole—Criticism and
interpretation. 6. Tutuola, Amos—Criticism and interpretation. 7. Agent (Philosophy) in
literature. 8. Decolonization in literature. 9. Poststructuralism—Africa. 10.
Postcolonialism—Africa. 11. Nigeria—In literature. I. Title. II. Series.

PR9340.5 .G46 2002
820.9'896—dc21

                                                                                    2002021022

10 9 8 7 6 5 4 3 2 1

To Evelyn Ugwu
and Ayodeji Timilehin

Contents

PREFACE

One of the most influential developments in contemporary Anglo-American literary theory and cultural criticism is the attention now being given to the issue of Europe's colonial past and its consequent imbrication, materially and epistemologically, with the "third world." An index to this development is the way in which the idea of modernity now occupies center stage in cultural criticism. The focus on modernity has led to fruitful debates that have significant implications for our understanding of cultural processes as well as literary structures. The issues devolve ultimately on the question of the human capacity to know (or transform) itself as well as its environment and productive abilities. On the one hand, theories associated with poststructuralism and postmodernism argue for an abandonment of the presuppositions taken to be the conceptual backcloth of the West's imperial past. These presuppositions include the following: the idea that human consciousness can master both its own internal mechanisms and the material, external world (that is, the idea of a centered subject); or, the notion that social history takes the form of a teleological evolution from nature to culture, from barbarism to civilization. Against these presuppositions, poststructuralist thinkers offer a wide-ranging critique of the notion of a centered subject as well as a teleological understanding of Enlightenment and progress. By contrast, others like Jürgen Habermas and Charles Taylor suggest that the poststructuralist critiques go too far and thereby end up championing an unacceptable relativism.

If there is an underlying concern that links the different theories and theorists, it has to do with the human capacity, or the extent of it, to understand itself and—perhaps based on the rigor and lucidity of that understanding—to change its circumstances for the better. At the heart of the various battles in Anglo-American theory and criticism then, is a concern with the agency of human beings in culture and history. This book concerns itself with this discursive conjuncture by bringing to it the evidence of a related but nominally different discursive formation: that of African literature and criticism, a tradition I invoke under the broader term of African letters. On my reading, the epistemological lesson of African letters is the perspective on agency it implicitly offers. Posed simply, this perspective is that positive agency—in the domain of language or that of concrete politics—can emanate out of an act that is otherwise conceptually limited. African letters offer this perspective at the performative, not constative, level. That is to say, its testimony is to be found, not in what it says or understands about itself, but in how it unfolds as a historical phenomenon, a discursive practice.

This book, then, seeks to tease out the agency of African literature and criticism by situating it within the context of Anglo-American theory—and, more specifically, the influential strand within it that has come to be known as postcolonial theory. I begin with the premise that the predominant way in which the idea of agency is being framed in contemporary postcolonial theory cannot allow a strong understanding of the epistemological implications of African literature and the criticism it spawned from about the middle of the twentieth century. There are three layers to this argument. First, I argue that the most influential vectors in current postcolonial theory do not offer an adequate conceptual space within which the peculiar inflections of modernity contained in African letters can be fully appreciated. To make this appreciation possible, postcolonial theory needs to move beyond a covert rhetoric of global prescriptiveness that often characterizes it at the present time. Such a move makes it possible to identify, in the history of African letters, an instance of self-representation and knowledge production that proceeded on the strength of powerful conceptual leaps. The implication of the story I tell about African letters, then, is that positive agency can result from discursive or political acts that are otherwise conceptually limited. It is this lesson that current postcolonial theory and cultural criticism needs to take seriously, if it is to fully grasp the logic of African literary criticism as a component of African letters.

There are by now a significant number of books that take postcolonial theory and cultural criticism as their focus. Examples are Leela Gandhi's *Postcolonial Theory: A Critical Introduction*, Bart Moore-Gilbert's *Postcolonial Theory: Contexts, Practices, Politics*, Asha Varadharajan's *Exotic Parodies*, and Robert Young's *White Mythologies*. Like a number of others, these studies locate themselves primarily within the discursive terrain of Anglo-American literary studies and cultural criticism. My book's contribution differs from these studies because my engagement of postcolonial theory is accompanied by an additional field of vision—that of African literature and criticism as a distinct discursive formation. Aijaz Ahmad's *In Theory* and Satya P. Mohanty's *Literary*

Theory and the Claims of History both approach one level of the limitation my book sees in current postcolonial theory. But Ahmad's critique is mounted as a way of saying that poststructuralist, postcolonial theory is useless and inherently conservative. This book, by contrast, says that postcolonial theory is useful in some ways, limited in others. Mohanty's less polemical contribution is provocative as a way of boiling down the various issues being discussed and contested in current theory. For this reason, I engage his book directly in the opening chapter.

I use the idea of modernity as the common theme that unites both Anglo-American literary and cultural theory on the one hand, and African letters, on the other. Modernity is taken in its traditional philosophical sense, to imply a teleological movement of society from a "primitive" state to a "civilized," secular-scientific one. As already indicated of course, this teleological confidence has come under a range of critiques in contemporary theory. The continued centrality of the term in ongoing critical discussions is, however, what makes it useful as the conceptual ground upon which my book's argument is built. I proceed by first identifying a number of problems in the ways the idea of human agency—in the political as well as the intellectual-discursive realms—is being theorized in current literary and cultural theory. I then reconstruct a debate that occurred in anglophone African literary criticism in the 1970s. In doing this, I show the sense in which African literary criticism as a discursive practice can enrich our understanding of agency in the political and cultural spheres.

The first chapter discusses some illustrative instantiations, from Terry Eagleton, Homi Bhabha, and Satya P. Mohanty, of Anglo-American modes of theorizing about culture, change, and self-knowledge. The purpose here is to demonstrate that there is in current theory a recognizable discursive form, a way of thinking about things, a way of objectifying thought by means of words. This demonstration allows me to set the stage for a discussion of (i) Louis Althusser's theory of interpellation, and (ii) its instructive fate in contemporary theory and cultural criticism. The chapter closes with the suggestion that Althusser's account of ideology and interpellation remains a pertinent way of entering into the sort of analyses—of contemporary theory and African literary criticism—undertaken in the chapters to follow.

Chapter 2 is subdivided into two main sections. The first illustrates an unresolvable debate in Anglo-American theory, namely, that between poststructuralists and those who accuse them of unacceptable relativism. I do so by staging an encounter between Jürgen Habermas and Jean-François Lyotard. The chapter demonstrates the sense in which, although both thinkers differ with regard to their view of the tasks of critical thinking in the "postmodern" era, they both rely on a static non-West to enable their theorizing. This non-West is an "other" in the phenomenological sense; it is a fossil drawn from the ethnographic archives of the West's imperial past. In this sense, the debate between them cannot illuminate the location—within global modernity—of black Africa, still less the discursive formation called African letters. What it can do is to reinforce a conceptual field where "Africa" never emerges as a "coeval" entity—to borrow Johannes Fabian's term—but only as a pre-constituted signifier: it enables thought to proceed, but is itself neither the occasion nor the referent of the thinking.

The emergence of theories of postcoloniality in literary and cultural studies is an offshoot of the ongoing reassessment of the claims of Western rationality exemplified in the work of Habermas and Lyotard. In this development, critics like Edward Said, Gayatri Spivak, and Homi Bhabha are the acknowledged forerunners. These scholars attempt to remedy the sort of blind spot exemplified by Habermas and Lyotard. For them, the reality of the colonial encounter can teach us a lot about problems inherent to the West's understanding of itself, of other societies, and of the human mind's capacity to produce knowledge. Their theories of postcoloniality rely heavily on poststructuralist premises. The second segment of this chapter takes up the contributions of Spivak and Bhabha, primarily because (i) Said's work has been extensively discussed by scholars, and (ii) Spivak and Bhabha exemplify poststructuralist postcolonial theory more fundamentally than Said ever did. I am concerned with the seminal essays of these theorists from the late 1980s and early 1990s—the work that essentially set the terms for what we now call postcolonial theory. I argue that, in the poststructuralist vector invented by Spivak and Bhabha, literary theory offers a number of helpful insights. I show that their achievements are accompanied by problems that can be delineated with the conceptual apparatus of poststructuralist theory itself. Finally, I argue that Spivak and Bhabha display inadequate attention to third-world literatures as well as the trajectory of their criticism prior to the moment of poststructuralism in Britain and the United States. The result is that their writing tends to be thick on global generalization and prescriptions, but thin with regard to the cultural products of specific postcolonial contexts.

Chapter 3 directs attention to the history of African letters as a discursive attempt, before the emergence of Anglo-American theories of postcoloniality, to contest the objectification of the non-European world in Western critical discourses. The criticism of African Literature is predicated on a twofold and valid assumption: that a major consequence of black Africa's colonization by Western Europe is the forced march toward modernity, and that creative writers posit their mission to be that of facilitating and witnessing to the forms, contents, and tensions of that march. The prevalent tendency among Africanist critics is to operate with a teleological grid such that modernity is conceived as a progression in social and cognitive being, while the term "Africa" and what it means to be African are assumed to be self-evident—at times, even ontologically given. Thus, the "emergence" of anglophone African literature is often located in the late 1950s—precisely at the point of the publication of Chinua Achebe's *Things Fall Apart* (1958). By a consensus so influential as to have become a truism, Achebe's novel is said to inaugurate a self-consciously decolonized and decolonizing literary tradition in anglophone Africa. Feminist work has decisively contested this construction by showing its gendered basis and substantive elisions (Cobham "Revisionism," Ogunyemi, Stratton). Chapter 3 uses Althusser's notion of *méconnaissance* to criticize this gendered and teleological view of African literature, not so much to denounce it as to unpack its ideological sources. Basing my discussion on anglophone literary criticism from the late 1950s to the early 1980s, I show that major Africanist critics were methodologically tied to a reflectionist view of literature—namely, the idea that literary structure corresponds to social structure in a one-to-one relationship. Flawed though this understanding of literature happens to be, the agency of African letters as a discursive intervention resides precisely there. That is to say, it is in immersing itself in an inherited, conceptually flawed, understanding of literary representation that Africanist literary criticism offers a concrete instance of agency-in-motion.

The fourth and fifth chapters take off from there to show the sense in which this immersion, its contingencies and limitations, can be found coded into two literary texts by the Nigerian writers D. O. Fagunwa (1903–63) and Wole Soyinka (1934–). Fagunwa is generally classified as a "preindependence" author, while Soyinka belongs in the postindependence generation: that is to say, the generation that "came of age" in the late 1950s. Conventionally understood, Fagunwa's *The Forest of a Thousand Daemons* and Wole Soyinka's *Death and the King's Horseman* are creative literary texts: fictional material upon which criticism or theory work in the search for substantive—that is, nonfictional—truth. My own approach is to read the texts as themselves self-conscious theories elaborated in the idiom of fiction and drama. In this way, agency as a problem turns out to have been theorized in Fagunwa's novel and Soyinka's play. Chapters 4 and 5 are thus designed to set out a way in which African literary texts theorize themselves and comment on the issue of human agency in discourse as well as in politics. My readings of *The Forest of a Thousand Daemons* and *Death and the King's Horseman* are the centerpieces of chapters 4 and 5 respectively, but along the way, I discuss other works by both authors as well as by two of their contemporaries and fellow Nigerians, Amos Tutuola and Chinua Achebe.

To fully appreciate why I have chosen to write this kind of book, it is helpful to make three clarifications at this point. The first has to do with the way the chapters relate to each other. The common practice in contemporary criticism is to begin with a "theory" chapter and then proceed to the "application" chapters. The nature of my project necessitates a different procedure, hence the structure I have adopted. The first two chapters are devoted to Anglo-American theory, but they are not prolegomena to the remaining ones devoted to African letters. That is, chapters 3, 4, and 5 are not "raw materials" upon which the theoretical discussion conducted in chapters 1 and 2 go to work. In analyzing the theorists that engage my attention, I do not seek in their writing some prescriptive truth—either on reality, or how to get on with the job of literary interpretation. Very much to the contrary, I read theory as one more act of language and gesture of will. Theoretical writing differs from creative literature in the grammar that organizes it, not the dynamic of desire at work in it. Consequently, Chapters 1 and 2 proceed with step-by-step attention to *how* the theorists say what they have to say. On this book's argument, it will not do to accuse Habermas of "ethnocentrism," Spivak with "obscurantism," some other thinker with some other "ism," as a step toward settling on the theory that gets it "right." When, therefore, we confront Althusser in chapter 1 or Bhabha in chapter 2, I am interested in explicating the story of desire discernible in their arguments, not simply endorsing or rejecting what they have to contribute. Perhaps there is indeed some theory out there that gets it right, but what counts as "right" will then have to be further clarified.

In this sense, this book's contribution is not conceived to lie in offering a new theory of modernity. What I attempt to do is to deploy a very familiar understanding of modernity as philosophical discourse—that associated with Habermas's account and the Lyotardian assault analyzed in chapter 2—in order to develop and substantiate a cluster of related propositions. First, Habermas's and Lyotard's accounts of modernity are not only Eurocentric but also understandably so, since their elaborations are in response to "Western" sociocultural problems as the philosophers understand them to be. Second, far from repudiating the discursive frame inherent to such accounts as Habermas's or Lyotard's, current postcolonial theory has primarily tried to inhabit it from the margins, that is, to press it to accommodate the concrete fact of European colonialism. However, in doing this, the most influential trends in postcolonial theory have drawn primarily on poststructuralism, thereby giving short shrift to alternative discourses, such as African letters, that derive from or address the yearnings of non-Western societies. Viewed against this background, African letters constitutes an attempt to develop a discourse where "the modern" is not covertly associated with the West while the non-West is discursively frozen in the status of "the traditional"—regardless of whether the traditional is valued negatively, as in Habermas, or positively, as in Lyotard.

The term "African letters" as I use it follows Abiola Irele's usage in an important essay entitled "African Letters: The Making of a Tradition" (Irele "Letters"). In his use, the term refers to writings by black Africans in the European languages up to and beyond the "independence" era of the 1950s and 1960s. As already indicated, my own focus is on African literature and criticism in the English language by African as well as non-African critics. I say nothing about African writings in French or Portuguese, and nothing about missionary writings that can be dated farther back to the mid-nineteenth century. After such studies as Kwame Anthony Appiah's *In My Father's House,* Robert W. July's *An African Voice: The Role of the Humanities in African Independence,* and V. Y. Mudimbe's *The Invention of Africa,* it should be impossible to say that such broad-based projects are not available. Consequently, and as far as this book is concerned, my sense is that to have gone beyond anglophone African literature and criticism would have broadened the scope of materials adduced in aid of the argument, but it would not have changed in a significant way the logic of the inquiry or, for that matter, the substance of the argument.

If it could be shown that my position would have been significantly different had I dealt with other literary-linguistic traditions within Africa, or other non-literary discourses (say, nationalist political tracts, historiographic materials, or missionary writings), I should gladly welcome the correction. That a number of people—black and white, male and female—have been moved in recent decades to write about Africa using languages that are not native to Africa (languages that, not so long ago, defined Africa as ontologically other) is of course the first point of interest here. To the extent, then, that this book is intended to elaborate a metacritical, self-reflexive understanding of the place of Africanist writing in modernity, my hope is that my focus and conclusions will prompt further studies, studies designed to modify my assumptions or contest my conclusions.

A similar reasoning applies to the creative writers I discuss in chapters 4 and 5. *The Forest of a Thousand Daemons* is a high-school staple in Nigeria, read by generations of school children in the original or in translation. Likewise, *Death and the King's Horseman* is considered Soyinka's magnum opus and has been included in the latest edition of *The Norton Anthology of World Masterpieces,* as well as the *The Harper-Collins World Reader* (edited by Mary Ann Caws and Christopher Prendergast). Likewise, Tutuola's *The Palm-Wine Drinkard* is considered a classic (albeit an exotic one); and of course, in the current climate of literary and cultural criticism, to think African fiction is to think of Achebe and *Things Fall Apart.* These writers are thus secure canonical figures in Africanist studies, and they are becoming better known in "postcolonial" and "world literature" classrooms.

Beyond this, there is the personal factor. As a Nigerian myself, the immediate cultural context that a Wole Soyinka or a Chinua Achebe addresses is familiar to me. As an educated Nigerian, one trained and professionally based in the Western academy, and one who wants literature and its reading to mean something, I belong exactly in their class. By and large, I am implicated in the questions of identity and sociocultural change that they articulate so eloquently. That I am drawn to their texts is therefore self-serving in a sense that I hope has not proven to be unproductive. Whether or not it has, I must leave to the reader's judgement. I would have loved to extend my close readings to texts by such writers as Ngugi wa Thiong'o, Buchi Emecheta, Tsitsi Dangarembga, or Nuruddin Farah. It would have been worthwhile, for instance, to consider Ngugi's *Petals of Blood* in intertextual dialogue with Achebe's *No Longer at Ease,* or Dangarembga's *Nervous Conditions* in dialogue with Ngugi's *Weep Not Child.* These are exciting avenues of inquiry that I regrettably could not get into in this project. It is my hope that the book makes up for its narrow choice with adequately detailed analysis of the selected texts, and reasonable persuasiveness of the overarching theoretical argument.

Similarly, although I believe that my argument applies to the "extratextual" realm of the creation of viable and prosperous societies, this book has little to offer in the way of hard-core political theory. To be sure, I can share my hard-core political analyses with friends, or in opinion letters to newspapers. But I lack the competence to mount such an argument as the substantive contribution of an academic book. Fortunately, Mahmood Mamdani's *Citizen and Subject* does what I am not equipped to do with the academic discipline of political theory. The reader who wants his politics straight up—that is to say, without the tedium of textual explication, the fluffy apparatus of rhetorical criticism—should benefit from Mamdani's book. And precisely for that reason, I feel justified in invoking disciplinary specialization to limit my object of analysis to the domain of literary theory and criticism.

That my conclusions and their rhetorical tenor have implications for such "extraliterary" domains as anticolonial or other struggles makes it plausible that readers may object to my self-serving circumscription. I can only promise that one of the aims of this book is to make visible, and argue against, the conceptual confusion from which such an objection draws its passion. For on the argument of this book, every act of a linguistic or concrete-political nature belongs to a specifiable discursive domain, and is thus bound to a conceptual topography and a protocol of enunciation. In this sense, a concern with the agency of linguistic actions is exactly a concern with the limits imposed by historic—Euromodern—delineations of the public sphere. As a taxpayer and wielder of a passport, I will vote when the time comes so to do. Perhaps I may also be sighted at political rallies if I happen to have no classes to teach at that hour. But this book is not designed for a political rally, not will it do anything to lessen the pain of that maimed woman or starving child we have come to associate with modern Africa. It sets forth an outlook on the world and may modify, or even change, our outlook on that world and the texts that witness to it. But that is the extent of it. Like all books, this is, finally, no more than a book.

ACKNOWLEDGMENTS

In a way, this book is an attempt to assemble and reassess the intellectual currents that have so far shaped me. Consequently, my debt to people and institutions is more extensive than I can possibly recall here. I will, however, try, in the hope that some sense of the depth of my gratitude will register, however imperfectly.

I am grateful to my teachers in the Department of English at the University of Ibadan, where I did my undergraduate work: they got me going, so to speak. I am also grateful to the English Department at Cornell University, where I did my graduate work, for making available a most stimulating environment and graduate student body. My sincere thanks to Anne Adams, Laura Brown, Walter Cohen, Jonathan Culler, Henry Louis Gates Jr., Peter Uwe Hohendahl, Biodun Jeyifo, Satya Mohanty, Harriett Mullen, and Mark Seltzer.

An NEH award enabled me to spend 1995–96 as a fellow of the School of Social Science, Institute for Advanced Study, Princeton, New Jersey. A University of Oregon Humanities Center fellowship enabled me to spend the fall of 1996 working on the project. I thank both organizations for extending financial support at crucial points in the evolution of this project.

I am grateful to colleagues at the University of Oregon for their support and encouragement. Linda Kintz and Tres Pyle read an early version of the manuscript and offered much-needed advise. Julia Lesage's pruning of chapter 3 helped me to overcome—I hope!—my tendency to use big and idle words. My discussions with John Lysaker, in and out of PLC Hall, have been tremendously helpful. My discussions with Joe Fracchia in the spring and summer of 1998 enabled me to turn a pivotal corner in the writing of the book. Many friends and colleagues read portions or earlier versions of the manuscript in its path to becoming what it has turned out to be: thanks to Lékè Adéèkó, Loren Kruger, Teju Olaniyan, Ato Quayson, and Alok Yadav. Patrick Mensah's twelve-page response, laced with good-natured jabs and general mischief, made this book better than it might have been. Abiola Irele and Françoise Lionnet continue to be valued sources of advice, for which I am sincerely grateful. Special thanks are due to Simon Gikandi, Isidore Okpewho, and Ken Warren, who helped me to isolate what I was trying to say, and gave me models of incisive criticism to which I aspire. Of course, the flaws to be found in this book are my sole responsibility.

I owe a million thanks to Madhu Dubey for her friendship and intellectual example over the years. And I will forever be grateful to Kofi Agawu for his searching questions and unwavering concern. Without our telephone conversations, I doubt if I would have kept on with the project. I hope I can be presumptuous enough to thank him for being a mentor, friend, and no-nonsense interlocutor—all at once. Finally, my sincere thanks to Jane Bunker and Diane Ganeles of SUNY Press for their seasoned editorial guidance.

This book is dedicated to Evelyn Obiageli Ugwu, whose wisdom and strength guide my thinking and make it all worthwhile. It is dedicated also to our son, Ayodeji Timilehin, merry one, offspring of the kolanut field, for becoming part of our life.

CHAPTER ONE

ISSUES AND CONTEXT:
ON KNOWLEDGE AS LIMIT

Often on television screens across North America, a peculiar kind of drama is played out in the service of a conceivably important cause. This drama involves images of poverty, disease, and what is seen as fratricidal war in places like Bangladesh, Sudan, or more recently, Rwanda and Burundi, images that humanitarian organizations beam into North American homes as part of their drive for donations. In these sequences, the setting is all so familiar, and yet, all too distant. It may come in the form of dilapidated tenements or mud huts that stretch their bleak countenances forth to announce a contemporaneity, a modernity, that is everything but modern. It may take the form of scorched earth filling the air with dust (evidence of uncontrolled desertification and failed harvest), a recent bloody confrontation between rebel guerrillas and some government or another, or erstwhile neighbors who now are bitter enemies on account of "primordial" tribal differences. At any rate, the pictorial eloquence in these sequences often resides, not in the singular historicity of each moment and space, still less in the complexity of each such historicity.

Solemnly and skillfully, the camera lingers over a wreckage of dead, bloated animals or abandoned armored tanks. It crawls with sympathy over tired mothers, half naked, emaciated; and then it rests on the child, now no longer a backcloth but foregrounded, powerfully, as the final center of narrative pathos. We see a crying child, but she is in fact too tired to cry: only the clotted mixture of tears and mucus signals an anguish too deep to sustain the exertion of a normal three-year-old's cry. As she cries by the fact of being too weak to cry, even so does she sleep in her very wakefulness. Her eyes, glazed, stare at us without effort, plaintive because she can no longer really cry. Her silence and physical disintegration convey a distance that is urgently intimate. For if sound-lessness announces her confoundment in the face of tragedy, her physical disintegration calls on a superior knowledge to comprehend her plight. And so the camera speaks what she cannot say, knows what she cannot know. It traces the evidence of her predicament on the visible rib cage and the leathery skin continuously visited by buzzing flies and other curious bugs. It closes in on her distended stomach; in contrasting so crassly with the frailty of the rest of her, her stomach bears witness—with the power of grim hyperbole—to the utter starvation at the root of its prominence. The camera, intimate cognitive subject, distances her tragedy onto the remote but legible plains of the "third world." By imaging the raw obscenity of her situation, the camera knows what she cannot know, while the voice-over, by imploring all humanity to help save a child, speaks what she cannot say.

Hopefully, the foregoing account strikes us as patently superfluous, for this may in turn enable us to appreciate, in a concrete way, the latent work of these images. In other words, my description's excess is intended to exhibit in words the concentrated abundance of the camera's images. For with just a little risk of overstatement, one can say that the camera rarely *ponders* such scenes beyond the assumption of a familiar logic of causality: it merely represents, dutifully, intensively. However, what may pass unnoticed in such representations is the displacement of the complex questions away from the daunting realm of political economy and its sociocultural sign-systems, onto the gripping telepathy of the suffering body. At such moments, it is the terrible corporeality of her victimization that the camera disseminates—a corporeality so terrible that the network of relations that determines (and thereby, narrativizes) the body in pain cannot be visible, dares not be visible, in the time of the viewer's empathy. These enactments constitute explicit dramatizations of the ideology of modernity in the face of the postcolonial problematic.[1]

There are a number of ways of responding to such dramas. One would be to stress that this demonstration is extreme, because its medium belongs in what is called popular culture. Here, the assumption is that in the specialized discourses, one encounters a more sophisticated and illuminating understanding of the ideology of modernity and its intersection with the postcolonial problematic. A variation of this response would insist that such demonstrations have a pragmatic utility for which one should overlook their naiveté. On this view, the philanthropic end is laudable and—in any case—it is wrong to expect a ten-minute sequence on the T.V. to display the kind of critical self-awareness one expects from specialized disquisitions. The other response would be less charitable, more morally outraged. It would draw attention to the complicity of mass culture with the "imperialist" designs of late capitalist Euro-America; it would denounce the capitalist world system that organically needs the precritical humanism of philanthropic agencies to mask its impact; and it would end with a declamatory exhortation as passionate as it is familiar: namely, that the third world needs (or, alternately, is destined) to break the shackles of "oppression" and "neo-colonialism."

Now, the first two options merely rationalize away the drama by stressing its pragmatic necessity. The third merely reinscribes the very mechanism it seeks to read through and beyond: in denouncing the ideological innocence of the cinematic gaze, it merely shifts attention from the pathos of the suffering body to the so-called evil of the imperialist eye. In this vein, all three reactions tell us rather less than their passion suggests. Much too little, since they move too anxiously—as the case may be—to a moralistic recuperation of, or an equally moralistic indignation at, the ideology of modernity dramatized by the cinematic eye. Certainly, such narratives often function, for the potential donor(s), as closed invitations to self-validating philanthropy and an equally self-validating paternalism—both at once. Yet this seems to me to be ultimately uninteresting: its own frame remains moral, its force rests too heavily on the very category it takes for granted—namely, the "self" that is being validated. But what if, in order really to learn from such sequences, we embrace them with incisive cultural criticism in our thoughts? What if, beyond moral outrage or evasive defense, we accord them the status of a drama that encodes large issues of epistemology, issues at the heart of some of the liveliest currents in Anglo-American literary theory and criticism?

Clearly, a double presupposition is at work in these sequences. First, the third world exists as an other, where the first world is the Self.[2] Second, the materiality of the third world thus imaged simply bears witness to an aberration. Where the first world silently intones its objective approximation to the promise of modernity, the third world comes across as not quite modern—still behind, alas, in humanity's march towards modernity's lofty promise. What this indicates is that there is a knowledge, as confident as it is compassionate, that guides the camera's eye: its humanist calling is simply to represent, to evoke—through motion, color, and sound—that which its knowledge already renders transparent. Under the sway of the ideology of modernity, then, these sequences perform a systematic repression as means to an arguably ethical end. This ideology, which is at the same time a knowledge (*méconnaissance*, in the Althusserian sense) is so sure of its self-evidence that the humanist gaze it underwrites performs a systematic reductionism with sincere compassion.

This brings us to the suggestion that a more complex and rewarding understanding can be encountered in specialized discourses. At least in part, contemporary literary theory and cultural criticism is concerned with images such as we have been discussing and, even more directly, theories of postcoloniality concern themselves with their determinations and meanings. If media images of third-world poverty tend to freeze the latter as radically other, one consequence of the freezing is that the object thus frozen can never be conceived as a subject with agency. One of the aims of this book is to suggest that current postcolonial theory risks replicating this maneuver in the way it approaches cultural-nationalist discourses of the postcolonial world. I would like us to keep the import (such as I suggested above) of these media images centrally in mind as we step onto the terrain covered in this book. The concerns we shall be addressing can be located at the intersection of two discursive sites: (i) contemporary literary and cultural studies—specifically, theories of postcoloniality and debates around what Habermas has called the philosophical discourse of modernity; (ii) African literature and criticism as a component of what Abiola Irele designates as "African letters." Using the question of modernity as the common ground of both discursive configurations, we shall try to develop a systematic and what I see as a productive dialogue between them. Thus in structure and argumentation, our discussion is designed to speak to Anglo-American postcolonial studies as equally as it addresses African studies. Investigating the possibilities theory offers for explicating the problems with which African writers and critics are grappling, this book demonstrates the ways in which the adventure of African letters illuminates the strengths and limitations of some contemporary theorizations of postcoloniality.

The purpose of this chapter is to spell out the terms and ramifications of three key questions. In a general way, these questions can be formulated thus: To what extent are the questions energizing some of the influential debates and perspectives in Anglo-American literary theory and cultural criticism relevant to the problematic of African letters? Is it possible that in some of its motions, theories of postcoloniality unwittingly replicate the logic of repression and decontextualization more unselfconsciously dramatized in media homilies about the third world? And in what ways can the framing of the question of agency—discursive as well as concrete-political—in contemporary theory benefit from direct engagement, such as this book undertakes, with a discursive phenomenon like African letters? As indicated earlier, the major issues of contention in current theory can be said to devolve ultimately on the question of subjectivity and agency, specifically, the human capacity to know (if not master) itself as well as its environment. This chapter illustrates and reflects upon some exemplary responses to this issue as a way of laying out how I intend to approach it in the chapters to follow. I begin by discussing an exchange on the question of subjectivity between Terry Eagleton and Homi Bhabha. I then move on to consider Satya P. Mohanty's contribution in his book, *Literary Theory and the Claims of History*. Although Eagleton and Bhabha are arguing from two putatively opposed standpoints (the former from the perspective of Marxism, the latter, poststructuralism), their shared commitment to a *theoretical* resolution of the status of the subject in cultural as well as discursive practice results in a situation where they both risk obscuring the reality of concrete subjects in datable interaction with specific historical challenges. Mohanty's "post-positivist realism" promises greater attention to the history and context of specific human endeavors or, on my terms, discursive formations. However, I argue that, in spite of itself, Mohanty's undertaking shares the sort of theoreticism he ascribes to poststructuralism. Finally, the chapter revisits Louis Althusser's theory of ideology in order to formulate the substantive premises that will inform our exploration of, on the one hand, postcolonial theory and, on the other, African letters, in the rest of the book. The chapter suggests that, applied to the problem of discursive formations—our specific area of concern in this book—Althusser's account of ideology and interpellation can be read in a way that makes it serviceable for a productive apprehension of the implications for cultural studies of African letters.

On the Problem of the Subject

The meaning of the third world and its inter-relationship with the first is currently at the center of a number of discussions in Anglo-American literary theory and cultural criticism. In these discussions, there appears to be a broad consensus around the basic idea that the dynamics of imperialism, and the discourses that witness to it, are being sorted out by the practitioners of cultural studies and, as a subspecies of that general category, critics who work under the rubric of postcoloniality. The consensus points to a certain confidence that the illumination promised by or actually offered in, the sorting out, has important ramifications for literary theory and cultural criticism in general. One of the aims of this book is to inquire into the basis of this confidence as well as the extent of payoff it offers. I take postcolonial theory as an influential rubric within the broad discursive configuration we have generally come to call cultural studies. Into this configuration, I intend to introduce a related but not entirely commensurate one, namely, African letters. The term African letters here designates the adventure of mind that is exemplified in African literature and criticism, as well as in other broadly cultural-nationalist writings. One of the questions this book explores, then, is the following: set off against the evidence of African letters, could we fully endorse the preoccupations and findings of postcolonial theory and come off rigorously vindicated?

This question is called for in light of the kind of interaction that postcolonial theory has tended to have with non-Western literary and critical traditions. It is well known that what is currently referred to as postcolonial theory gets its institutional baptism in the wake of Edward Said's *Orientalism* (1978) and is overwhelmingly poststructuralist in premises or reference. The genealogy of the broader terrain of cultural studies is, of course, more complicated. But it remains the case that the kind of cultural studies that is at present most influential in the academy tends to be influenced by poststructuralist premises. Under the language of ratification, continuation, qualification, or outright rejection, post-structuralist theory can legitimately be said to be the single most recognizable context and flashpoint of contemporary postcolonial theory and cultural criticism. To be distinguished from this configuration are the critical discourses that comment upon, speak to, or otherwise draw meaning out of, say, African or Caribbean literary texts. The latter often use conceptual tools that remind one of Lukács or Leavis, rather than Derrida or Lacan.

In light of the impact of poststructuralist theory on the way we think and talk about history, culture, and language, the high visibility of post-structuralist postcolonial theory is altogether to be expected. Going strictly by the rhetoric and overt claims in contemporary theory and cultural criticism, one might expect a warm friendship with "third world" and "minority" literary and critical traditions. This is however far from the case: often in African literary criticism, theory is cast as a "first-world" preoccupation, Eurocentric and self-mystifying—ultimately irrelevant to the passion of African letters. At one level, this accusation may appear to have some merit. For although a central idea in current theory is that third world literatures have a lot to tell us, it is hard to be certain of the conviction behind the idea. Despite the general celebration of otherness, the literatures emerging from the former European colonies seem not to be as securely in the forefront of analytical attention as the abstract theoretical claims made about them (see Slemon and Tiffin, "Introduction").

Current literary theory and cultural criticism, then, appears to have enemies (or at best, polite fellow travelers who smirk at every available opportunity) where one would expect allies. This scenario is not altogether new. As is well known, theory has proven to have a remarkable capacity to draw an unhelpful kind of reaction: namely, that its label (i.e., this or that theory, or this or that theoretical affiliation) elicits more or less reflex rejection, where what is being rejected is a label that is conflated with a content. From ongoing complaints about philistines and the trauma that culture is supposed to suffer at the hands of postmodernists and canon-busters, it would seem that wherever two or more are gathered in the name of theory, there you will find some cursing or gnashing of teeth. The matter is quite often compounded by the preeminence of theoretical camps that seem foremost to operate on the strength of slogans and declarations. Thus, for instance, it is sometimes taken for granted that to announce one's camp as poststructuralist entails a standpoint in favor of cosmopolitanism and opposition to nativism or essentialism. By extension, to be for cosmopolitanism is to be conceptually more up-to-date and global, committed to transnational solidarity as against narrow parochialism (see Benita Parry, "Cheers").

One of the aims of this book is to show that poststructuralist postcolonial theory can be most useful if its implicit opposition to certain kinds of (non-poststructuralist) third world discourses is dialectically superseded. On this view, not only is it more interesting to grant labels and slogans less weight than they may otherwise acquire, doing so actually rescues theory from itself. To undervalue (let alone reject) Anglo-American theory because it is a first world preoccupation is to misconceive a lot that is of value in it. Whatever they happen to be (and we shall be elaborating on some of them), the limitations of Anglo-American theory cannot be made visible from a standpoint that withdraws from it on the basis of, as it were, its place of birth. Consequently, this book seeks to develop and exemplify a critical vocabulary that can make a genuine interaction between Anglo-American postcolonial theory and African literary criticism possible and productive. This involves developing a way of thinking and talking about literature, culture, and history that speaks to mainstream theory as well as African literary criticism at once.

It might be helpful to proceed by rehearsing a genealogy of sorts. Around the turn of the twentieth century, and more comprehensively after the Second World War, global politics took an epochal turn with the consolidation of nationalist movements in the colonized world, movements that combined sustained—sometimes, armed—activism with a passionate interrogation of the colonizer's claims about culture, social organization, and the epistemology that is taken to underpin these two. If the concrete struggle of nationalist movements in the colonized world aimed at political emancipation, never was there any doubt about the necessity of an epistemological liberation—hand in hand with such political emancipation. In this respect, a large part of the intellectual energy of what in this book we shall be calling African letters has been devoted to the project of establishing the difference—cultural and epistemological—of the postcolonial subject from its Western counterpart. Less a discourse of global, magisterial ambition, these discourses tend to pursue a truth that is avowedly circumscribed as historical, framed—as it were—with the vision of an explicit project. The impetus is that of understanding the colonial and neocolonial moment in African history, and the project, that of contesting negative representations generally associated with European imperialism.

If these epistemic developments first took root in the colonized world, the impulse has by now taken some hold in Euro-American literary theory and cultural criticism. One significant contribution of poststructuralism is the basic proposition that the world has at the present time become a village. As we shall see in chapter 2, this spirit energizes Jean-François Lyotard's account of the "postmodern condition." Such an account posits the mutual imbrication of such binary opposites as first world/third world; it suggests, in other words, that we recognize the interpenetration of economic, political, and cultural systems that may otherwise be seen as radically disparate. In this sense, the angle from which someone like Lyotard joins the project of epistemological decolonization would seem to be dated. Rendered schematically, the interdependence that Lyotard points up has always been taken as a self-evident subtext in African letters, so self-evident as not to merit belaboring. On this view, it would follow that the burden of analysis, in African letters, tends most often to be placed in identifying the contours of that interpenetration. We have then a complex and problematic intersection. On the one hand, first world critical thought seeks to expose epistemic imperialism by destabilizing the logic of binarisms while, on the other, Africanist discourses appear most often to retain that binarism in order to underscore the different knowledge of the colonized—the knowledge that had to be suppressed so the West can understand itself and ratify its sense of human potential and epochal advance.

The basic project shared by all strands of Anglo-American radical thought—namely, the critique of foundationalist philosophy—sets out to undercut the epistemic cartography of the Enlightenment, where true cognition (i.e., science against myth, culture against nature), and the global advancement it promises, was attributed to the European genius. Rejecting the ethnocentrism of this presumption, contemporary theory sets out to demystify its assumptions and claims. And so it is, that the critique of Enlightenment foundationalist thought becomes an interdisciplinary stimulant, a way of bringing to light the evidence of erstwhile suppressed concerns such as race, gender, or sexuality. The routine way of referring to this trend is to cast it in terms of the "death of the subject." Generally, everyone agrees that the rise of the West, and its subjectification in discourse, has been accompanied by a good many contradictions. But this is where the divergences arise. At the level of theory, how do we go about rethinking our traditional (preconstituted) knowledges and ways of knowing? Some would charge others with throwing away the subject altogether, insisting—as a more politically serviceable move—on the construction of "other" subjectivities as a strategy, precisely, of resisting the actually existing imperialism of the West. The debates rooted in this basic site of contention take various forms. For our first illustration, let us examine an exchange between Homi Bhabha and Terry Eagleton on the pages of *ICA Documents* entitled "Identity." The particular exchange discussed here appears in short pieces by both Eagleton and Bhabha, but it concisely dramatizes an observation that deserves to be put in place.[3]

Eagleton's short piece presents a general account of the debate around the question of the subject. There are those for whom, to quote Eagleton, "the theoretical decentering of the subject, the prising open of its fetishized self-identity to the powers of dissemination and self-subversion signals an unqualified triumph" (47). At the other end are those who view this dissolution as a symptom of political quietism; for this group, the "dispersed, ungrounded, non-autonomous subject is less the potential negation of patriarchal capitalism, than the graphic image of its very victim" (47). Both views, Eagleton contends, have a case. However, he argues for "a political theory, or theory of the subject, which is capable . . . of grasping social transformation as at once diffusion and affirmation, the death and birth of the subject" (48). What he misses, then, is a *dialectical* (his own word) conceptualization of the status of the subject in political engagement and social transformation. By contrast, Bhabha expresses less disenchantment with the assaults on the subject. For him, it is precisely "the dialectical hinge between the birth and death of the subject that needs to be interrogated" (10). Invoking Eagleton's worry over the "vacuously apocalyptic" cast of most of contemporary radical theories, Bhabha counters that the "compensatory and vicarious processes of signification" of these modes of thought "are a spur to social action; the production of something else besides which is not only the cut or gap of the subject but also the 'intercut' it produces across social sites and disciplines" (10). "This hybridity," he concludes, "spatialises the project of political thinking by continually facing it with the strategic and the contingent" (10). The undermining of the subject thus constitutes, for him, a timely and valuable project.

Both Bhabha and Eagleton share a number of basic assumptions. Both agree that critical thought can participate in social transformation via an epistemological revolution, a theoretical witnessing of the forms and strategies of political or cultural struggle. They do not deny the value of constructions of imaginary identity, neither do they deny that expediency should not lead to the elevation of such constructions to the level of the natural. Where they part ways is with regard to the alloca-tion of priority. Are we serving the revolution better, so to speak, by belaboring the imaginary status of identity, or is it enough to admit that insight and then concentrate on what specific movements and forma-tions achieve via such imaginary constructions? These are interesting questions, but it should be noted that they presuppose the possibility of conceptual, transhistorical, resolution. However, the occasion of medi-tation derives from the pressures of a particular cultural and political conjuncture, a recognizable moment and space.

Paradoxically, it is this moment and space that may remain hid-den because it is taken for granted. When Bhabha writes: "[w]hat must be left an open question, *post* postmodernism is how we are to re-think 'ourselves' once we have undermined the immediacy and auton-omy of self-consciousness" (10), he begs the question of who the "we" denotes, as well as the substantive purchase of the temporal scheme (post-postmodernism) the formulation presupposes. Are "we" to be persuaded that all thoughts and actions based on the illusion of self-consciousness should be adjourned while "we" figure out exactly how to think and act henceforth? And till when might this adjournment be expected to last; when, in other words, is "post-postmodernism"? The risk in a discussion framed in these terms is that, caught up in ques-tions of how the subject should be theorized in order to serve our understanding of social practices, what may be occluded from view is the reality and shape of specific instances of subjectification that sur-round and impact us.[4]

The adventure of African letters constitutes a specific instance of subjectification in the realm of discourse, and should therefore be seen as a case of agency-in-motion. We shall see, in chapters 3 through 5, a process of self-construction, one that subsists on a number of conceptual leaps and discursive imagination of community. I shall be arguing that the achievement of African letters, its agency as an activity of human minds in concrete history, resides in these conceptual leaps and con-structions. I shall be suggesting that as critics, we need to attain a more modest apprehension of what human agency involves in cultural as well as political practice. We need to distinguish between agency as, on the one hand, a historical category tied to specific contexts and ends, and on the other, a formal abstraction. While the latter should have a place in cultural criticism, it should not be posed in ways that become covertly transcendental and prescriptive.[5] Where cultural processes and discursive formations are concerned, our understanding of agency is at its richest if we work with the hindsight of history and context, rather than with normative (transhistorical) prescription or speculation.

A recent book that argues for a similar orientation in literary and cultural criticism is Satya P. Mohanty's *Literary Theory and the Claims of History*. In his book, Mohanty undertakes to reconsider positivism as well as relativism in order to show that one does not need the latter in order to transcend the former. In a critical climate where concern with such notions as "human nature," or a "real world" independent of discourse are seen as old-fashioned (except as signs of a repressive and deluded past) Mohanty urges that we cannot afford to give them up so easily. Mohanty uses hermeneutics and Anglo-American philosophy against poststructuralism, especially as the latter has blended with a broader postmodernist current in literary studies. His understanding of postmodernism as an epistemological position makes it synonymous with poststructuralist thought. In his account, this position characterizes an entire range of theoretical strands and self-identifications in literary theory, and so much is this the case that even the Marxisms of Louis Althusser and Fredric Jameson are presented as instances of postmodernism.

Mohanty argues for an approach to cultural criticism that begins with the premise that there is in what humans do a cognitive basis, a logic, and that this logic can be understood to varying degrees. The tools with which we seek to achieve this understanding can thus be made stronger, more refined. The real force of his contribution, then, is with regard to our commitment to developing finer methodological equipment, the language to describe and seek to understand cultural processes as they take shape on the ground. For him, it is in doing this that we will be better placed to recognize the agency of individual or collective adventures in the domain of culture. Mohanty's account of postpositivist realism grants (like poststructuralism) that cultural processes are contingent in a way that ontological facts of nature are not. However, historical and contingent though they are, Mohanty's point is that human affairs and cultural practices are not simply arbitrary or devoid of logic and pattern. Further, he is in agreement with the poststructuralist claim that such realities as identity or cultural change do not exist in a transparent realm where they can be accessed "directly," that is, without the mediation of theory, inherited beliefs, or institutional ideologies. For him, the problem with postmodernism is that it too quickly gives up on this logic, preferring instead to dwell on the ruptures of pattern, the moments where knowledge comes up short against the dense opacity of contingent history.

Mohanty's argument hinges on the need for the building of communities, the need for communication and persuasion. However, a certain deployment of "we" anchors much of his argument without getting adequately specified. In arguing for a hierarchy of truths among competing languages and sites of truth seeking, he shifts between a "we," understood as a community of intellectuals who are trained and paid to look for truth in specific disciplinary formations, and a "we" that surreptitiously denotes human beings in their day-to-day confrontation with reality. We shall see in the next chapter that although he would set his version of community and persuasion apart from the notion of communicative rationality and consensus that Habermas is known for, Mohanty's account recalls the latter's on at least this count. I am persuaded that issues like identity, value, etc., can be rationally understood precisely because of (not despite) the mediation of theory. However, the idea of theory mediation implies that there could be a variety of such theories, such mediations. Seen from this perspective, we immediately grant the inherent relativity of each particular theory, insofar as each is mediated by such things as history, institutional, or disciplinary parameters. For Mohanty, cultural studies needs to go beyond this first-level relativism, so to speak, and entertain the possibility that the truths that different mediations generate can be hierarchically judged. If we judge one truth to be closer to reality, and if this judgement is well justified within the norms of the community making the judgement, then we can call the judgement objective. This definition of objectivity thus depends on a sense of institutional norms that Mohanty implicitly grants, but performatively brackets. And yet, it is this implicit subtext of institutions that requires explicit thematization, if the agency of African letters is to be fully appreciated.

How is it possible for Mohanty to hold the two positions indicated above—namely, (i) that truth does not reveal itself in lightning flashes sent by God, and (ii) that truth claims are objective to the extent that they satisfy prevailing norms of knowledge production? The answer lies in his use of scientific knowledge and its justification as an analogy for knowledge of human actions and sociocultural processes. There is an analogical parallelism set up between the natural and human sciences, and it is here that Mohanty's argument meets its ultimate limitation. Here is a good passage for isolating this limitation:

the fact that in a prescientific time all humans who cared to think about diseases might have held the "folk legend" explanation of them does not invalidate our current belief that we now have a better explanation, and one that matches the way the world is. To believe that we do, we do *not* need to subscribe to the idea that the world-as-it-is can be completely described once and for all in one neutral language, but we do subscribe to the very different idea that the external world exists and might reveal regular processes of functioning which could be identified as "lawlike" by our best scientific procedures of observation and systematization. (165, emphasis Mohanty's)

The claim being made here seems to be that, for instance, the explanation that science has for the cause and progress of a disease may change with time and new evidence, but the objective fact and source of causation remain constant. However much our understanding of the causes of a disease changes or gets better, whatever it is that really causes it will always be "there."

If we accept this, and I see no reason not to, we are still left with something unique to cultural processes as opposed to the object of the natural sciences. Human interactions happen in time, and so does our understanding of those interactions. In the domain of human actions, understandings, and representations, things are not just there or not there. We can use as an example a novel Mohanty discusses, Toni Morrison's *Beloved*. One cannot understand slavery as history and culture, or Sethe as body and mind, by approaching her infanticide with any "either-or" problematic. Examples of the either-or propositions I have in mind include: is the attack she mounts on her daughter—ostensibly to protect the daughter from enslavement—"rational" or not; is Sethe's sense of herself adequate to her situation or not, and so on. However one wishes to pose and answer these questions, the understanding of slavery as a historical reality with a "causal structure" has little to do with the ontological or moral status of the killing itself. So much is this the case that the killing is itself contingent: as the novel demonstrates, the second time she finds herself in what appears to be a similar situation, Sethe's attack is directed outwards at the threat, not inwards at the child.

A similar logic would be applicable to an issue that continues to exercise the attention of philosophers, namely, whether or not one can validly evaluate the practices or norms of an alien culture, even when these appear to be entirely incommensurable with the evaluator's own culture. A particularly instructive scenario is the practice of human sacrifice that used to be common in prescientific societies. It seems to be the case that many such cultures also have a concept of human beings as essences—in other words, they have posed the question of why and how humans are different from stones, or why life is deeply numinous and thus to be nurtured and revered. Obviously, there is a contradiction between this view and human sacrifice, so one can say that the practice is wrong. But again in this case, the wrongness is exhibited in the fact that the culture itself has posed the question. Yet another clue may be found in the fact that our hypothetical prescientific peoples often appear to engage in the practice within powerful cults that exclude a sizeable number of the population. In other words, it would appear that the cultures tacitly recognize the contradiction but repress it by means such as exclusion.[6] Approached in this way, it could be said that all cultures immanently carry the grounds and terms for their own critique. If I am right, a critique of "prescientific" culture that proceeds from the grounds and self-understanding of a scientific one can only be most persuasive if it relativizes its own motions. In this sense, Kant's categorical imperative, or Althusser's account of ideology and superstructures, equips us to *articulate* the wrongness of human sacrifice. But precisely because of this, our articulation is neither "objective" nor transhistorical. Rather, it is, as the case may be, "Kantian" or "Althusserian," where both qualifiers designate products of specific human minds under specifiable cultural conditions and pressures.

Of course, the examples of Toni Morrison's Sethe, or prescientific peoples immolating fellow human beings in the name of culture, are extreme cases. I raise them mainly to indicate that there is something to be said for the poststructuralist suspicion of truth claims that seek to hide the mode of operation through which the particular truth is apprehended and represented. Mohanty shares this general suspicion, granting as he does that much wrong has been perpetrated, conceptually and concretely, in the heyday of Eurocentric positivism. The most important difference between him and his object of critique, then, is to be found in where he wants us to invest conceptual and analytical energy at the present time. Where poststructuralist criticism focuses on the obstacles to knowledge as a way of avoiding the naive confidence of foundationalist epistemology, Mohanty insists that we should hold these obstacles as the threshold, rather than the culmination, of our inquiries. Posed this way, his position holds some promise. But as Mohanty himself grants, poststructuralism proceeds from a salutary attempt to avoid the ethnocentrism of much of Western theorizing about culture and civilization. Although he grants this much, Mohanty does not confront its implications as squarely as is necessary. It is on the strength of this evasion that he is able to categorize the anti-ethnocentric impulse as a sign of liberal pluralism, one that can only culminate in sophisticated (but no less unacceptable) relativism. I should like to suggest, however, that a lot depends on how the relativist perspective presents itself in particular analytical situations. On this view, if Mohanty's commitment to incremental knowledge marks, at least in principle, an advance over poststructuralism's focus on opacity, his impatience with cultural relativism may generate a regression.

Our approach in this book is to retain Mohanty's caution regarding the excesses and lacunae of some *deployments* of poststructuralist insights, while purging his own "postpositivist" alternative of the possibility of ethnocentric regression. In order to spell out how this purging might be achieved, I should like to return to one of the figures Mohanty identifies with poststructuralism/postmodernism, Louis Althusser. In the next section, I want to show that one can use Althusser's theory to account for agency within the parameters and concepts of poststructuralist theory.

SUBJECTIVITY, AGENCY, KNOWLEDGE

We have already noted that Mohanty's reading of Althusser is tendentious. We also suggested that his position is not well served by the turn to the philosophy of science, and the notion of postpositivist realism. There is a sense, indeed, in which his postpositivist realism can be transcoded into a Foucauldian or Althusserian register; that is, the position he wants to elaborate can be elicited from within the logic of poststructuralism itself. It is this line that I wish to explore here with reference to Althusser. As is well recognized, practically every strand of contemporary theory and cultural studies proceeds from a broadly Althusserian frame. In the late 1980s, Michael Sprinker claimed that "[t]o the extent that the current horizon of understanding [in literary theory] is demarcated by the relationship between the aesthetic and the ideological, it can be said with justice that we remain determinately within the Althusserian problematic" (2). I want to argue that this seemingly old-fashioned claim remains valid even now.[7] Implicitly or explicitly in the course of this book, we shall be encountering the ghost of Althusser, specifically his theory of ideology and the epistemological position it entails. Of course, Althusserianism has been declared dead for some time now. The fact indeed that it suffered this fate in our poststructuralist climate may index the possibility that, against Mohanty's reading (wherein Althusser is cast as a full-fledged poststructuralist), the latter's theory retains a dimension that not all poststructuralists recognize in themselves.

For example, to compare Althusserian theory in its "raw" form to the work of post-Marxists such as Ernesto Laclau is to see that, at the least, what the former offers cannot simply be subsumed under post-structuralist social theory and cultural criticism. Althusser's theory rewrites the Marxist totality as a structural, rather than expressive, totality, and he saw his project as a direct onslaught on the idea of a self-sufficient subject that is at the heart of, for instance, Sartre's existential-ism or Lukács's account of proletariat consciousness. But if these strike us as familiar postmodern themes, his deployment of relations of pro-duction as the analytical category that underpins all others marks a dimension that is not necessarily postmodern. This dimension leads to a rather remarkable situation where Althusser's theory draws formally similar criticism from ideological quarters that are otherwise opposed on substantive issues. Thus he is attacked—as Mohanty does—for proposing a concept of the subject that is ultimately too determinist, too skeptical, to be truly useful for an explanation of human agency.[8] From what Mohanty will call a postmodern standpoint, however, Laclau and Chantal Mouffe fault Althusser for the same limitation; indeed for them, a good account of agency requires a deeper deconstruction of the sub-ject and subjectivity, deeper, that is, than Althusser's tentative gesture in that direction. For the post-Marxist theorists, Althusser cannot go the required distance because he also operates with a traditional Marxist tool, namely, a reductive subordination of social relations to economic determination. On this view, his notorious "last instance," or the insis-tence on a pure theoretical realm that transcends ideology, betray a view of the process of knowing that flies in the face of his own flirtation with Lacanian psychoanalysis. On this score, both Marxists and post-Marx-ists or, in Mohanty's terms, realists and non-realists, fault Althusser on the same grounds, but for antithetical reasons. Where for Mohanty Althusser goes too far with the decentring of the subject, for Laclau and Mouffe he doesn't go far enough. We need, then, to consider the possi-bility that Althusser's theory may be useful precisely because it invites and sustains the pulling and shoving bestowed on it by mutually opposed ideological interlocutors.

Althusser is most notorious, perhaps, for his notion that history and social processes unfold in a multilevel structure that is somehow ultimately determined, "in the last instance," by the economic level. At this point, I am not concerned with whether or not this claim is correct. What I should like to do for now is to focus on the epistemological side to Althusser. In the section that follows, I elaborate the sense in which, whatever other problems his theoretical system contains, Althusser's account of ideology and subjectivity retains two crucial promises for postcolonial cultural criticism. First, it opens up a way of thinking and talking about human agency and cultural practice that accommodates Mohanty's reservations about the temptations of simplistic relativism. Second, it does so in a way that can survive the force of the "post-Marxist" critique of such poststructuralists as Laclau and Mouffe. I do so by locating Althusser in a nexus that takes off from Antonio Gramsci and leads onto the project of radical democracy associated with the poststructuralist theorists Laclau and Mouffe.

But first, a couple of qualifications. My discussion is based primarily on the famous ISAs essay, and my interest is in the *logic,* rather than argumentative tightness, of its claims. Put differently, I begin with the premise that the essay is neither timeless in its substance, nor watertight as a piece of argumentative exposition. As Warren Montag has suggested, however, to the extent that it is subtitled "Notes Towards an Investigation," we can from this temporal distance learn from it despite, or indeed, because of, its weaknesses.[9] For our present purposes, the promise of the ISA essay lies in its account of how we know what we claim to know. Whether or not Althusserian theory fails as a Marxist theory of capitalist society and socialist struggle, my contention is that its account of ideology offers, first, a valuable materialist epistemology, and second, a basis for thinking through the dynamics of struggle—be this in the discursive or the concrete political domain.[10]

The crucial term to begin with is, of course, hegemony. Gramsci's use of the notion of hegemony is geared towards a conceptualization of the workings of society in its totality, insofar as society is seen as a relational structure composed of distinct and diverse, but interactive units or levels. For Gramsci, society at the height of capitalist production is based on a logic of hegemony. Gramsci worked and thought against a background of liberal political science and economics. In the terms of the liberal framework, the State is the arm of society created by society for the welfare of society. The process has a passive, agent-less provenance: the development of society via the economy ("its needs") finds expression in the order and organization of civil society; civil society, in turn, consummates its development in the establishment of the State, which then functions to keep civil society in order.[11]

Into this narrative, Gramsci introduces agency and conflict. First, the development of society itself feeds on contradiction and intersubjective conflict, and second, this conflict, resulting in a war of interests, accounts for particular configurations in the evolution of state and civil society apparatuses. In the well-known military metaphor, a society with a well-entrenched bourgeoisie and state apparatuses represents that phase of the war when the dominant class has a hegemonic control of

the apparatuses that serve its interests. In his words, "the massive structures of the modern democracies, both as State organisations, and as
complexes of associations in civil society, constitute for the art of politics as it were the 'trenches' and the permanent fortifications of the front
in the war of position" (243). Civil society therefore denotes the site
where hegemony can be glimpsed, where domination, or the dominant
view, exerts its hand such that reality appears given—just the way things
are or, the best of possible worlds.

Thus in the passage below, Gramsci is discussing what he called
the "educative and formative role of the State":

> [The state's] aim is always that of creating new and higher types of
> civilisation; of adapting the "civilisation" and the morality of the
> broadest popular masses to the necessities of the continuous devel-
> opment of the economic apparatus of production; hence of evolving
> even physically new types of humanity. But how will each single
> individual succeed in incorporating himself into the collective man,
> and how will educative pressure be applied to single individuals so
> as to obtain their consent and their collaboration, turning necessity
> and coercion into "freedom?" (242)

In one sense, the question Gramsci poses in this passage may be said to
constitute the point of departure for Althusser's theory of ideology. As is
well known, Althusser's reading of Marx insists that the latter's conception of society is spatial, and the base-superstructure idea works as an
architectural metaphor.

But Althusser sees the classical Marxist formulation as being limited by its descriptiveness. On the one hand, it may encourage an occlu-
sion of Marx's fundamental break with Hegel, namely, the difference of
his conception of society from the Hegelian totality. Further, its spatial
formulation, and the metaphoricity of that formulation, makes it inca-
pable of accounting for the workings of society as a structure. To this
end, Althusser contends that we cannot know the internal workings of
the structure unless we look at it from the perspective of *reproduction*.
His notion of the state apparatus and its complementarity with the ideological state apparatuses is his way of looking at society from the point
of view of reproduction. The social machine needs a mechanism that will
ensure that the worker, first and foremost, perceives his cycle of walking
through the factory gates every morning as an instrumental positioning,
necessary to the natural, pragmatic course of things. Where the state
repressive apparatus keeps him in line through force when necessary, the
ideological state apparatuses (churches, schools, philanthropic/patriotic
clubs, etc.) keep him in line by inducing his consent to stay in line.

But he does more: his definition of *ideology* marks another significant contribution. To get at this significance, let us look again through Gramsci. Gramsci relates the workings of state apparatuses clearly to ideology—the latter being the most effective and insidious weapon of the former. He saw full well that ideology is a representational category: an objectification through practices, norms, etc. of the specific network of social configurations. Gramsci went far enough as to posit that ideology exists only as practice, in and through which historical entities—individual and collective—perceive their world and their relation to that world. For Gramsci, classical Marxism erred insofar as it viewed ideology as being external to the structure of society, an externality which is then taken to mean that ideology is "off the mark"; that is to say, illusory and mired in false consciousness as far as the true structure of society is concerned. On the contrary, ideology is in Gramsci's view very much a necessary coordinate of every social system; it needs therefore to be analyzed "historically, in the terms of the philosophy of praxis, as a superstructure" (376).

On this score, Gramsci made a distinction between what he called "historically organic ideologies, those, that is, which are necessary to a given structure," and those "that are arbitrary, rationalistic, or 'willed'" (376–77). Two consequences derive from this. First, Gramsci's distinction between organic as against arbitrary ideologies presupposes the precision of the one, as against the imprecision, the relative error, of the other. "To the extent," wrote Gramsci, "that ideologies are historically necessary they have a validity which is 'psychological'; they 'organise' human masses, and create the terrain on which men move, acquire consciousness of their position, struggle, etc. To the extent that they are arbitrary they only create individual 'movements,' polemics and so on (though even these are not useless, since they function like an error which by contrasting with truth, demonstrates it)" (377). Gramsci's notion of ideology implicitly maintains the true/false binarism central to the classical Marxist conception. The difference is that, whereas classical Marxism worked with the "scientific versus ideological" schema, Gramsci redesignates the categories. The result is that he admits ideology as necessary to the structure but inscribes a distinction between "organic" versus "arbitrary" ideologies—thereby leaving us with a true/false dualism.

According to Althusser, ideology is a representational category. It is representational because it exists as practice—in beliefs, norms, rituals, etc.—in and through which subjects represent to themselves their world and their relation to that world. However, what is represented in ideology is not the "real" relation between subjects and their world.

Althusser grounds this proposition in Lacan's schema of the imaginary, the symbolic, and their relationship to the "real."[12] For Lacan, the real is that sphere which lies beyond the subject's grasped reality and which therefore eludes absolute apprehension. As Alan Sheridan has observed, Lacan's real "is not to be confused with reality, which is perfectly knowable: the object of desire knows no more than that, since for it reality is entirely phantasmatic" (*Écrits*, x). That knowable reality, however, comes to us only through the "imaginary": that is to say, only through perceived "images." In other words, we grasp reality only by means of image and concept.[13] The symbolic, on the other hand, denotes the realm of language, of relational activity; it is the order wherein the reality of every given thing establishes itself in differential relation—and, by definition, only as such—to every other thing.

If we combine these two planes, the situation we get goes something like this: the individual who grasps reality via the mechanism of the imaginary does so because the symbolic order confers on him or her the sense of self (i.e. the subjectivity) on the basis of which he or she can then delimit, in the very act of grasping, the object that is being grasped. Consequently, while the imaginary denotes a site where perception itself occurs; and while the symbolic facilitates the mechanism of the imaginary because it is only through its (i.e., the symbolic order's) differential effects that the subject registers what it will thenceforth take to be the substantiality of reality, the real is the order that the symbolic cannot reach. The real, in other words, is constitutively precluded from the cognitive mastery of the imaginary mechanism: "the real [is] that which is lacking in the symbolic order, the ineliminable residue of all articulation, the foreclosed element, which may be approached, but never grasped: the unbilical cord of the symbolic" (*Écrits*, x).

By couching his account of ideology in psychoanalytical terms, Althusser seeks to rearticulate Marxism such that ideology remains integral to the structure of society while also transcending the true-false binarism. Bearing the Lacanian schema in mind, it becomes easy to see that the representation of reality in and as ideology necessarily belongs to the imaginary plane, and the representation achieved on this plane is enabled by the symbolic order. As Jane Gallop has argued, "If the difference between the imaginary and the symbolic is understood as an opposition between two identities, we can be sure we have given an imaginary reading of the terms. It could be said that the symbolic can be encountered only as a tear in the fabric of the imaginary, a revealing interruption. The paths to the symbolic are thus *in* the imaginary. The symbolic can be reached by not trying to avoid the imaginary, by knowingly being *in* the imaginary" (60).

Another consequence of the imaginary-symbolic terrain on which Althusser places the workings of ideology can be found in his notion of interpellation, that is to say, the process by which ideology constitutes individuals into subjects. The "subjectification" of individuals (i.e., interpellation) lies squarely in the Lacanian symbolic plane, since the individual becomes a subject who "comprehends" himself and others only through the effects of the symbolic order. Caught in the trace effect of the imaginary and the symbolic orders, in the overdetermined sociality in which he functions, the worker conceives of his reality within such terms as are inscribed in the symbolic order. He conceives of himself as a subject who consciously works for his employer (consent); what he does not know—and cannot know—is the "real" fact that the structure has always already interpellated him, has always already constituted him into a subject whose self-apprehension is to participate in a constructed inscription rendered natural and transparent. For Althusser, "The reality in question in this mechanism, the reality which is necessarily ignored *(méconnue)* in the very forms of recognition . . . is indeed, in the last resort, the reproduction of the relations of production and of the relations deriving from them" (182–83).

Of course, there is an interesting problem in the theory as I have just set it out. The problem lies in Althusser's attempt to hold within the same argument a constructivist notion of ideology and a scientistic claim that relations of production constitute the overarching analytical category, the ultimate determinant of social relations. For one, and at the most basic level, Althusser's interpellation comes across as a totally encompassing mechanism, one which the subject cannot escape. His account makes the structure, and the ideologies that keep it in place, into a watertight machine that so heavily overdetermines subjects that there can be no way out. Patrick Brantlinger has thus argued that Gramsci's ideology offers a stronger vision because it leaves, in its very formulation, an active space for agency.[14] For Brantlinger, the very language of "positioning," or "movement" suggests that Gramsci is as interested in how individuals are subjected as he is in how they struggle against their subjection. Gramsci does not confer on ideology an absolute status whereby it simply acts on subjects, leaving no room for what Laclau and Mouffe are later to call "counter articulation."

We shall presently see that this problem can be resolved without giving up what may be called the fundamental logic of the Althusserian account of ideology. To this end, it is best to pose the problem as an epistemological one: how is it possible for Althusser himself to theorize ideological overdetermination if he is himself an overdetermined subject? How is it possible to set out the form of a system in which—by the terms of one's theory—one is always already mired? This problem is linked to Althusser's celebrated privileging of dialectical materialism as the mode of thought adequately equipped to apprehend the historical process with scientific precision, that is to say, beyond ideology. Opposed to ideology, theory here passes over into the view from above, a purchase on objective truth that transcends the misrecognitions of ideology. On this view, Marxist "science" represents the perspective on society and the historical process that captures "the real," escaping thereby the circumscription of the imaginary/symbolic mechanism.

From a poststructuralist perspective, it is easy to see the problem in this aspect of Althusser. However, as Gayatri Spivak has suggested in her interview with Walter Adamson, Althusser later came to modify this position, granting more complexity to the force-field of ideology and conceding the necessity of constant revision to a claim he had posited with eloquent self-assurance earlier in his career (Spivak, "Postcolonial Critic," 50–58). Spivak approaches Althusser's legacy from this direction, claiming that the latter "did keep on saying that one must continually rethink the distinctions between ideology and history, ideology and science, ideology and philosophy, and he finally came out recommending a *pratique sauvage*, a wild practice, a wild philosophy" (54). She goes on to suggest a way of relating to the Althusserian problematic: "we have the task of re-inscribing the Althusserian insight there [i.e., in the Althusser who is less comfortable with bipolar distinctions] rather than throwing him away as a closet idealist" (54).

I agree with Spivak's suggestion, noting at the same time that we have here moved from the grand question of society and change (as phenomenal realities), to a narrower one of epistemology—how we know these realities that we do, somehow, more or less, know.[15] Looked at this way, the problem in Althusser's theoretical system may reside in a peculiar interaction, within it, of (i) an account of social and cultural processes, and (ii) an account of how the mind comes to know those processes. This is a way of formulating the distinction that Mohanty makes, between Althusser's substantive claims about social structure and the epistemological theory that subtends that claim. Against Spivak's suggestion that "Althusser was ill-served . . . by turning to Lacan in order to develop his notion of the primacy of interpellation," my claim is that Althusser's Lacanian predication of interpellation is precisely what makes the epistemological logic of his theory useful for an analysis of disparate (but ultimately kindred) discursive formations such as this book undertakes.

To formulate this value, let us turn to the path pursued by Ernesto Laclau and Chantal Mouffe in *Hegemony and Socialist Strategy*.[16] Their theory undertakes to facilitate a new conception of the social, one that transcends both Hegelian Marxist and Althusserian privileging of class and relations of production. The rethinking of Marxism that they offer is meant to facilitate what they call radical democracy. Admitting Gramsci's notion of hegemony, Laclau and Mouffe uncover in it an ultimate essentialism, for class remains Gramsci's "single unifying principle." Although Gramsci sees society as being run via a logic of hegemony, and although he grants—through his concept of "collective wills," or that of the "historical bloc"—that a simultaneous articulation of diverse elements constitutes the struggle for hegemony, he still subsumes everything under the umbrella of class, thereby getting stuck with an essentialist residue.[17]

This critique of Gramsci is to be expected, since a crucial part of their argument rests on the ineliminable multiplicity of overdetermined identities. For this reason, class has to undergo "de-essentialisation" in Laclau's and Mouffe's hands in order that the multiplicity of subject positions that crisscross even within the same class can receive adequate attention—indeed, can *transform* the entire theoretical ensemble. In the same vein, they reject Althusser's concept of determination in the last instance: "If the concept of overdetermination was unable to produce the totality of its deconstructive effects within Marxist discourse, this was because, from the beginning, an attempt was made to render it compatible with another central moment in Althusserian discourse that is, strictly speaking, incompatible with the first: namely, determination in the last instance by the economy" (98). Within the terms of *Hegemony and Socialist Strategy*, Althusser's theory of overdetermination is useful only to the extent that it is not qualified with the radically incompatible notion of an economic determination in the last instance.

The authors of *Hegemony* proceed on two levels. First, they retain Gramsci's formulation of hegemony without his underlying privileging of class; and, second, they hold on to Althusser's psychoanalytic formulation of overdetermination—rescuing it, in their view, from the regression that would qualify it with a determination in the last instance. Armed with these reworkings of Gramsci and Althusser, their model of hegemony is couched in terms of discursivity. *Discourse* designates for them an existent or a hoped for articulatory practice, the network of relations that exists (or is hoped for) as the "status quo." The different positions in this network, "insofar as they appear articulated within a discourse" (105), they call *moments*. They use *element* to designate any difference that has not become a "moment," any differential position that is suppressed in order for the articulated practice that keeps "discourse" in place to be realized. What this means is that, (i) the social is constructed as articulatory practices whereby subjects are "assigned" absolute places in the articulated whole, but (ii) this assignment of subject-positions within the articulated whole can never be as total as Althusser's model suggests, for that would mean that there will only be moments and no elements: "The transition from the 'elements' to the 'moments' is never entirely fulfilled. A no-man's-land thus emerges, making the articulatory practice possible. In this case, there is no social identity fully protected from a discursive exterior that deforms it and prevents it becoming fully sutured. Both the identities and the relations lose their necessary character. As a systematic structural ensemble, the relations are unable to absorb the identities; but as the identities are purely relational, this is but another way of saying that there is no identity which can be fully constituted" (110–11). On their terms, identity does not pre-exist the moment of struggle, the moment of articulation; and this is because it is in and through the system of differences activated at the site of struggle that identities acquire what may be called the agency of signification. Posed this way, Laclau and Mouffe have a good case in pointing to the problem in any essentialist or totalized notion of identity. Let us isolate a couple of its uses.

Nobody would disagree with the proposition that no single class constitutes a homogenous unit: one needs only to recall empirical instances of intraclass struggles, say, between immigrant workers and the "native" workforce, or over differentials relating to racial supremacy or sexual orientation, to entertain the import of their position. Marching as workers in some rural logging company or urban corporation, the black marcher, his gay sister, and the young man beside them who happens to belong to the Aryan brotherhood can occupy the same subject-position: that is, make meaning as workers, without each losing his/her other identities, identities that in different circumstances will translate into a different set of subject-positions. This provides a way out of the straitjacket of interpellation in Althusser's theory; with the theory of subject positions, it becomes possible to think of subjects as individuals who are, in every given social formation, hailed into heterogeneous identity locations along such axis as race, class, gender, or nationality. Since these locations are not necessarily coextensive with one another, the hailing of individuals into them is never total and inviolable: the racial subject is crisscrossed, its straitjacket potentially undermined, by the complexities of class or gender. The recasting of Derrida's notion of a "surplus of meaning," namely, the idea that there are always differential subjects and subject-positions constitutively outside the hegemonic network of moments, has value as a way of drawing attention to what or who is left out in a society's reckoning of itself and its values.

In this sense, *Hegemony* marks a refinement of Althusser, for whom structural ensembles interpellate so seamlessly that there can only be moments and no elements: no room, on the terms of *Hegemony*, for disarticulation or counterarticulation. Concretely, this means there cannot be social change or even contestation of the dominant (hegemonic) system. It is important to say "refinement" because the theory of radical democracy remains in a fundamental sense within an Althusserian frame. That is, the insistence on overdetermination, and the deconstruction of the notion of a fully sutured identity or totalized knowledge, do not constitute a total break with the space opened up in Althusser's concept of interpellation. In a sympathetic assessment of Laclau's and Mouffe's theory, Slavoj Žižek has observed that although it "presents perhaps the most radical breakthrough in modern social theory" (Žižek 251), the argument of *Hegemony* is weakest in its conceptualization of the subject. Žižek endorses *Hegemony*'s dispersion of the unitary subject, achieved via the concept of subject-positions, but he insists that there remains something fundamentally Althusserian. For him, "such a notion of the subject-positions still enters the frame of the Althusserian ideological interpellation as constitutive of the subject: the subject-position is a mode of how we recognize our position of an (interested) agent of the social process, of how we experience our commitment to a certain ideological cause" (251). In other words, Žižek stresses in Althusser's theory its Lacanian predication of subjectification. According to him, if indeed the process of subjectification entails misrecognition; if, "as soon as we respond to . . . interpellation and assume a certain subject-position, we are a priori, *per definitionem* deluded . . . it is precisely the Lacanian notion of the subject as 'the empty place of the structure' which describes the subject in its confrontation with . . . antagonism" (251).

Žižek's claim is important in one basic respect: it suggests that, regardless of other problems in the Althusserian system, the narrative of ideology developed in the psychoanalytical register of the ISA essay can be isolated and taken on its own merit. This is where we are brought back to the claim Mohanty makes, that Althusser's theoretical system fails on account of its marriage of a scientist thesis to a constructivist epistemology. We are now in a better position to pose Althusser's problem in the most penetrating way, with regard to my own specific concern in this book: he offers an epistemological thesis and contradicts that thesis in the account of social structure and intersubjective relations that the thesis was meant to serve. As an account that claims to make known the totality of existing social structure(s) and practices, Althusserian theory is internally contradicted by his definition of ideology as a process of interpellation by means of which subjects enter sociality, as well as the field where practices unfold. For as Laclau's and Mouffe's contribution shows, the way subjects enter social relations is indissociable from the relations themselves: it is indeed the particular relation that constitutes the subject as such. And yet, insofar as every particular (contingent) relation is based on the constitution of individuals into subjects, Althusser's Lacanian predication of the process of subjectification remains in force. Laclau and Mouffe make sense, but precisely in making sense, they make Althusser more intelligible and serviceable.

We may thus grant Laclau's and Mouffe's dispersion of the Althusserian unitary class subject and still remain with a refined but fundamentally Althusserian narrative of subjectification, or the subject's road to knowledge. In this sense, the theory of radical democracy explains agency (that is, why human beings are able to change their outlook as well as their world) in a way that Althusser's theory, insofar as its claim to be a theory of the social totality remains unqualified, cannot manage coherently. But if Althusserianism falters as social theory, because it does not persuasively explain how subjects are able at times to change their world, its account of ideology and interpellation remain sound. The social theory may falter, but when pressed in a direction logically immanent to it, the epistemological thesis that accompanies it is serviceable. Against Mohanty's view, then, Althusser's epistemological thesis can be refined and extended (as Laclau and Mouffe have done, in my analysis) in a way that entertains and explains human agency. On this view, Althusser's "the real" is neither reality as it is perceived by the subject of ideology, nor "scientific truth" as the early Althusser tended to insist.

It may be objected that there is a fundamental inconsistency in the fact that Althusser's theory uses Lacanian apparatus—that is, a theory of constitutive lack—to elaborate a materialist theory that wants to claim a measure of epistemological certitude. In our view, however, there is a basic but decisive response to this sort of objection. Skepticism about the reach of knowledge need not be understood to mean skepticism about the human capacity to know things. We can know many things about an object, but we cannot know all there is to be known about that object. Moreover, knowing a lot (however much that happens to be) does not mean that there is only one way, one language, in which the object should or could be known. As I argued in my analysis of Mohanty's contribution, human beings are subjects with agency to the extent that they are capable of doing (or knowing) things that are yet to be thought, things that cannot be thought, until the event of the doing. This is not to say that the doing happens in a vacuum or without precedence; very much to the contrary, it is to say that human actions happen in space and time, but cannot simply be correlated, in a relationship of immediacy and simple causality, to the social density that underpins them. Likewise, actions always draw on or model themselves after prior actions by the same or another agent; nonetheless, the shape of a particular action in the context of the social density that subtends it cannot be traced in a linear fashion from the trajectory of its prehistory. In familiar poststructuralist idiom, there is repetition to be sure, but the repetition comes with its difference.

REPRESENTATION AS IDEOLOGY

Our concern in the preceding section was to zero in on Althusser's account of ideology and subjectification and draw out its implication as a theory of knowledge. This book deploys a crucial insight at the heart of Althusser's definition of ideology as material practice. For Althusser, as we have indicated, ideology is at once a representational category and a material practice. Thus understood, ideology straddles two indissociable levels: there is, first, the *representational* level—what we are told we are and what we thereafter claim to be. In turn, both subsist and persist because we perform these representations (inherited as well as actively constructed) as much in our daily business of living as in our context-specific contemplation of that life.[18] On this view, ideology is representation that endures because it constitutes subjects and subjectivity, and because it is inscribed in rituals and institutions. Insofar as one cannot act and think on that act in the same temporal moment, the very inscription of ideology in material practice is what makes action possible and at the same time marked by a constitutive incompletion, a lack. Posed as an epistemological claim, what this means is that the self that acts does so on the basis of a knowledge that is at the same time a misrecognition. By pressing a conceptual distinction between reality (as it is accessible to us via the mechanism of the imaginary and the symbolic), and the real (as that which eludes the self-assurance of the absolute)—a distinction that Althusser's text invites—we open up a space where knowledge becomes historicizable as achievement and lack, agency and limit.

My concern in this book is to use this account of ideology and interpellation (and the logic of knowledge production it opens up) to enter into a dialectical analysis of current theory and African letters. As already stated, my contention is that if it rests at a simple rejection of the nativist limitations of third world discourses, current poststructuralist theory in its postcolonial vector is not consistent with its own (fundamentally Althusserian) premises.[19] The next chapter, then, concentrates on the debate around modernity and postmodernity between Habermas and Lyotard, and concludes with a discussion of poststructuralist theories of postcoloniality. The discussion is necessary because the purpose of this book is to provide an "appropriate representational milieu," to borrow from Kofi Agawu, for African letters.[20] For the agency of African letters to be adequately rendered and appreciated, it is essential to have a clear picture of this representational milieu. This is because it is within this milieu, this context, that African letters acquires the kind of discursive significance or agency that I claim for it.

CHAPTER TWO

CONTEMPORARY THEORY
AND THE DEMAND FOR AGENCY

The first chapter set out a basic outline of some of the issues at stake in recent discussions of modern (or postmodern) culture and the study of culture. Looked at from the perspective of current literary theory and cultural criticism, it seems fair to say that a crucial task for cultural studies is generally seen to lie in casting a backward glance at what the West has wrought, so to speak, in the process of its self-constitution as a civilization as well as a "civilizing" influence on others. Involved in this glance is the impulse to reassess the "status of the subject," as it has come to be called. Whether understood in collective terms or in the narrower sense of the individual consciousness that thinks and, in thinking, fashions or contributes to collective living and knowing, the postindustrial Western subject has emerged as a crucial concept—up for grabs, for or against—in contemporary theory.

It should be of real consequence, then, that if one comes at the issue of culture and its study from the perspective of African letters and its creators, all the fuss about and around the subject would appear to be beside the point. If there is any concern with that subject to be discerned, it is a concern that is by and large polemical, one that fixes the West as a steady, recognizable monad to be transcended. In other words, the point is not to figure out anew what exactly the concept means, meant, or should/can be made to mean; very much to the contrary, the West is here grasped as a fully historical, directly meaningful idea *and* reality. On these terms, what is at stake is how to transcend the shadow of that idea and the reality it has engendered. What is at stake is the rediscovery of what, in black Africa, the West had to misunderstand or misrepresent in the heady movement of its own self-constitution. In the next chapter, we shall discuss this scenario by examining the case of Africanist literary criticism as one instance of this impulse in African letters. To be well placed to grasp the full import of this scenario when we come to it, however, it is crucial to try to understand what indeed is involved in the reassessment of the Western subject as it is currently being carried out in theory and criticism.

The argument of this chapter is developed in two steps. First, I take up the debate around "postmodernism" as it has developed in the intertextual dialogue and, at some points, direct confrontation between Habermas and Lyotard. In a second step, I turn to discussions of "postcoloniality" as this has been elaborated in the work of Homi Bhabha and Gayatri Spivak, on the one hand, and some of their critics, Benita Parry and Helen Tiffin, on the other. By starting with the debate around postmodernity in the social theory of Habermas and Lyotard, our aim is to explore the way non-Western otherness figures in the interstices of their positions. Both thinkers require the figure of the non-West as a contrastive enabler of their meditation on the West's specific condition in modernity. The unavoidable consequence of a conceptual field mapped in this way is that the non-West cannot be seen in its own specificity, still less in the complex historicity of its imbrication with the West. This imbrication is willy-nilly material and conceptual, body and mind; consequently, it has the status of a germinal node in modernity's contours. Whatever insights issue forth from a social theory that overlooks this node are thus constitutively flawed. To mix metaphors, insofar as a crucial (even if unwilling) actor in the drama of modernity is not allowed to speak its lines, the action can neither be substantively comprehensive nor fully rewarding.

In this direction, it is an important achievement of poststructuralist postcolonial theory that in the work of Bhabha or Spivak, social and cultural theory is challenged to face the materiality of our benighted actor. And yet, the theories of Bhabha and Spivak invite, precisely by their own logic, an overcoming. In seeking to compel "mainstream" theory to acknowledge the challenge of otherness, current postcolonial theory is pressed to speak the language of "the mainstream" as it is presently configured. To be sure, this is not necessarily a problem (to a large extent in fact, it is unavoidable); it becomes a problem for our understanding of cultural practice, however, when the forms and contents of previous challenges (such as one finds in third world cultural nationalist discourses) are inadequately rendered. My argument in this book is of course that, to facilitate genuine and productive dialogue between contemporary Anglo-American theory and African letters, it is necessary to render the latter in its specificity. For that very reason, it is equally necessary to explore the claims and counterclaims in Anglo-American postcolonial theory on the terms of the theories themselves. The present chapter aims to do this.

The sense of modernity with which we shall be working is the sociophilosophical one, and perched at the tip of such an account would be Max Weber's notion of rationalization and instrumental reason. For Weber, if medieval and pre-Reformation European civilization rested upon a steadfast religiosity, an autocratic Christian episteme, what distinguishes modernity is a secularization of civil society in both the political and the epistemological realms.[1] Weber's formulation contains two implications. First, it conflates both the cognitive-epistemological and the concrete-political, the latter being the objectification of the spirit entailed in the former. Second, it assumes the moment of modernity as the result of a ferment that is unique in its essence and impact, and that is exclusive to the history of the West. In the first lecture of *The Philosophical Discourse of Modernity,* Habermas constructs a genealogy of this term, linking it to its current resonance in the concept of modernization—with a technical, primarily sociological connotation.[2] "Modernization," writes Habermas,

> was introduced as a technical term only in the 1950s. It is the mark of a theoretical approach that takes up Weber's problem but elaborates it with the tools of social-scientific functionalism. The concept of modernization refers to a bundle of processes that are cumulative and mutually reinforcing: to the formation of capital and the mobilization of resources; to the development of the forces of production and the increase in the productivity of labor; to the establishment of centralized political power and the formation of national identities; to the proliferation of rights of political participation, of urban forms of life, and of formal schooling; to the secularization of values and norms; and so on. (2)

This redeployment extends the range and promise of modernity beyond its Weberian European peculiarity, constituting it into a larger dynamic that encompasses the modern world in general. As is well known, the distinction Habermas points up, between an understanding of modernity as, on the one hand, a philosophical-epistemological category, and on the other, a practical political objectification, goes back to Kant. As Ernst Behler has observed, it was Kant who, "[t]hrough his three critiques ... subdivided reason onto the faculties of theoretical reason *(Critique of Pure Reason),* practical reason *(Critique of Practical Reason),* and aesthetic judgement *(Critique of Judgement)* and thereby established

special courts for the three cultural spheres of philosophy and metaphysics, morality and law, and aesthetics and poetics (17). Habermas
may well be right in insisting, contra Weber, that the philosophical discourse of modernity should not be hastily held accountable for the con-
crete-sociological phenomena that characterize the contemporary scene;
that is to say, that the concept should not be collapsed into a reality,
however construed, in a relation of immediate referentiality, a relation
of pure objectification. Nonetheless, it is the case that in both realms, the
West occupies center stage: it inaugurates modernity as we now understand it, both as an "objective reality," and as the concept that attempts
to grasp that reality.

Contemporary critiques of modernity engage the concept in one of
three senses: either as a philosophical discourse, or as a sociopolitical objectification, or in these two senses conflated (whether or not problemati-
cally). For our purposes, the term "modernity" is to be understood as
straddling the dual senses of philosophy and metaphysics, and morality and
law (that is to say, theoretical, and practical-sociological). Using the term in
this third sense will afford us an opportunity to think about the conceptual
problems that might be entailed in their conflation. Throughout this book,
I shall be suggesting in various ways that there are significant problems
involved in a conflation of the theoretical with the concrete-practical, of
thought with objective reality. But for now, let us proceed with the third
sense of modernity just isolated. In this third sense, modernity is a state of
social and cognitive being, and this state is also a trend: it carries an evolutionary connotation whereby social collectivities are assumed to be
involved in a progressive evolution toward full maturity, or taken to be
regressing from that fully evolved ideal. This evolution, its stresses and conflicts, becomes the object of theoretical discourse—the latter witnessing to,
participating in, or influencing the adventures of the former.

Where Lyotard emerges from a conceptual backcloth we can generally call poststructuralist, Habermas struggles with a background in
Frankfurt School Marxism, a tradition he wants to transcend by means
of an eclectic synthesizing of insights drawn from sources such as systems theory, hermeneutics, and linguistics. In considering both of them
together, I am not seeking to dwell on the substantive purchase of their
different accounts.[4] What I wish to do is to abstract the basic lines of the
divergent arguments presented, and to highlight the conceptual and
rhetorical operations at play therein. My claim is that beyond the divergences between the two thinkers on the theme of modernity, they share
a similar angle of version. The angle of vision that they share cannot use-
fully illuminate the peculiar inflections of modernity to be found in
African letters.

HABERMAS AND COMMUNICATIVE CONSENSUS

Habermas is one of the most celebrated opponents of poststructuralist thought and the very idea of a postmodernity. In his view, those thinkers generally referred to as poststructuralists are in fact neoconservatives who are simply re-enacting a familiar and, by now, tired undertaking. As he puts it in "Modernity—an Incomplete Project,"

> The "young conservatives" recapitulate the basic experience of aes-
> thetic modernity. They claim as their own the revelations of a decen-
> tered subjectivity, emancipated from the imperatives of work and
> usefulness, and with this experience they step out of the modern
> world. On the basis of modernistic attitudes they justify an irrecon-
> cilable antimodernism. They remove into the sphere of the far-away
> and the archaic the spontaneous powers of imagination, self-experi-
> ence and emotion. To instrumental reason they juxtapose in
> Manichean fashion a principle only accessible through evocation, be
> it the will to power or sovereignty, Being or the Dionysiac force of
> the poetical. In France this line leads from Georges Bataille via
> Michel Foucault to Jacques Derrida. (14)

Habermas's case is at its best when he takes the issue at stake back in time to the tangled era of its prior eruptions: when he historicizes the "post" in postmodernism to show that its problematic was once that of the moment in relation to which it claims its naming. For him, the proclamations of postmodernist thinkers merely recall the claims of the proponents of a rebellious aestheticism beginning in the eighteenth cen-tury and culminating in Baudelaire and the surrealists; the "post" in postmodernism merely recalls similar dramas of self-representation, where the "new" radically requires the "old" to be able to delineate itself. "With varying content," he observes, "the term 'modern' again and again expresses the consciousness of an epoch that relates itself to the past of antiquity, in order to view itself as the result of a transition from the old to the new" (3).

Habermas feels that in their attack on Enlightenment rationality, the poststructuralist philosophers paint too uni-dimensional a picture of their object of critique. Although Foucault explicitly sees his project to be an attempt to destabilize what he calls a "calm, continuist image"[4] of the Enlightenment epistemological order, Habermas would insist that his (Foucault's) project cannot proceed without such an image: that is, an erroneous uni-dimensional and continuist characterization of Enlighten-ment discourse. Thus, in "An Alternative Way out of the Philosophy of the Subject: Communicative Versus Subject-Centered Reason," he insists that the poststructuralists "do not see that the philosophical counterdis-course which, from the start, accompanied the philosophical discourse of modernity initiated by Kant already drew up a counterreckoning for subjectivity as the principle of modernity" (295).[6] For him, "the basic conceptual aporias of the philosophy of consciousness, so acutely diag-nosed by Foucault in the final chapter of *The Order of Things,* were already analyzed by Schiller, Fichte, Schelling, and Hegel in a similar fashion" (295).

Kenneth Lea has observed that the "peculiar 'objective' form, the appropriation of pragmatic linguistic theory, and [the] conceptual orga-nization" of Lyotard's *The Postmodern Condition* "all indicate that the book is aimed specifically at Habermas" (102). It is easy to see why Lyotard and Habermas cannot see eye to eye on the issue of modernity or the claims of a postmodernity. Even when they confront a third party, as in their divergent readings of Theodor Adorno, the event emerges with considerable symptomatic value. In "Adorno as The Devil," Lyotard argues that Adorno's critique of instrumental reason stops short because he (Adorno) failed to really exorcise the demon of a residual utopic yearning. By contrast, Habermas contends that Adorno fled too quickly from the task imposed on us precisely by that demon.

If Horkheimer's and Adorno's *The Dialectic of Enlightenment* (1944) is generally acknowledged as powerful deconstructive thinking before deconstruction became a buzzword in American literature departments, Habermas is not too impressed with the forerunners. "How can these two men of the Enlightenment (which they both remain)," he wonders, "be so unappreciative of the rational content of cultural modernity that all they perceive everywhere is a binding of rea-son and domination, of power and validity?"[6] The thrust of Habermas's claim here is twofold: (i) that Adorno and Horkheimer presume the pos-sibility of a self-positioning *outside* of modernity, and (ii), that to see reason as bound up with domination necessarily amounts to being "unappreciative of the rational content of cultural modernity." It is use-ful to note that even if it can be shown that Adorno and Horkheimer are "unappreciative" of the rational content of modernity, it is not clear how that amounts to a critique of their position. To charge a theoretical position with moral error (here, lack of due appreciation) says nothing about the internal consistency of that position. This example is not for-tuitous: it sets the stage for the drama that unfolds in Habermas' con-frontation with so-called poststructuralist ideas. To start with, the pre-suppositions   and   project   that   Habermas   imputes   to   the poststructuralists is often not what they conceive their project to be. When, for instance, he observes that what they advocate is an "antimodernism," or that the substantive revelations they claim as their own are self-avowedly "emancipated from the imperatives of work and use-fulness," such a characterization can only stick if it is argued out as a blindspot in the logic of their project, rather than as its predicative prin-ciple—whereas Habermas presents the charge as if it were the latter. On this count his attack is often reductionist and, therefore, constrained from the outset. But this is not the place to explore these issues. What follows is rather an account that takes Habermas at his word. Our pri-mary aim, let us remember, is less a matter of adjudicating between him and the poststructuralists, than it is of illustrating how Habermas con-ceives and elaborates the need to resume the incomplete project of Enlightenment rationality.

In the essay on Horkheimer and Adorno cited earlier, Habermas's reading of *The Dialectic of Enlightenment* proceeds by teasing out and comparing the impulse behind the book to that which underpinned the later work of Nietzsche. He adopts this strategy to enable him to distin-guish between the critiques of Enlightenment rationality initiated by the Frankfurt School and that which is now generally associated with post-structuralism. He writes: "On their [Horkheimer and Adorno] analysis, it is no longer possible to place hope in the liberating force of enlight-enment. Inspired by Benjamin's now ironic hope of the hopeless, they still did not want to relinquish the now paradoxical labor of conceptu-alization. We no longer share this mood, this attitude. And yet under the sign of a Nietzsche revitalized by poststructuralism, moods and attitudes are spreading that are confusingly like those of Horkheimer and Adorno. I would like to forestall this confusion" (106). It is as if, dis-turbed by the likes of Foucault or Lyotard claiming an affinity between their work and that of the Frankfurt School, and further alarmed that a hasty reading of, say, Adorno may indeed give the appearance of such an affinity, this heir to the tradition of critical theory finds it necessary to set the records straight. By reading Adorno and Horkheimer in the light of Nietzsche's passion, Habermas wants to demonstrate that the struggle of the two men to "enlighten the enlightenment about itself" is activated by an impulse that is significantly different from that of the poststructuralists. To watch him do this is to eavesdrop on a veritable drama. Habermas's account comes across as a narrative of epic quest-ing; the thinkers who people his thinking emerge as protagonists seeking a lost treasure, a reassuring perspective on modernity and its conflicts.

Let us follow him as he follows the questers. According to him, in setting for themselves the task of demystifying reason, Nietzsche, Horkheimer, and Adorno confront a paradox. This paradox is inherent to any such undertaking, for its very performance presupposes the faculty of reason itself. He calls this predicament one of performative contradiction, "the embarrassment of a critique that attacks the presuppositions of its own validity" (127). This contradiction leaves only two options left for the three protagonists. Nietzsche chose the first option: he attempted to avoid the devastating implication of the contradiction by resorting to a theory of power. Such a theory is for Habermas actually a non-theory: "It is without basis as a theory, if the categorical distinction between power claims and truth claims is the ground upon which *any* theoretical approach has to be enacted" (127). The categorical distinction Habermas here insists on, between "truth claims" and "power claims," is of crucial significance. We will defer it for now in order to consider the option taken by Horkheimer and Adorno; in doing this, we shall be brought back to the truth/power distinction so crucial to Habermas's rejection of Nietzsche and poststructuralism. According to Habermas, Horkheimer and Adorno are forced to elevate that contradiction itself to the status of a critical strategy; in other words, they could do no better than to thematize the performative contradiction involved in their project *as the point* of the project itself. Consequently, they ended up implying that the only effective way of countering the reifications of modernity is by "stirring open, holding open, and no longer wanting to overcome theoretically the performative contradiction inherent in an ideology critique that outstrips itself" (127).

Unlike Nietzsche—and by extension, his poststructuralist continuators—Horkheimer and Adorno do not attempt to outdo Enlightenment rationality and instrumental reason by developing a "better" theory. If anything, *theory* itself—the very act of developing a theory, and the confidence presupposed by the act—stands as integral to, and a symptom of, the disease they seek to expose. In Habermas's words, Horkheimer and Adorno realized that "[a]ny attempt to develop a theory at this level of reflection [i.e. where critique turns back on itself, thereby incurring a performative contradiction] would have to slide off into the groundless; they therefore eschew theory and practice determinate negation on an ad hoc basis, thus standing firm against that fusion of reason and power that plugs all crevices" (127–28). Put differently, what this claim entails is that Horkheimer and Adorno's critique of totality involves a conception that the will to theory *per se* marks a will to totalization. Although he disagrees with both men's choice, he also seems to want to recuperate them. For he readily historicizes their scepticism, noting that it was a reaction to "the state of the question by which Horkheimer and Adorno saw themselves confronted at the beginning of the 1940s" (129). He grants that they were right in concluding that critical theory could no longer rely on ideology critique as an effective procedural choice: conditions under Nazism rendered immanent critique impossible. The problem, however, is that the "uninhibited scepticism" to which they resorted was too extreme: "like historicism, they surrendered themselves to an uninhibited scepticism regarding reason, instead of weighing the grounds that cast doubt on this scepticism itself. In this way, perhaps, they could have set the normative foundations of critical social theory so deep that they would not have been disturbed by the decomposition of bourgeois culture that was then being enacted in Germany for all to see" (129).

At this point, it is helpful to reprise Habermas's moves so far. First, the project embarked upon by Nietzsche and the authors of *The Dialectic of Enlightenment* can only land them in an embarrassing predicament, that of a performative contradiction. Second, the latter do not follow the path Nietzsche trod in his doomed struggle to overcome the contradiction. Therefore, instead of Nietzsche's will to power, they end up at the dead end of an ad hoc critical procedure that Adorno was later to christen "negative dialectics." We are brought back, then, to the overall project of *The Philosophical Discourse of Modernity*, namely, that of exposing the weakness of poststructuralist theory. For what is being played out here is a systematic reclaiming of the Frankfurt School from the clutches of poststructuralism. Habermas's account enables him to focus not exclusively on the flaw in Adorno and Horkheimer's position, but also on the extreme withdrawal from social trauma that it symptomizes. It achieves two things: it tells us where Horkheimer and Adorno took a wrong turn, and—as Habermas would have it—warns us that we can learn from their predicament.

In effect, Habermas is jabbing at poststructuralism, telling us that we can do better. If we grant that, faced with the delicate moment of the 1940s, Horkheimer and Adorno took a wrong turn; and if we grant that even their wrong turn is more consistent than Nietzsche's before them, we would in effect be conceding the heart of Habermas's argument, namely, that there is a confusion somewhere if, late in the twentieth century, a Nietzschean resurgence aligns its passion with the Frankfurt School's. But we would also be conceding that it will be a regression to go back to Nietzsche when we can retrace Horkheimer's and Adorno's adventure back to the moment of their wrong turn. As already indicated, of course, that moment is the point where Horkheimer and Adorno found themselves confronted with a performative contradiction and stood right there, casting contradiction itself as critical procedure *and* substantive end. On Habermas's terms, this negative dialectics is at least consistent because it does not seek to dismantle Enlightenment Reason by replacing it with a "counter-Enlightenment" theory. That is to say, it does not fuse knowledge with power, paradoxically banishing theory to install counter-theory. But negative dialectics is limited because it wrongly assumes that its culmination in contradiction is the only option available: "Anyone who abides in a paradox on the very spot once occupied by philosophy with its ultimate groundings is not just taking up an uncomfortable position; one can only hold that place if one makes it at least minimally plausible that there is *no way out*. Even the retreat from an aporetic situation has to be barred, for otherwise there is a way—the way back" (128). It is to *the way back* that Habermas wants us to look. He is intent on reconstructing what Horkheimer and Adorno too quickly gave up on in order to restore critical theory to what he sees as its true vocation, to give it back its cutting edge. As he himself might put it, what he wants is a theory that would "set the normative foundations of critical theory so deep" (129) that critique does not surrender to scepticism—whether in the form of negative dialectics or of power. His theory of communicative action, elaborated in the two volumes of *The Theory of Communicative Action*, is an attempt at such a reconstruction. At the beginning of the first volume, Habermas makes it clear that his reconstruction requires the figure of an other; "the presuppositions of modern thought," he notes, "should become visible in the mirror of mythical thinking" (44). To represent prescientific, "mythical" thinking, he turns to the archives and retrieves Zande witchcraft practice.

This move is a familiar one, for the belief system of the Azande of central Africa have over the years become a ready instance of mythical rationality. In cultural anthropology, E. E. Evans-Pritchard's research among the Azande has generated a range of perspectives on the rationality or otherwise of prescientific magic and ritual.[7] If the Zande belief system has become a classic case study, it would seem that Peter Winch's "Understanding a Primitive Society" is the classic exemplar of relativistic thinking with regard to prescientific ritual practices. Winch's argument is that we cannot judge prescientific practices by the terms and standards of scientific ones because these practices may operate on fundamentally different logics.[8] Assessing Winch's argument, Habermas comes to the conclusion that Winch's relativistic stance compels us to take seriously the premise that "modern Western societies promote a distorted understanding of rationality that is fixed on cognitive-instrumental aspects and is to that extent particularistic" (*Communicative Action*, 66). But to that very extent, Winch also reveals—without meaning to—that the Zande concept of witchcraft bears the mark of a limited rational system, in contrast to which the modern system can validly claim universal applicability. Winch's arguments, Habermas suggests, "are too weak to uphold the thesis that inherent to every linguistically articulated worldview and to every cultural form of life there is an incommensurable concept of rationality; but his strategy of argumentation is strong enough to set off the justified claim to universality on behalf of the rationality that gained expression in the modern understanding of the world from an uncritical self-interpretation of the modern world that is fixated on knowing and mastering external nature" (66). By uncritically deploying Evans-Pritchard's Zande culture—univocal and static—Habermas uncharacteristically forgets that no cultural unit exists that can validly be defined in static, or what Paulin Hountondji would call "unanimist," terms.[9]

Enlisting a static, nonhistorical "Zande culture" serves his argument well, for it enables him to elaborate a theory of rational communicative action that would be adequate to the complexity of modern society. But it also reenacts a conceptual maneuver that Johannes Fabian criticizes in his book *Time and the Other: How Anthropology Makes Its Object:* in elaborating a theory by means of which modern societies can work towards a better model of interaction, Habermas thinks "in terms of the non-West."[10] But on these very terms, the non-West can neither have any interior depth nor substantive history. Habermas thus enacts a mode of thinking that purports to address the "modern world" posed at a high level of abstraction while concretely abjecting the non-West. In this way, the textually pre-constituted non-West has to be the outside that enables the inside to think itself.

This is all the more ironic because Habermas's theory is intended to work out a model of communication and relational consensus. It is good to seek, as Habermas does in *The Philosophical Discourse of Modernity,* a "paradigm of mutual understanding" (296)—a theory of intersubjective communication that would rest on consensus among the participants of diverse cultural units. But the communicative unit presupposed in Habermas's theory appears not to be of this world; that is to say, not of the contemporary world where large-scale immigration or multinational trade relations make it absurd to speak of social interaction in terms of a coincidence of interests while conceptually reducing entire hemispheres to the status of an outside that enables the inside to constitute itself.

Even if we imagine a society still untouched by the complexities of postindustrial culture and multinational capital, Habermas's communicative unit remains conceivable only as a discursive invention that lacks any material referent. His theory turns on an abstract and Eurocentric understanding of communication and mutual understanding. This charge speaks to the conceptual, not existential or moral, dimension of the loaded term "Eurocentrism." That is, the discursive frame

that subtends Habermas's account, one the account ends up reproducing, is unselfconsciously Eurocentric. So narrow is his deployment of the
notions of communication and consensus, that he is able to elide the
concrete fact that conflicting interests among participants of specific cultural spheres often define the realm of culture. Let us consider the following passage:

> Fundamental to the paradigm of mutual understanding is . . . the
> performative attitude of participants in interaction, who coordi-
> nate their plans for action by coming to an understanding about
> something in the world. When ego carries out a speech act and
> alter takes up a position with regard to it, the two parties enter into
> an interpersonal relationship. The latter is structured by the system
> of reciprocally interlocked perspectives among speakers, hearers,
> and non-participants who happen to be present at the time. On the
> level of grammar, this corresponds to the system of personal pro-
> nouns. *Whoever has been trained in this system* has learned how,
> in the performative attitude, to take up and to transform into one
> another the perspectives of the first, second, and third persons.
> (296–97, my emphasis)

This passage sheds light on two significant conceptual leaps. In the first
sentence, the "plan for action" that Habermas mentions may precisely
be what constrains the possibility of consensus. Participants in the same
cultural realm may have such incompatible understandings about the
"something in the world," that the plan of action that would follow
from each such understanding becomes mutually antagonistic rather
than coordinate. Further, the claim in the last sentence ("whoever has
been trained in this system has learned how . . . etc.") underplays the
possibility that the pragmatics of training may itself be a site of contestation. For unless one is preaching to the choir, the Christian Bible cannot be a self-evident source for teaching the ecumenical greatness of the
prime mover. To entertain this possibility is to open up an analytical terrain wherein one can see in, say, the pragmatics of education in specific
systems an index of exclusions and ideological inducements that often
characterize social fields.

It may of course be said that it is precisely this ideal field that
Habermas has in mind. On this view, his position would be that modern
society requires in theory an ideal communicative unit against which the
determinate performances of specific sociocultural fields can be read.
However, Lyotard might object that this view presupposes an equally
idealist deployment of the very category "theory." As we shall see in a
moment, if for Habermas theory requires a distinction between "truth

claims" and "power claims," for Lyotard that distinction is ultimately flawed: the only factor that legitimates truth claims themselves, that is to say, theory as such, is power. It is on this point, then, that we should turn to Lyotard's version of the challenge of postindustrial modernity.

LYOTARD AND THE PRAGMATICS OF DISCOURSE

We have already noted that, in direct contrast to Habermas, Lyotard suggests that Adorno's critique of modernity and the modern predicament did not go far enough. For him, Adorno still retains a utopic vision: he immolated God merely to install the devil as the authentic purveyor of emancipation. In turn, if he takes Adorno to task for not going far enough in his critique of instrumental reason and the metanarratives that legitimate it, he seeks to explode the very core of a value-neutral account of science. Couched in Marxian terms, one might say that if in traditional positivist accounts of scientific knowledge, use value is a byproduct rather than definitive constituent of theoretical (scientific) inquiry, Lyotard suggests that use value has always been integral to the labor of science. As Kenneth Lea has observed, for Lyotard the use value of science progressively devolves into exchange value as the modern world careens deeper and deeper into a postindustrial modernity.

In *The Postmodern Condition,* Lyotard writes: "It is widely accepted that knowledge has become the principle force of production over the last few decades; this has already had a noticeable effect on the composition of the work force of the most highly developed countries and constitutes the major bottleneck for the developing countries. In the postindustrial and postmodern age, science will maintain and no doubt strengthen its preeminence in the arsenal of productive capacities of the nation-states. Indeed, this situation is one of the reasons leading to the conclusion that the gap between the developed and developing countries will grow ever wider in the future" (5). This formulation immediately poses the "developed" countries side-by-side with the "developing" ones. The framing therefore replicates a conceptual operation we saw at work in Habermas's expository procedure, one wherein the shadow of the non-West rears its head at the scene of any attempt to think categories like science, knowledge, or modernity. This point becomes even more crucial because *The Postmodern Condition,* commissioned by and initially presented to the "Conseil des Universites" of the government of Quebec, takes for its direct object the "developed" societies. The very first paragraph of the Introduction establishes its focus: "The object of this study is the condition of knowledge in the most highly developed societies. I have decided to use the word *post-modern* to describe that condition. The word is in current usage on the American continent among sociologists and critics; it designates the state of our culture following the transformations which, since the end of the nineteenth century, have altered the game rules for science, literature, and the arts" (xxiii).

For Lyotard, postmodernism is a furtherance of modernist developments; in his words, postmodernism "is not modernism at its end but in the nascent state, and this state is constant" (79). He takes for his point of departure Habermas's notion of a "legitimation crisis" that confronts postindustrial society. This crisis arises in the wake of transformations in such terrain as science, literature, or the arts, transformations that put into question the claims of the traditional (Western) epistemological order. Lyotard wants to "place these transformations in the context of the crisis of narratives" (xxiii). The introduction of the narrative paradigm points to the other dimension of the text—namely, that of linking the transformations with which he is concerned to coterminous, or what he seems to wish were coterminous, transformations in the reality of social structures and the politics that would respond to such reality. As Fredric Jameson observes in his preface to the English translation, the reach of Lyotard's text assumes that "doing 'normal' science and participating in lawful and orderly social reproduction are . . . two phenomena—better still, two *mysteries*—that ought to be able to illuminate one another " (*Condition,* viii).

In Lyotard's account, the social bond exists under a model of discourse; and discourse, in its turn, exists under a model of language games. He uses the scientific community as his central exemplar of a terrain fashioned on this model. The scientific institution, functioning as it does under a model of language games, appears as a microcosmic window on society and its regulation: "It should . . . be clear from this perspective why I chose language games as my general methodological approach. I am not claiming that the *entirety* of social relations is of this nature—that will remain an open question. But there is no need to resort to some fiction of social origins to establish that language games are the minimum relation required for society to exist: even before he is born, if only by virtue of the name he is given, the human child is already positioned as the referent in the story recounted by those around him, in relation to which he will inevitably chart his course" (15). Marked by massive computerization and its foster child—corporate multinationalism—postindustrial culture engenders greater international mobility of capital and information. Progressively, therefore, individual nation-states are drawn into relations that transcend state boundaries.

For Lyotard, this implies a rearrangement of power and legitimation; it points to a new cartography of the social, thereby witnessing to
the multiplicity, the heterogeneity, of frequently incommensurable language games. Having less hold over the new multinational networks that
constitute the major consumers of computer knowledge, the state can no
longer legitimate its power through a recourse to the old language game,
the old narratives. On these terms, narratives of universal peace, the
capacity and necessity of the individual and societal body to achieve full
self-knowledge; or, for socialism, the self-knowledge and consequent
dictatorship of a global proletariat: these narratives of emancipation
should be considered obsolete. The project of the Enlightenment, in
short, is obsolete. Always under attack under the critical restlessness of
high modernism, these narratives now need to be confronted with even
more forceful intellectual skepticism. And if computer culture and
postindustrial fragmentation of society make this irreversible, postmodernism is the name of the new reality. Our historical moment, then, calls
for a different epistemological standpoint: one that avoids totalizing
metanarratives and their attendant totalitarian consequences. On this
basis, Lyotard insists that the communicative consensus that Habermas
wants to theorize is politically regressive.

Lyotard presents multinationalism as the mark and cause of an
unprecedented sociocultural dispersion and fragmentation. Methodologically, this move is fundamentally important as a cause-effect
ground for his theory of antitotality. Put differently, it is by means of the
notion of social dispersion and fragmentation that Lyotard grounds his
critique of totalizing aspirations in political organization, in epistemological systems, and in artistic invention. For our purposes, this raises
two crucial issues. First, a Habermasean will quickly object that there is
nothing new in the fragmentation that Lyotard cites as mark and cause
of his theory of postmodernity. The Habermasean might call Lyotard's
attention to the fact that the theme of social fragmentation is a familiar
one—that successive generations from Greco-Roman antiquity have
talked of one fragmentation or another—thereby canceling out the *post*-
modern specificity Lyotard wants to claim. Our Habermasean might
even add that there is a methodological inconsistency here: as we have
seen, *The Postmodern Condition* develops a cause-effect (that is, a historicist) analysis as premise for what purports to be a specifically postmodern antihistoricism.

In response to this charge, we may say that, despite its faulty
methodological predication, Lyotard's transhistorical thesis can still
stand because concrete historical experience bears it out. By this I mean
the conception of history that Nietzsche had offered in his time, namely,

its recurrent, cyclical tendency. In this sense, it becomes possible to read Lyotard's use of advanced technocracy as being mainly heuristic—one choice out of many social transformations that history readily offers. Such a reading makes fragmentation itself a transhistorical phenomenon, thereby justifying Lyotard's transhistorical theory. But this reading does not quite touch the precise location of Habermas's bite. In fact, it only opens it up further, for to agree with Lyotard that fragmentation and dispersion constitute the ubiquitous, ineluctable reality of social formations and experience is to underplay the historical specificity that his theory wants to claim.

Second, Lyotard's theory of antitotality is so expansive in its rhetoric that it slips into a paradoxical totalizing frame. We have seen Habermas exploit this line of critique when he argues that, with poststructuralist thinkers, the impulse of antitotality paradoxically ends up in yet another totalizing theory—albeit in reverse. Various critics in search of strategies of liberation for third world societies—or racially, ethnically, and sexually oppressed groups within first world societies—have raised similar objections.[11] Lyotard seems intent on repudiating any and all instances of social theory grounded in a totalizing frame. An instance of this can be found in the book's very final moment: "Under the general demand for slackening and for appeasement, we can hear the mutterings of the desire for a return of terror, for the realization of the fantasy to seize reality. The answer is: Let us wage a war on totality; let us be witnesses to the unpresentable; let us activate the differences and save the honor of the name" (82). At a moment like this, Lyotard's rhetoric suggests that his rejection of metanarratives of emancipation is a sweeping one—not limited, that is, to the historical trajectory of the First World since the so-called era of Enlightenment philosophy. In other words, Lyotard is not too eager to circumscribe the purchase of his discomfort with totalizing narratives. To be sure, *The Postmodern Condition* posits the "most highly developed societies" as its object, and explicitly claims to be speaking on behalf of subjugated knowledges and groups. In a passage like this, however, it is almost as if *any* attempt to seize reality is both a fantasy and a "desire for a return of terror," that all nationalisms have to be inherently totalitarian. Habermas can hold on to moments like this, pointing out that it demonstrates such skepticism toward positive agency as can only translate into quietism at the political as well as discursive levels. Lyotard concedes that one of the challenges of the postmodern moment is to transcend the "discovery of the 'lack of reality' of reality," and go further to "(invent) other realities" (*Condition*, 77). A Habermasean will be justified in holding the poststructuralist down to this concession. On this view, over and beyond Lyotardian antitotality, theory can legitimately emphasize the constructive (or reconstructive), without giving up on the deconstructive moment.

At any rate, what I wish to stress here is that as far as cultural representation is concerned, Habermas and Lyotard share a discursive frame that needs to be thematized for the non-West to emerge with coeval agency. We can demonstrate this by considering the role of non-Western mythology and the discourse of cultural anthropology in Lyotard's text. In the section subtitled "The Pragmatics of Narrative Knowledge," Lyotard suggests, via a reading of story telling protocols among the Cashinahua, that knowledge in primitive societies is explicitly codified in narrative forms. In his view, the hierarchies of authority on the basis of which primitive society is constituted are codified in myth. Every narrative event wherein such myths are narrated then becomes a communal ritual of self-preservation, for, integral to the narrative of communal myths is a legitimation of that community's organizational formation and epistemological order. This feature of primitive societies runs counter to scientific cultures where consensus or performativity—surreptitiously undergirded by metanarratives of emancipation—constitute the criteria by which knowledge is legitimated.

Between the pragmatics of legitimation in primitive cultures as against modern scientific ones, then, what we have is a situation of incommensurability. And for Lyotard, incommensurability denotes radical difference: "It is . . . impossible to judge the existence or validity of narrative knowledge on the basis of scientific knowledge and vice versa: the relevant criteria are different"(26). It is a legacy of modern history that the scientific cultures missed the import of incommensurability and, instead, saw primitive cultures as less rational. This, for Lyotard, is one locus of colonialist narcissism:

> narrative knowledge does not give priority to the question of its own legitimation and . . . it certifies itself in the pragmatics of its own transmission without having recourse to argumentation and proof. This is why its incomprehension of the problems of scientific discourse is accompanied by a certain tolerance: it approaches such discourse primarily as a variant in the family of narrative cultures. The opposite is not true. The scientist questions the validity of narrative statements and concludes that they are never subject to argumentation or proof. He classifies them as belonging to a different mentality: savage, primitive, underdeveloped, backward, alienated, composed of opinions, customs, authority, prejudice, ignorance, ideology. Narratives are fables, myths, legends, fit only for women and children. At best, attempts are made to throw some rays of light into this obscurantism, to civilize, educate, develop. (27)

By means of such appeals to the history of imperialism, Lyotard locates one impulse of his antitotality in the necessity of rethinking the categories and assumptions of Enlightenment rationalism in the face of our contemporary reality. In "Universal History and Cultural Differences," he confirms such a reading even more explicitly. The essay's title recalls Kant's "On the Idea of a Universal History with a Cosmopolitan Purpose."[12] It is as if Lyotard wants us to recognize the immensity of the distance between Kant and us. If Kant in that essay registers an optimism with regard to the possibility of a universal history, Lyotard's essay attests to the error of that dream and the necessity, now, of fashioning a different project.

Here, then, lies the epistemological significance of Lyotard's antitotality, namely, the discursive frame he shares with Habermas. In contrast to Habermas, Lyotard would want a mode of seeing that pays due attention to the unique features of our contemporary climate, a major aspect of which is the legacy of imperialism and the upsurge of multiple local nationalisms. Along this line, his skepticism towards grand narratives may be said to be predicated on an impulse to respect the legitimacy of subordinated modes of seeing. At this level, his position marks an advance beyond Habermas's Eurocentrism. But if he differs from Habermas on this point, he joins him on the implicit conceptualization of the non-Western other that he deploys. To serve his purpose, the "Cashinahua," like Habermas's "Azande," need to be present, but only as static incarnations of otherness.

MARLOW'S PRECEDENT

At the beginning of *Heart of Darkness*, we meet Marlow "upon the lower reaches of the Thames." There, in the company of friends, he contemplates the "great spirit of the past" (Conrad, 8). It occurs to him that imperial Britain, Lord of entire hemispheres symbolically watched over by the grandeur of the Thames, was itself once subject to the brutal might of Rome. For Marlow, if Rome signals the very quintessence of territorial ambition and ruthless plunder of subjugated lands, spoils of conquest also characterize the imperial Britain that he contemplated at the turn of the twentieth century. As he puts it in one of the novella's most famous passages, "The conquest of the earth, which mostly means the taking it away from those who have a different complexion or slightly flatter noses than ourselves, is not a pretty sight when you look into it too much. What redeems it is the idea only. An idea at the back of it; not a sentimental pretence but an idea; and an unselfish belief in the idea—something you can set up, and bow down before, and offer a sacrifice to . . ." (10). Between classical imperialism and modern civilizing missions, the only difference is that the latter is underpinned by an *idea*. This idea, in his view, outweighs the subject's self-possession: it is "unselfish," and works compellingly as "something you can set up, and bow down before, and offer a sacrifice to" (10).

Significantly, Marlow cuts himself short at the very moment of this insight. In the nameless narrator's words: "He broke off. Flames glided in the river, small green flames, red flames, white flames, pursuing, overtaking, joining, crossing each other—then separating slowly or hastily" (11). It is as if Conrad's alter ego is terrified of his own observation; and so, he stops himself, trailing off on an insight that could otherwise be the starting point of *renewed* meditation. Marlow averts his gaze from the legions of Rome and the merchant ships of King Leopold's Belgium, and instead focuses on the riot of colors that adorned the mercuric face of the Thames. As he accomplishes this retreat, Conrad is careful to register its suturing effect, for the very next sentence informs us: "The traffic of the great city went on in the deepening night upon the sleepless river" (11). In other words, the peace of the great city, watched over by the sleepless river, remains undisturbed: life goes on as usual. Faced with the constancy of night traffic and the seductiveness of colorful flames on eternal landmarks, an uncomfortable thought has to trail off, or retreat to the background.

The preceding pages constitute an attempt to begin at the point of Marlow's retreat. We have sampled two contemporary perspectives on "modernity" as a social and epistemological category. Like Marlow's scurrying flames on the face of the Thames, the divergent elaborations we have been exploring offer much that is useful regarding the condition of modernity. But the conflict of vision and priorities they exemplify can also divert our attention away from alternative ways of telling the story of "modernity." This book is interested in ways that stress the priorities, inspired choices, or false starts, of non-Western pagan cultures: those cultures that often exist in our libraries as always-already-known signifiers of "myth" and "non-science." I have chosen to use Habermas and Lyotard to suggest that alongside the substance of their positions, postcolonial criticism can learn something from a close attention to the way both thinkers articulate those positions. We can learn a lot from the substantive issues at the center of the intertextual dialogue between both theorists; but for my purposes, we can learn even more from the procedural dimension of their thinking. Lyotard, we saw, could not think modernity without seeing the mutual imbrication—consequent on imperialism and the internationalization of capital—of the West and the non-West. On the other hand, however, although Habermas would not contest the pertinence of such an insight, he insists on distinguishing between modernity as encoded in philosophical discourse from the eighteenth century on, and modernity as objective structural reality—economic and political. In this, we encounter one tension at the heart of the Habermas-Lyotard dialogue: is modernity as objective reality coextensive with modernity as the philosophical concept that seeks to grasp that reality? If it is, will it not imply that any contemporary perspective on modernity that seeks to be rigorously materialist should pay more attention to the complexity of the non-West than both thinkers do in the texts we've been discussing?

This leads to the other lesson I want to foreground. As the texts we examined struggle either to contest the claims of modernity or to recuperate and point up its residual, yet-to-be-exhausted possibilities, the status of the non-West is, at best, ghostly. In these texts, the West emerges as subject precisely in its difference from the non-West, regardless of whether one is in support of, or in opposition to, the much-maligned enlightenment rhetoric. This last point does not imply an "us-them" scheme; that is, it goes beyond whether the representation is being done by an insider as against an outsider. Indeed, to understand the effects of the ideology of modernity fully is to recognize that even "natives" participate in some way in it. One of the productive aspects of poststructuralist accounts of the postcolonial condition is to be found in the approach of a Bhabha or a Spivak to this issue.

With characteristic flourish, Adorno began *Negative Dialectics* with an attack on the Kantian and Hegelian system. Citing Molière, Adorno writes: "When something that is to be conceived flees from identity with the concept, the concept will be forced to take exaggerated steps to prevent any doubts of the unassailable validity, solidity, and acribia of the thought product from stirring. Great philosophy was accompanied by a paranoid zeal to tolerate nothing else, and to pursue everything else with all the cunning of reason, while the other kept retreating farther and farther from the pursuit. The slightest remnant of nonidentity sufficed to deny an identity conceived as total" (22). It would be reductive to read this to imply, either that no attempt to formulate an account of modernity can be "adequate"; or that, this being the case, concept and "real life" should be left alone to go their incommensurable ways. Theory is inescapable, and we cannot do without concepts. Adorno's announcement becomes useful, then, specifically as a clearing of the grounds. Rather than an anti-intellectual rejection of concepts (theories) as such, it becomes a cautionary flag that we might carry along as we seek more concepts and invent more knowledge. For if they are anything at all, terms like "postcoloniality," or the "Africa" in African letters, are concepts whose meaning cannot be dissociated from modernity itself. The adventure of the notion of postcoloniality, its specific elaboration in current literary theory and cultural criticism, is the subject of the next section.

THE SIGNS IN "POSTCOLONIAL THEORY"

It is helpful to use the term "postcolonial theory" with initial scare quotes, if only to indicate that there is need to be guarded with its use. There is a level of imprecision in what it entails, and growing carelessness in the purposes it is invoked to serve. Given this situation, and because the term "postcolonial theory" is by now securely in the vocabulary of Anglo-American criticism, it is useful to begin by further clarifying the sense in which I intend to use it. I shall be suggesting that the imprecision is due to a certain entanglement of substantive content with institutional context; and further, that a productive unraveling of the lessons of postcolonial theory requires a double maneuver, for where the former (content) is best approached by means of an immanent reading, the latter (context) can be achieved only by means of a historicizing procedure. For much of what I have to say to make sense, then, I should like here to set some terminological delineation that will hopefully give shape to what I have been calling postcolonial theory, and advance my aim of grounding the theory in its measure and limits.

In his book *White Mythology: Writing History and The West,* Robert Young offers an excellent assessment of the impact of Edward Said in the efflorescence of colonial discourse analysis, namely, the critique of preconstituted Western assumptions about history and the place of the West in human self-understanding. Young follows the chapter on Said with separate chapters on Homi Bhabha and Gayatri Spivak: the trio, it would seem, speak to Sartre, Foucault, and others in a way that offers a nice scaffold for the story Young seeks to tell. Yet, in anchoring his undertaking on Said, Spivak, and Bhabha, Young privileges these figures as definitive of the moment of postcoloniality; unwittingly or not, he thereby locates previous anticolonial efforts only as, at best, ancestral efforts.[14] More immediately, current work (on the culture of colonialism or its aftermath in writings after the end of formal colonial rule) that does not speak with a poststructuralist accent cannot find a respectable space in the topography of Young's story.

And yet, I would argue that Young's topography is altogether valid; its validity is indeed crucial to historicizing the discursive formation we primarily have in mind when we invoke the term "postcolonial theory." The story of this discursive formation would have to begin with Edward Said's *Orientalism,* a book that traces in discourse the story of Europe's adventure into the sociopolitical and psychic space of the Orient. What *Orientalism* demonstrated is as much an intellectual direction as a fusion of political commitment and formal-disciplinary erudition; what it spawned is a specific way of framing questions about colonial history and representation. At this conjuncture, then, whatever takes for itself, or is endowed with, the tag of postcolonial theory follows Said's trail, or is understood to be doing so. In this sense, antiimperialist writings that pre-date *Orientalism* are, strictly speaking, only good old antiimperialist writings, not colonial/postcolonial discourse analysis in the specific sense given to it by Benita Parry (more on this later).

There is an immediate oddity here, one that takes us a bit closer to the conceptual and institutional delineations I am struggling to mark: why would George Lamming's *The Pleasures of Exile* (1962), or Okot P'Bitek's *African Religions in Western Scholarship* (1970), be antiimpe-rial writing, not "colonial discourse analysis"? The reason is ready and waiting in the underlying assumption and consequence I pointed to ear-lier in Young's book: the term "colonial discourse analysis" passes over into postcolonial theory, both deriving their meaning from a specific institution and a specifiable conjuncture. That institution is the Anglo-American academy, and that conjuncture is broadly speaking the post-1960s era, which is to say, the era following Vietnam and the civil rights struggle. And so it is that within the discursive formation that can gen-erally be called postcolonial criticism, the most visible and prestigious vector—that which we call postcolonial theory—traces its conceptual roots to *Orientalism*'s Foucaultian texture, radicalizing it with Derrida and Lacan.[15] Postcolonial theory, then, unfolds at the point in literary and cultural criticism where deconstruction intersects with psycho-analysis, the point where—shall we say—Derrida and Foucault sit at table with Lacan. If Derridian deconstruction and Lacanian psycho-analysis have both come to be called—not necessarily by hostile com-mentators—"high theory," then, it seems apt to delineate the postcolo-nial vector within it as postcolonial high theory, if only to mark my contention that there is theory and there is theory.

The single most far-reaching impact of literary theory generally has been its recasting of the entire edifice of literary structures and their tra-ditional reading in the academy as one of cultural nationalism that is dressed up in the rhetoric of humanism and universalism. As an out-growth of theory in this general sense, postcolonial theory participates in this questioning of traditional protocols of literary study. But where theory in general identifies its target in the various tags that have entered the domain of mass culture (such as logocentrism, phallocentrism, and so forth) postcolonial theory packages all of these tags under an overarching name: "colonial." This is to be expected; that is, for the term "postcolonial" to make sense as an epistemological, and not simply temporal, adjective, the theory it designates has somehow to be different from, beyond, something else that came before. The "colonial" that postcolonial aims to dislodge is thus said to be the very epistemological foundation of literary criticism, from its European provenance to its various satellites across the contemporary global village. Here, a second layer of the "something else" to be transcended can be found. For, the important whipping boys of postcolonial theory are cultural-nationalist discourses wherever they are to be found (Lazarus *Postcolonial*; Miller *Nomads*; Ann DuCille). It is asserted that the discourses of nationalist movements that fought to liberate colonized societies from European rule often preserve the "us-them" dichotomy that originally underwrote Europe's violent advance into the lives and minds of the non-West. As the story gets told, in contesting the claims of imperial Europe, third world nationalist discourses (or at least those labeled "nativist"—a term that soon reads like a catch-all synonym for nationalistic rhetoric anyway) seek a narrative of emancipation wherein the native self is restored to its true light, but that restoration necessarily needs a coherent and self-contained West as its point of reference.

From the evidence of African letters, the story of nationalist discourses has to be told with greater discernment and nuance. For instance, (i) the discourses enact an *agon* more interesting and instructive than a simple replication of classic Western binarism, and (ii) even where such replications are to be found, where nativism is to be encountered, robed in raffia skirts and bearing jungle drums, it will still be too hasty to conclude that a specific theoretical lesson automatically follows or should follow from that discovery. In the poststructuralist context that postcolonial theory inhabits, nativism has become something of a pariah.[16] One way of articulating and engaging the various positions in contemporary postcolonial theory is by confronting the basis of the differences between them. As I have already noted, the ascendancy of postcolonial studies has had its share of turbulence and controversy. Preeminently at stake is the status of the subject in the constitution of discourse and, by extension, its subversion. At the risk of some schematism, we can say that on one side are those who (purportedly) are satisfied simply with decentring the subject, while on the other are those who want to retain some space for agency—the latter arguing that to decenter the subject without qualification is to foreclose, or demonstrate an inadequate commitment to, the necessity of subject constitution in any political movement or project.

As can be expected, the critics who belong to the first camp profess an allegiance to poststructuralism. Opposed to them are those who admit the basic premises of poststructuralism but perceive a problem in the dynamics of bringing those premises to bear on the postcolonial scene. The result is that, if with the first group the study of colonialism follows from the poststructuralist critique of power and knowledge, the other group insist that poststructuralism did not invent such a critique, that anti-imperialist work predates it by at least half a century. For this second group, poststructuralism is a product of the advanced capitalist first world; consequently, to pursue—without qualification—the concerns of a Derrida or a Foucault in the postcolonial space is to reconstitute the imperial relation at the level of theory.

As with all bipolar characterizations, the one I have been erecting is arguably problematic. Quite apart from the fact that the dichotomy is not as neat as the account above suggests, many critics who work within a poststructuralist frame accent and thematize the topographical provenance of poststructuralism itself, modifying and extending, even as they deploy, its premises. What delineates the contending positions is less the incompatibility of the substantive issues, than it is the conceptual pedigree and critical idiom they claim or reveal. For my purposes, it is not productive to engage Anglo-American theorists of postcoloniality on the basis of theoretical labels, or the "subversive" value ascribed to those labels in a relationship of hard-wired causality. Rather, I should like to read postcolonial theory from the inside out, so to speak. I want to explicate what some of the more influential figures have to say on their own terms. I want to do so in part because there are countless students, undergraduate and graduate, in anglophone Africa as much as in other parts of the English-speaking world, who want to be able to understand what all the glamour and gore of postcolonial theory is about. They deserve to do so, in language that is more inviting than intimidating, and in a tone that tolerates conceptual weaknesses; for as Kwame Anthony Appiah writes, "we are, after all, fallen creatures" ("Tolerable," 78). Just as importantly, I want to demonstrate that in some crucial ways, postcolonial theory—in its poststructuralist vector—replicates a discursive structure whose inner logic is parallel to that which animated Africanist literary discourse from about the late-1950s. And yet, paradoxically, the latter tends to be characterized as unselfconscious cultural nationalism (which is to say, that it lacks adequately "subversive" theory and consequence). I will thus be following the logic of the figures I cite as this reveals itself from within the terms of their own rhetoric. To do this is to take the theory so resolutely on its own terms that one is able to begin to tell a story that might transcend the circumscription of the theorists' overt intentions.

I begin with two self-avowedly "non-poststructuralist" (or, more accurately, anti-poststructuralist) versions of postcolonial theorizing. I then move on to examine the work of two defenders of poststructuralism's value for postcolonial criticism, Homi Bhabha and Gayatri Spivak. My specific contention is that the debate around agency is not too promising, as long as the concept is pursued in abstract terms. In other words, as long as the agency of human minds (and bodies) in concrete historical situations is conceived as an issue that can be theorized outside of those specific contexts, the debate around agency cannot produce genuine knowledge about African literature and criticism as it took shape from the 1950s. I should like to stress that any final statement on the work of the figures I discuss is, at this point, premature. Each of them is still active and productive, and one expects ever more productive developments in their work. I concentrate on their essays that first appeared in the 1980s because I think it necessary to go back to the founding moment of what has today become established as postcolonial theory. My discussion of these critics and theorists, then, is intended to be searching and critical, not polemical.

WITNESSES AND COUNTER-WITNESSES

Stephen Slemon, Helen Tiffin, and Bill Ashcroft espouse a measured anti-poststructuralist position and have done very valuable work in that direction.[17] The value of their work lies in bringing so-called "elite" postmodern theories into dialogue with "peripheral" cultural productions and conceptualizations from the postcolonial world. Helen Tiffin articulates a shared agenda in her Introduction to *Past the Last Post* (1990): "Whatever the fate of textual/literary Studies in the twenty-first century, postmodernism, or specifically post-structuralism in alliance with post-colonialism has determinedly and successfully eroded the centrality of British literature and canon-based studies within academic institutions. But as well as the positive effects of alliance, we must also understand the tensions and stresses, the power relations within and between the two discourses if we are to chart the course of literary history and its relationship to world cultures and politics this century" (Adam, xv). The introduction to *After Europe*, which Tiffin coauthored with Stephen Slemon, can serve to concretize a number of the tensions she indicates in the passage above.

Tiffin and Slemon identify two methodologies that have achieved something of a hegemonic stature in the analysis and critique of imperialism and colonial discourse. These methodologies "tend to classify themselves under the rubric of 'deconstructive' or 'new historicist'" (Slemon et al., xiv). According to Tiffin and Slemon, "[t]here are important differences between these two forms of theoretical practice (not to mention important differences within each of them); but what they share is an attempt to carry a critique of 'the imperialism of the signifier' forward towards . . . a 'disclosure of complicities where a will to knowledge would create oppositions'" (xiv).

I want to isolate two directions from which Slemon and Tiffin launch their critique of the "elite" perspectives on the critique of colonialism. First, they argue that the deconstructive or new historicist angle on colonial discourse can only end up privileging textuality, thereby foreclosing any focus on the concrete materiality of colonialism. Second, and relatedly, the elite critics of colonialism end up limiting themselves only to analyses of colonial texts, that is, the texts of the colonizer. For Tiffin and Slemon, since Homi Bhabha and Gayatri Spivak—the two figures they persistently cite—are intent on deconstructing the texts of imperialism, or more accurately, pointing up the self-undoing interiority of the colonial text, the two cannot foreground the agency of the texts of the colonized, texts that have always provided a counterarticulation, an-Other way of seeing, to subvert the precarious power of colonialism's narcissistic address: "[W]hen theoretical practice amounts, in (Benita) Parry's words, to the 'obliteration of the role of the native as historical subject and combatant, possessor of an-Other knowledge and producer of alternative tradition,' it inherently joins hands with that neo-colonizing apparatus which post-colonial criticism . . . always sets out to subvert" (xvi). For them, the political urgency built into postcolonial literary production, the explicit "extratextual" codes that underpin literary output in the postcolonial space, can neither be adequately thematized nor worked through within a theoretical grid that glibly dismisses referentiality. The operative qualification here should in my view be the qualifying "glibly." In addition, they are interested in stressing the anticolonial effort of the colonized themselves in their own accents, rather than through the elite grid of poststructuralism.

I agree with these concerns. Let us re-examine the suggestion that "mainstream 'critical theory' . . . locks into an ironic relation with postcolonial critical practice" (xvi) because in it, "the cultural, historical agency of colonized and of postcolonial peoples is simply written out of the equation of power" (xv). Were this to be accurate, the irony would be that whatever insurgent potential a new historicist or deconstructive

approach carries, its consolidation within the academy makes it vulnerable to the danger of co-optation. Thus co-opted by the traditional
Eurocentric academy, it becomes disabling to the very epistemic
rearrangement it set out to achieve. In this particular text, Slemon and
Tiffin are ambiguous as to whether deconstructive theory applied to
postcolonial studies has reached the stage where it has become disabling,
or when it can be said to have reached such a stage. But they rightly signal that a theory that set out to demystify establishments or ideas based
on power and inequality may in time end up on the side of power.

Tiffin and Slemon predicate their critique on grounds staked out in
Benita Parry's important essay, "Problems in Current Theories of Colonial Discourse." Like them, Parry argues that "[t]he significant differences in the critical practices of Spivak and Bhabha are submerged in a
shared program marked by the exorbitation of discourse and a related
incuriosity about the enabling socio-economic and political institutions
and other forms of social praxes" (43). But Parry distinguishes between
Bhabha and Spivak on the question of their different attitudes towards
the subversive agency (voice) of the colonized. She praises Bhabha for
his recovery of the (immanent) subversiveness of the native whose labor
of appropriation deconstructs colonialist claims. "Bhabha's theorizing,"
she writes, "succeeds in making visible those moments when colonial
discourse already disturbed at its source by a doubleness of enunciation,
is further subverted by the object of its address; when the scenario written by colonialism is given a performance by the native that estranges
and undermines the colonialist script" (42).

By contrast, she accuses Spivak of a "deliberated deafness to the
native voice where it could be heard" (39). In Parry's reading, Spivak's
project takes the notion of epistemic violence to the point of absurdity
such that "[w]here military conquest, institutional compulsion and
ideological interpellation was, epistemic violence and devious discursive negotiations requiring of the native that he rewrite his position as
object of imperialism, is; and in place of recalcitrance and refusal
enacted in movements of resistance and articulated in oppositional discourses, a tale is told of the self-consolidating other and the disarticu-
lated subaltern" (36). Parry's essay raises important issues with regard
to the theories of colonial discourse, but her findings conflict with
mine in two respects. First, while Bhabha may indeed be charged with
an "exorbitation of discourse" at the expense of the lived materiality
of the colonial event, Spivak is to my mind not susceptible to that
charge. Second, Parry moves too quickly to praise Bhabha for recovering the voice of the native, and to fault Spivak for not making space
for such a recovery.

The basis of my divergence from Parry is linked to what Henry Louis Gates Jr. has called a critical double bind. Gates poses the nature of this bind in the following way: "You can empower discursively the native, and open yourself to charges of downplaying the epistemic (and literal) violence of colonialism; or play up the absolute nature of colonial domination, and be open to charges of negating the subjectivity and agency of the colonized, thus textually replicating the repressive operations of colonialism" ("Fanonism," 462). Gates is pointing to a conceptual tangle that is often acted out in theoretical debates about colonial or postcolonial agency. It is a tangle that should be fairly central to the entire project of a postcolonial studies, yet it is not often broached. However, to adapt Gayatri Spivak's metaphor, instead of continuing the argument over whether or not the subaltern can speak, it may be just as interesting to spend time with specific conjunctures where the subaltern did or did not "speak." That way, we will be better placed to argue over which acts of speaking denoted freedom, which didn't, and what our findings tell us about history and freedom. I need now to turn to the poststructuralist theorists at the center of the debate indexed in Parry's discussion. I shall begin with Homi Bhabha.

MIMICRY AND POSTCOLONIALITY

Bhabha's work is powered by a Lacanian deconstructivist perspective on language and social organization, and he brings this logic to his analysis of colonial discourse and contemporary cultural politics. Bart Moore-Gilbert has classified Bhabha's work thus far into two phases: the first phase focuses on "the cultural exchanges involved in the history of British rule in India," while the second addresses "issues raised by the cultural consequences of neo-colonialism in the contemporary era" (114). But as Moore-Gilbert also notes, this division should be seen as a way of sorting out a particular methodological impulse that may otherwise appear bewildering. Since Bhabha's theorizing seems to be at once focused on the past (what happened or had to have happened) and the present (what is happening *now* and how we should therefore read our past and our present), his rhetoric has a certain capaciousness that is suggestive but disorienting. This aspect of Bhabha's theorizing is based on his attempt to pay attention to what he has called "the temporality of repetition that constitutes those signs by which marginalized or insurgent subjects create a collective agency" (Bhabha, *Location,* 199). Our discussion here focuses on the interventions that first appeared as journal essays in the 1980s. If there is a *poststructuralist* postcolonial theory now, it is in part due to the theory of colonial discourse and pathology that Bhabha formulated in the work that Moore-Gilbert identifies as the first phase.

At the center of Bhabha's theory of the colonial relationship is the notion that the legitimating principle of colonialism is that of modernizing the non-West, that of transforming the latter, through a process of "refinement"—from nature to culture, from primitivism to enlightenment—into a copy of the former. However, were this dream to be actualized, the categories "West" and "non-West"—or what we now refer to as first world as against third world—would become meaningless, for the non-West would then have been effectively transformed into a copy of the West. And yet, in the colonialist discursive order, the burden of this noble mission falls on Europe because of an *essential* quality of the European genius. Whichever way one chooses to grasp this genius, its singular discursive role is to place the West at center stage in the teleological drama that constitutes what Habermas calls "modernity's self-reassurance." The West, in other words, oversees the arduous journey of the non-Western Other toward the promise of modernity.

Having thus set for itself the task of enabling the dark races to catch up with modernity, Bhabha argues, colonialism rests on a deep contradiction: its avowed dream can come to pass only at the cost of self-annihilation—that is, the canceling out of its claim to an essentialized genius. For Bhabha, this tension at the heart of colonial logic explains why colonial discourse *and* society emerge with the characteristic perversion that Frantz Fanon has called a "Manichean delirium." In Bhabha's words, "The representative figure of such a perversion . . . is the image of post-Enlightenment man tethered to, *not* confronted by, his dark reflection, the shadow of colonized man that splits his presence, distorts his outline, breaches his boundaries, repeats his actions at a distance, disturbs and divides the very time of his being" (*Location*, 44).[18]

Homi Bhabha derives two implications from this premise: one is sociopolitical, the other, psychic—that is to say, representational. Let us first consider this dual discursive/sociopolitical implication as Bhabha undertakes to work it out. As I've indicated, the contradiction facing colonialist rationality, for Bhabha, is that it needs to insist on a "natural" hierarchy between colonizer and colonized in order to justify its mission. In the same breath, it needs to presuppose the dismantling of that hierarchy as its mission. In this sense, even as colonialism seeks to justify its play of power via a logic of the natural, that justification makes sense only insofar as it presumes the eventual deconstruction of naturalness. Thus, for Bhabha, it is only logical that colonialist discourse yields profound moments of rhetorical suturing. To carry the impossible

burden of humanist coherence in a discourse necessarily hinged on contradiction, colonial discourse resorts to the sheer passion of enunciatory
will, covered over by familiar declamations of progress and civility, but
objectively held in place by dissimulated power. In colonial society,
writes Bhabha, "The barracks stands by the church which stands by the
schoolroom; the cantonment stands hard by the 'civil lines.' Such visibility of the institutions and apparatuses of power is possible because the
exercise of colonial power makes their *relationship* obscure, produces
them as fetishes, spectacles of a 'natural'/racial pre-eminence. Only the
seat of government is always elsewhere—alien and separate by that distance upon which surveillance depends for its strategies of objectification, normalization and discipline" (83). For Bhabha, then, to look
closely at colonialist prose is to observe the intrigue of power and the
durable impoverishment of colonialism's rationality—the very things its
self-contradictory address seeks to hide.

But such a venture has another potential value: it may serve to
shed light on the predicament of postcoloniality and the burden of a
politically astute oppositional discourse. That is, the drama of colonial discourse can be harnessed to sharpen the critical edge of a truly
post-colonial discursive practice. Homi Bhabha therefore reads colonial bureaucrats and other witnesses of colonial authority both to
demonstrate the contradictions inherent to their rhetoric and to signal a space wherein a specifically postcolonial discourse can proceed.
As he argues in "The Other Question," "In order to understand the
productivity of colonial power it is crucial to construct its regime of
truth, not to subject its representations to a normalizing judgement.
Only then does it become possible to understand the *productive*
ambivalence of the object of colonial discourse—that 'otherness'
which is at once an object of desire and derision, an articulation of
difference contained within the fantasy of origin and identity. What
such a reading reveals are the boundaries of colonial discourse and it
enables a transgression of these limits from the space of that otherness" (67). This passage captures one aspect of Bhabha's project that
I find worthy of attention. First, it suggests that the contradictions
inherent to colonial discourse served the productive purpose of secur-
ing the far-reaching practice of colonial power; that an impoverished
argument (or pseudo argument) was made *productive* of an insidious
political practice. Second, it suggests that understanding this dynamic
promises a subversive strategy. For if the ambivalences of colonial discourse were deployed for the exercise of colonial power, those very
contradictions limit colonial power from within, thereby making it
possible for an anticolonial articulation.

Homi Bhabha develops this suggestion further in his concept of mimicry. Here he considers the immanently contradictory process whereby colonial discourse figures the colonized subject as a "mimic man"—a subject who is normalized towards a standard that, by definition, must not be attained. Afterall, Englishness only retains a naturalized valence if the native—who is colonized so as to attain it—can only be by nature Anglicized but not quite English. "The line of descent of the mimic man," writes Bhabha, "can be traced through the works of Kipling, Forster, Orwell, Naipaul, and to his emergence, most recently . . . as the anomalous Bipin Chandra Pal. He is the effect of a flawed colonial mimesis, in which to be Anglicized is *emphatically* not to be English" (87). In Bhabha's reading, this enabling contradiction (enabling because it serves, at the discursive level, the practice of colonial subjugation) becomes the locus of a counter insurgency. The more effectively colonialism produces a "mimic man," the more immanently that product deconstructs its authority and regime of truth: "it is as if the very emergence of the 'colonial' is dependent for its representation upon some strategic limitation or prohibition *within* the authoritative discourse itself. The success of colonial appropriation depends on a proliferation of inappropriate objects that ensure its strategic failure, so that mimicry is at once resemblance and menace" (86).

This celebration of the potential of mimicry opens up a problem. When, for instance, Bhabha says that "[t]he *menace* of mimicry is its *double* vision which in disclosing the ambivalence of colonial discourse also disrupts its authority" (88), it is not clear whether this reading of colonial mimicry (that is, as a locus of immanent critique) works only as a retroactive, explanatory postulate as against a normative prescriptive one. In the theory of the colonial subject worked out by means of the tropes of "the mimic man," "hybridity," or "sly civility," it is unclear whether we are dealing with a substantive narrative of emancipation—valid historically across diverse sites of colonial interaction—or a specific, historical but not historicist, perspective on determinate moments and texts of the colonial encounter. Put differently: is the figure of the mimic man to be understood as a truth brought to light by Bhabha's labor of reading, and limited to the specific moment of colonialism and its address? Or is it to be understood as a permanent signifier of transgression, to be found as much in the historic instance of colonialist address as in the contemporary moment of neo-colonialism?[19]

If the former, the force of Bhabha's theory would be that, as colonial discourse put ambivalence to use in the exercise of colonial power and thereby immanently restricted the absoluteness of that power, so too should we now, in the postcolonial moment, hold onto that immanent limitation in order to make it the basis of a counterarticulation. This would amount to a retroactive attempt to explain the past and make its lessons usable for the present. If the latter, Bhabha's point would be more ambitious. It would mean that colonialism's mimic man is, even in our neocolonial dispensation, always already a menace, that the mimic man always already subverts colonialism from within. Here, the agency of the critic as the one who reads that transgression into the figure of the mimic man becomes immaterial—or, more correctly—is occluded. Bhabha's mimic man thereby becomes transcendental; and his theory, a resounding announcement of transgression, inevitable and always already at play.

In this second sense, Homi Bhabha would be ontologizing mimicry as subversion, giving an ahistorical twist to mimicry as well as political subversion. In my view, Bhabha is quite right in noting the way in which the West is necessarily "tethered to" the non-West as a legacy of colonialism; quite right that formerly colonized societies have to be "dark shadows" of their former colonizer, shadows that repeat the actions of the colonizer at a distance. But it does not necessarily follow that in so doing, the colonized distorts the outline of the colonizer. I am suggesting, then, that Bhabha's notion of mimicry works as a retroactive explanatory paradigm, but breaks down if posited as a normative prescriptive model. In the heyday of colonial rule, the mimic man may have been what Bhabha calls a "sly," subversive figure (*Location*, 93–101). One can profitably test the postulate against specific historical contexts. But in our contemporary moment, mimicry cannot be posed as revolutionary. At a sociopolitical level, all that Bhabha's model points up would be why in contemporary times, the political structures and institutions of postcolonial societies—institutions modeled on those of the West—are burdened with problems that the West itself has supposedly transcended. In other words, Bhabha's model would indicate the economic dependency of the nominally postcolonial nation-state—a situation no one would call subversive or desirable.

The problem is that Bhabha's notion of the mimic man as a figure of menace and transgression is formulated in psychoanalytical terms. However, although Bhabha's critical vocabulary suggests a strictly psychoanalytical delimitation, and although he often appears to circumscribe his explorations and its theoretical purchase within the level of the psyche, his lyricism, especially in his more enthusiastic moments, pushes him squarely onto the level of the sociopolitical. A dual tension thus attends Bhabha's account of postcoloniality. First, it enacts a tension between a retroactive, explanatory mode and a normative, prescriptive one. That is, Bhabha reconciles neither himself nor his auditors to the issue of which mode his theory purports to be invested in. Second, with regard to the applicability of his postulates, Bhabha conflates the psychic terrain with the sociopolitical, even as his own moves tend to insinuate that any attempt at such a conflation is conceptually flawed. He wants to reach the sociopolitical via an investment in the psychic, and does so simply by conflating them in rhetoric.

This double tension accompanies all of Bhabha's work thus far. It is dramatized well in his sustained engagement with Frantz Fanon's theory of colonial society and subjectivity.[20] For Bhabha, Fanon's genius is that "He may yearn for the total transformation of Man and Society, but he speaks most effectively from the uncertain interstices of historical change: from the area of ambivalence between race and sexuality; out of an unresolved contradiction between culture and class; from deep within the struggle of psychic representation and social reality" (40). In this, Bhabha recognizes that, at the least, Fanon's work is marked by a tension between, on the one hand, "psychic representation," and on the other, "social reality." He makes it very clear that he prefers those moments where Fanon speaks "from the uncertain interstices of historical change," rather than those moments when he yearns "for a total transformation of Man and Society." For Bhabha, the former Fanon is more effective than the latter, the latter being constrained by "an existentialist humanism that is as banal as it is beatific" (61).

Writing on Bhabha's reading of Fanon, Gates has argued that "Bhabha may be Fanon's closest reader, and it is an oddly touching performance of a coaxing devotion: he regrets aloud those moments in Fanon that cannot be reconciled to the poststructuralist critique of identity because he wants Fanon to be even better than he is" ("Fanonism," 460). Bhabha, Gates observes, "wants Fanon to mean Lacan rather than, say, Jean-Paul Sartre, but he acknowledges that Fanon does tend to slip" (461). Other commentators have suggested a similar reading. My question is the following: why does Bhabha find himself in this "pulling and pushing" (Gates's words) with Fanon? For him, Fanon strays at those moments when he tries to think the social with the psychic, when he attempts to restore "the dream to its proper political time and cultural space" (Location, 60). I agree with this reading of Fanon, in whose conceptual field Marx and Freud are made to clash. Desperately seeking the concepts and the vocabulary to grasp the colonial pathology—psychic and social—Fanon attempts to articulate the psychic, via Freud, with the social, via a Marxism saturated with Sartrean Hegelianism. Fanon is for this reason most insistently stimulating when his philosophical tools prove inadequate to the political reality he is addressing.

Certainly, Bhabha is more comfortable with the Freud he finds in
Fanon, than with the Sartre. It is of course perfectly legitimate for
Bhabha to prefer, so to speak, Freud over Sartre. The problem is that he
wants to claim that the psyche, which is his privileged arena of analysis,
sheds adequate light on the social. But he also wants to maintain—performatively through his critique of Fanon—that the two should not be
made to meet. When he observes that Fanon oscillates between
"ambivalencies of identification" and "antagonistic identities" (60) we
may conclude, purely by the logic of that formulation, that Bhabha
grants the following: the fact of the former does not imply the absence
of the latter. Indeed, he suggests that Fanon's politicization of the psyche
is inflected by and participates in a determinate context, "a state of
emergency" (60). Yet, Bhabha is in this encounter less interested in
exploring the complex of forces that subtend and give broader meaning
to Fanon's conceptual struggle. Rather, he grants those forces principally
to dissipate them into a transtemporal philosophic insight that is also a
moral-political caution: "Fanon must sometimes be reminded that the
disavowal of the Other always exacerbates the edge of identification,
reveals that dangerous place where identity and aggressivity are
twinned" (62). In this way, Bhabha's reading of Fanon goes against the
grain of his own rhetoric on two counts. First, he criticizes Fanon for
conflating the social with the psyche, even as his own rhetoric performs
something similar. And second, the element of pathos and sentimental-
ism that he rightly perceives in Fanon, one that he attributes to banal—
Sartrean—existentialism, returns to his own rhetoric in the moral caution he enjoins us to entertain: "the disavowal of the Other always
exacerbates the edge of identification, reveals that dangerous place
where identity and aggressivity are twinned."

In sum, Bhabha's work on colonialism and its discursive ramifications is accompanied by significant contradictions. The theory use-
fully exhorts us to face up to a bitter truth that the ideology of dialectic transcendence is ultimately a sedative hope, that culture subsists
only on the condition of conflict. But he gives short shrift to determinate sites of conflict and the discursive problematics they generate—in
this case, that of Fanon. While on the one hand granting the produc-
tiveness of contradiction, he does not entirely grant the contradictions
(of a Fanon) their materiality and implications for current postcolonial
thinking.[21] And while he identifies the limitations of Fanon's writing to
occur at those moments when Fanon wants to link the psychic with the
social (thereby implying that such transcoding is conceptually flawed),
he somehow wants his own theory to be at once a vision of the psychic
and the social-political.

CRISIS AS ENERGY

I want now to take up the contributions of Gayatri Spivak whose work, although explicitly poststructuralist, differs from Bhabha's in a number of respects. Unlike Bhabha, Spivak claims not to be interested in proposing an overarching theory either of colonial discourse or of a singular postcolonial text. In this respect, Robert Young is correct in suggesting that Spivak's work is "best approached not through critical or historical labels, but in terms of the politico-theoretical difficulties which it raises" (158). Spivak illuminates the postcolonial condition *not* because of a consistent theory offered in her work, but because of the tensions that she brings to the surface, and in which she thereby becomes implicated, as she engages in her encounters with discursive formations.

If there is anything consistent about her work, it lies in her deliberate, self-assigned role of being the gadfly of discursive fields, interrupting and "bringing to crises" the uncritical edges of totalizing knowledge. Spivak most often operates by reading others reading, and thereby discloses what she calls "ideology in action": that is, the assumptions and dissimulations framed in our discourses and social texts.[22] In "A Literary Representation of the Subaltern: A Woman's Text From the Third World," she discusses Mahasweta Devi's "Breast Giver" by offering four propositions she aims to get the reader "to at least entertain" (*Worlds*, 241). These propositions encapsulate her overall critical project and point up her strategy:

a. The performance of these tasks, of the historian and the teacher of literature, must critically "interrupt" each other, bring each other to crisis, in order to serve their constituencies; especially when each seems to claim all for its own

b. The teacher of literature, because of her institutional subject-position, can and must "re-constellate" the text to draw out its use. She can and must wrench it out of its proper context and put it within alien arguments.

c. If thus placed in the arguments from Western Marxist-Feminism, Western Liberal Feminism, and French high theory of the Female Body, "Stanadayini" can show us some of their limits and limitations.

d. This might have implications for the current and continued sub-alternization of so-called "third world" literatures. (241)

Now, in proposition *a*, the notion that critical interruptions are necessary in order that varying subject positions can retain a spirit of dialogism and each would thus be unable to "claim all for its own" is a veritable counterhegemonic model. Proposition *c* goes further to suggest that a and b are posited in the context of a specific intellectual climate, namely, Euro-American critical theory: "Western Marxist-Feminism," etc, etc. It makes good sense, then, to surmise that Spivak locates her impulse and strategy in a precise politico-discursive space. The value she sees in her project is articulated in proposition d, namely, that her reading of Mahasweta Devi aims to further a broader project of bringing to light and critiquing "current and continued subalternization of so-called third world literatures" (241).

In this sense, Spivak's deconstructive strategy sets its immediate sights at a specific academic critical institution. However, proposition b also tells us that she has to pay a price: in seeking to "re-constellate" Mahasweta Devi's text as an intertextual interrogation of High Theory, she has to "wrench it out of its [Devi's text] proper context and put it within alien arguments." I respect the frank honesty of this concession; I recognize its value, even as I note that it remains a price. It is indeed true, as she writes in "Marginality in the Teaching Machine," that "[t]he persistent critique of what one must inhabit, the persistent consolidation of claims to founding catachreses, involve an incessant recoding of diversified fields of value" (*Machine,* 61). But to say this is immediately to grant that value ("diversified," marked by constant "recoding" as it is) cannot logically be hypostatized on the wings of a superintending gadfly, an all-encompassing diacritical procedure. We shall come to see the full implication of this observation.

If she dialogizes Euro-American critical wisdom with news from "other worlds," she is also interested in interrogating the news from that other world itself. As third world critical thought seeks to get out of the epistemic violence of imperialism, Spivak wants to keep an agile eye on the forms and results of that attempt. In this regard, the notion of "productive crisis" is very important to her. She sets out to interface seemingly disparate discourses, to make them bring each other to crisis. In bringing to productive crisis the attempts being made in the ex-colonial terrain to escape the epistemic violence of imperialism, she seeks to finetune them, make them more productive, by relentless deconstructive attention. In her words, "If academic and 'revolutionary' practices do not bring each other to productive crisis, the power of the word has clearly passed elsewhere" (53).

On this point, Spivak joins up with Bhabha for whom, as we have seen, the claims of postcolonial discourse need to be fine-tuned if the discourse is to remain self-aware and truly decolonized. Like Bhabha, too, Spivak turns to the discourse of colonialism to locate the contradictions that secured its supposed rationality and also to point up the contradictions that therefore, necessarily, attend the postcolonial condition. In this vein, Spivak coins the term "postcoloniality" as both a *conjuncture* and a *strategy*. For her, postcoloniality is that contradictory cultural and political moment where the formerly colonized finds him- or herself asserting an identity, a modernity, that is contingent on the colonial experience and indebted to the categories of the colonizer:

> Whatever the identitarian ethnicist claims of native or fundamental origin . . . the political claims that are most urgent in decolonized space are tacitly recognized as coded within the legacy of imperialism: nationhood, constitutionality, citizenship, democracy, even culturalism. Within the historical frame of exploration, colonization, decolonization—what is being effectively reclaimed is a series of regulative political concepts, the supposedly authoritative narrative of whose production was written elsewhere, in the social formations of Western Europe. They are being reclaimed, indeed claimed, as concept-metaphors for which no historically adequate referent may be advanced from postcolonial space, yet that does not make the claims less important. (*Machine*, 60)

Postcoloniality, according to this definition, is a state—a condition. Formulated concretely: what defines the Nigerian postcolonial subject is a citizenship—an institutional and juridical value-coding—whose genealogy goes back to Europe. This situation manifests itself in the overarching project of Africanist discourse as it unfolded in the second half of the twentieth century. It manifests itself as a muted contradiction, wherein great stress is placed on a discursive will to disengage from Europe in order to step up to modernity, a modernity that is defined as a teleological move from myth-based reason to secular-scientific rationality.

Consequently, postcolonial identity is the sign of a history, which is to say, its genealogy can be seen in discursive systems and effects. In Spivak's term, postcolonial identity is not an ontology but a concept-metaphor. By extension, insofar as concept-metaphors are purely conceptual and owe their meaning to discursive configurations, they are instantiations of catachresis: "A concept-metaphor without an adequate referent is a catachresis. These claims for founding catachreses make postcoloniality a deconstructive case" (60). Because the intelligibility of postcolonial identity ultimately rests on discursive rather than natural or unmediated content, identity lacks a referent in the ontological sense. By the same token, since the postcolonial quest for modernity hinges on trust—that is to say, trust in an ideal consecrated in Enlightenment or third world "development" rhetoric—the postcolonial condition entails investment in an absent referent.

From this premise, she derives a second, transitive definition of postcoloniality. In this second definition, postcoloniality is a strategy, a designation of agency: "Postcoloniality as agency can make visible that the basis of *all* serious ontological commitment is catachrestical, because negotiable through the information that identity is, *in the larger sense,* a text. It can show that the alternative to Europe's long story—generally translated as 'great narratives' is not only short tales *(petits récits)* but tampering with the authority of storylines" *(Machine,* 65). Two themes are worth noting in this passage: the first concerns her notion of text "in the larger sense," and the second relates to her claim that the alternative to great narratives does not lie simply in inventing short (or local, indigenous) stories. Lyotard is of course the most frequently cited exponent of the position that the notorious grand narratives are obsolete. For Spivak, however, the point is not simply to replace grand narratives with more localized ones, but to disrupt, tamper with, "the authority of storylines." One implication of this would be that it is not enough to have, as the phrase goes, "a literature of one's own," while accepting conventional mystifications of the status of literature in society.

If Marxism spells for Lyotard one instance of the grand narrative, Spivak insists that Marx's insights retain some validity that we will do well to re-thematize, not discard. In what is perhaps her most famous essay, "Can the Subaltern Speak: Speculations on Widow Sacrifice," she writes: "In the face of the possibility that the intellectual is complicit in the persistent constitution of the Other as the Self's shadow, a possibility of political practice for the intellectual would be to put the economic 'under erasure,' to see the economic factor as irreducible as it reinscribes the social text, even as it is erased, however imperfectly, when it claims to be the final determinant or the transcendental signified" ("Subaltern," 280).[23] Although she rejects the deterministic potential to which Althusser's model remains vulnerable when brought to bear on literary analysis—especially with regard to the notion of symptomatic reading— she retains from Althusser a complex commitment to the economic dimension in the interstices of the social text. This brings me to the question of textuality, or what Spivak refers to as text "in the larger sense." Spivak's use of the concept of textuality suggests that she does not construe colonialism as a linguistic inscription in the conventional formalist sense. Where Bhabha can be faulted on this charge for performatively fleeing from any attempt to locate colonial pathologies in a "political and cultural space" (even though he cognitively recognizes the socioeconomic as a factor in the structure of colonialism as history), Spivak attends to a *determinate* institutional conjuncture as one site of interaction in which we can contemplate the silent motors of a neocolonial order. Consequently, to charge her with ignoring the lived materiality of colonialism is to miss the fact that colonialism is, for her, nothing other than a lived, continuing phenomenon in which the intellectual willy-nilly participates. Casting our contemporary moment as a social text then becomes her way of disruptively returning that text to the table—without however making it the final determinant, the word that answers all questions. If, as pretty much everybody will agree, there is nothing outside of the economic order under capitalism, Spivak would be perfectly right in insisting that there is nothing outside the *socius*; it is this socius that opens itself up as text to be interrogated.

The elaboration of political economy worked into Spivak's understanding of postcoloniality, her attempt to think the latter along with the former, anticipates a cluster of concerns that will come to the surface in my discussion of Africanist criticism. For now, it may safely be granted that she registers a caution worth entertaining, namely, that literary theory and cultural criticism would do well to thematize the unequal relation between the peripheral economies and the central postindustrial economies the former function to consolidate in a relation of dependency.

This angle to Spivak's contribution tends to be overlooked in the discussion of the minimal prerequisites, so to speak, of a truly "subversive" discourse. We encountered one illustration of this in Benita Parry's critique cited earlier. For Parry, Spivak's notion of epistemic violence gives so much power to the systematic colonialist disarticulation of the colonized that it becomes impossible for her to notice or, indeed, recognize the latter's transgressive agency. In Parry's words, "the story of colonialism which [Spivak] reconstructs is of an interactive process where the European agent in consolidating the imperialist Sovereign Self, induces the native to collude in its own subject(ed) formation as other and voiceless" ("Problems," 35). As a consequence, "while protesting at the obliteration of the native's subject-position in the text of imperialism, Spivak in her project gives no speaking part to the colonized, effectively writing out the evidence of native agency recorded in India's 200 year struggle against British conquest and the Raj—discourses to which she scathingly refers as hegemonic nativist or reverse ethnocentric narrativization" (35). What this passage insists on is that Spivak underplays the subversive efforts of nationalist movements for being nativist and reverse ethnocentric, thereby consolidating the imperial self at the very moment of their anticolonialist affirmation. Like Bhabha as we have seen, Parry recognizes that subversion is never a tidy process. She contends that a discursive formation can subvert hegemony in the very motion whereby it also consolidates hegemony. As she writes, "Within another critical mode which also rejects totalizing abstracts of power as falsifying situations of domination and subordination, the notion of hegemony is inseparable from that of a counter hegemony. In this theory of power and contest, the process of procuring the consent of the oppressed and the marginalized to the existing structure of relationships through ideological inducements, necessarily generates dissent and resistance, since the subject is conceived as being constituted by means of incommensurable solicitations and heterogeneous social practices" (43).

On the force of this premise she argues, against Spivak, that some nationalist discourses can be read as being truly subversive. The possibility this raises is that agency may lie in the process through which the native occupies the space of the other that consolidates the imperial self. Thus, she writes in "Resistance Theory/Theorizing Resistance": "When we consider the narratives of decolonization, we encounter rhetorics in which 'nativism' in one form or another is evident. Instead of disciplining these, theoretical whip in hand, as a catalogue of epistemological error, of essentialist mystifications, as a masculinist appropriation of dissent, as no more than an anti-racist racism, etc., I want to consider what is to be gained by an unsententious interrogation of such articulations. . . . This of course means affirming the power of the reverse-discourse by arguing that anticolonialist writings did challenge, subvert and undermine the ruling ideologies" (Parry, "Cheers," 88). I want to suggest that Parry's strictures against Spivak on this issue can be made useful for further work. But in doing so, we need not jettison a crucial insight that we outlined earlier, apropos Spivak's definition of postcoloniality-as-agency. Parry's claim makes available a mode of criticism that explores determinate conjunctures and sites of contest, wherein nativism serves a transgressive purpose even as it remains within colonialism's epistemic structure. My claim is that Spivak cannot reject this commitment without violating her own idea of postcoloniality-as-agency. For her as we have seen, the constitution of colonial/postcolonial subjectivity is traceable to Europe's advance into the lives and minds of the colonized, and should be posed as such. As we have also seen, she insists that nobody escapes this scenario, and nothing can get done but within its material/textual organization—where text is understood "in the larger sense." If we accept this, it should follow that "subversion" is inconceivable unless the agent of subversion operates within the orbit of the colonial structure or text. On this issue, then, Spivak's thinking thus far is not radically incompatible with the concerns expressed by Parry. To pursue such a mode of critique, however, one would have to grant that agency cannot be definitively theorized in an aprioristic sense, that is to say, outside of specific historical conjunctures.

READING WITH THEORY

In "The Scramble for Post-Colonialism," an essay that appeared in 1994, Stephen Slemon provides a valuable account of the conceptual logic of the various contending vectors in contemporary postcolonial theory. He shows the ways in which Edward Said's *Orientalism* has been fleshed out in fruitful directions in the work of Homi Bhabha and Gayatri Spivak. He cautions, however, that the poststructuralist trajectory exemplified by Bhabha and Spivak need not be short-circuited by methodological turf battles. Echoing Gates's "Critical Fanonism," Slemon cautions that "academic interest in . . . the discourse of colonialism bids fair to become the last bastion for the project of global theory and for European universalism itself" (30). Asking "whether we really need to choose between oppositional critics whose articulations of the postcolonial institutionalize themselves as agonistic struggles over a thoroughly disciplined terrain" (30), Slemon argues for methodological tolerance and close attention to historical specificity. Ann duCille's argument for methodological tolerance is predicated on a similar line of thought. She focuses specifically on the tense relationship between nativist discourses of Afrocentricity on the one hand, and poststructuralist theory on the other. "If we could see beyond the tufts of straw and the feet of clay," she writes, "I wonder what practitioners of these three discourses—African American studies, postcoloniality, and Afrocentricity—might learn from one another, and in particular what we might teach one another about the white academy that claims and disclaims us. As we go about our intellectual business and launch our critiques, we would perhaps do well to be less suspicious of one another and more suspicious of the academy that promotes, demotes, and divides us" (135).

The claim that there is a "white academy" that promotes or divides us is problematic if understood within a frame of racialized abjection. But if understood in the Althusserian-poststructuralist sense I elaborated in the previous chapter, the white in "white academy" becomes no more than a synecdoche of Euro-American hegemony. The academy is an educational apparatus that interpellates all, and recruits those who are deemed "worthy." In this sense, we all—regardless of race and other markers of identity—participate in reproducing "the system," insofar as the academic institution is part of the larger capitalist society. The task I should like to stress, then, is less that of being suspicious of the academy conceived as an abstract synecdoche, than of demystifying the totalizing aspirations of academic discourses. Such demystification participates in the system of knowledge production and dissemination by critically reflecting on how knowledges operate and are reproduced. My argument in this chapter has been that poststructuralist, postcolonial theory can be useful wherever it facilitates this sort of orientation in cultural criticism. By extension, wherever the theory claims epistemological transcendence, it betrays inadequate attention to historical grounding, including its own, and thereby becomes vulnerable to criticism.

It is time now to reassemble the results of our exploration. First, I have argued that Spivak's insistent foregrounding of political economy, coupled with her explicit self-location in a determinate historical and institutional conjuncture, makes her analyses of the postcolonial condition less prone to the abstractions characteristic of Bhabha. The gain is that she yields a mode of thinking that can inform determinate conjunctural analyses. In addition, Spivak points up a promising direction for materialist analyses, one that goes deeper than simply remarking the economic overdetermination of the contemporary world system. One useful consequence of this is that it cautions contemporary criticism against idealistic celebration of the subversiveness of nationalist discourses or "third world" literatures.

On this score, the limits of Homi Bhabha's foundational work on colonial discourse are clear. Bhabha's theory of colonial discourse and his encounter with Fanon yield a two-fold problem. First, his findings claim at once a retroactive-explanatory and a normative-prescriptive salience. Second, he explores the workings of the psyche, resists the attempt to think those workings along with history and ideology, yet desires that his findings be held as an acceptable account of a determinate sociocultural event. Categories like mimicry, hybridity, or sly civility are elegantly protean. But, unwilling to historicize them within particular discursive fields—indeed, skeptical of the desire to do so—Bhabha often takes refuge in lyricism. The poetry takes flight and escapes the persistence of what brought his object (that is, the colonial condition) into being: history and political economy. If Spivak marks an advance on Bhabha in this direction, the price she pays is that her contributions can only be metacritical, locked into a performative contradiction she acknowledges but cannot thereby mitigate. Here lies the creative provocation that Spivak's work on postcoloniality offers so far. On her own terms, Spivak is productive precisely to the extent that her critical commitments, and the mode of thinking they mobilize, move pointedly towards crisis. But to do full justice to the logic of her position and prevent the stasis to which a weak mobilization of productive crisis might succumb, we need to turn the latter back on itself. Put differently, to remain consistent and rise above reification, the conceptual trajectory of productive crisis has to welcome its own crisis and supersession.

In the efforts of the poststructuralist theorists of postcoloniality, the non-West becomes part of the drama of modernity in a way it doesn't with Habermas or Lyotard. However, postcolonial theory can only get stalled if the lure of epistemic transcendence ("I am right, so others must be wrong") wins out. This tendency might be called a will to theory, understood as a search for aprioristic finality. Unchecked, this will to theory may encourage a scenario of circular claims and counterclaims, wherein what is at stake is simply the dismissal of one model and the installation of another. What may be lost are complex textual specificities that testify to complex colonial histories. In attending to diverse colonial histories in the richness of their textualization, we can borrow from Tiffin, Slemon, and Parry, without having to jettison Spivak and Bhabha. In an inherently comparative field like postcolonial criticism, one that is only just crystallizing out of a broader ferment in literary and cultural theory, such conceptual tolerance—perhaps even methodological promiscuity— can be enabling.[24]

In the present climate of postcolonial criticism and cultural studies, to understand African literature and criticism sensitively requires attention to history and context. By now it should be evident that I use the terms "history" and "context" with a specific conceptual frame in mind. The agency of African letters is available to analytical demonstration if it is grasped within this specific conceptual frame. As I argued in the previous chapter, epistemic or political statements emerge (and acquire meaning, if they do) because a relational context—a discursive web—occasions and apprehends them (or suffers them) as such. Indeed, the subject-position from which the epistemic or political statement derives is constituted by and within that relational context, that discursive web. On these terms, identity is a discursive subject-position, not a static or monolithic ontology. And for that reason, the epistemic or political articulation that emerges therefrom cannot be transcendental. The agent *becomes* and acts, only within a structure of predication and circumscription.

If this account is persuasive, discursive agency in particular moments and cultural formations can most productively be shown by means of dialectical reconstruction, not theoretical speculation or prescription. And so, in the next chapter, I should like to explore the criticism of African literature from about the 1960s onward. My concern is to show the ways in which the literature and the criticism offer an instance of discursive agency that is part of the broader struggle for discursive decolonization that had been taking place in sub-Saharan Africa since the 1950s. In this sense, the purpose of the next chapter is to demonstrate that the story that current postcolonial theory seeks to tell about agency can be more powerfully equipped if it is more finely tuned to the adventure of mind we are designating as African letters.

CHAPTER THREE

THE LOGIC OF AGENCY
IN AFRICAN LITERARY CRITICISM

The central preoccupation of African letters can be formulated as that of working through the tension between one cluster of values that is called "tradition," and another that is called "modernity." As indicated in the second chapter, I use the term "modernity" in its Weberian sense, that is, a mode of seeing that engenders a historically unique social organization, one grounded in instrumental reason and legitimated by the promise of "enlightenment" and universal emancipation. The purpose of this chapter is to consider the ways in which this working out has been conducted in an attempt to tease out a certain logic that is inherent to it. What this chapter tries to reveal is the *problematic*, in the Althusserian sense, of African letters.[1] Because this chapter aims to make this logic explicit, our task is a metacritical one, concerned as we aim to be with raising to the surface a subterranean logic immanent in the intellectual current we are calling African letters. And so to that very extent, a charge of theoreticism can invariably be raised. It is a familiar charge, and goes something like this: idle theorists stay locked at the metacritical level, parasitically fussing over what others are doing. It may be useful, then, to begin by indicating why an inquiry into the logic of African letters has significant benefits as much in its own terms as in the context of contemporary postcolonial theory and cultural criticism.

In the last chapter, we were concerned with establishing the proposition that the philosophical discourse of "modernity" subsists on a number of presuppositions that render it (i.e., modernity) inconsistent;

indeed, that its force as the West's self-representation seems to lie in the productive suturing of those inconsistencies. One of these inconsistencies—the one on which we particularly focused—is the dichotomization of "tradition" and "modernity," a dichotomization that serves to introduce an evolutionary logic. By means of this logic, the non-Western enters the field as an Other that needs to catch up. In Habermas and Lyotard, we encountered versions of this dynamic, even though both position themselves very differently as far as attitudes to the challenge of modernity are concerned. The conclusion we sought to set in place there is that a teleological grasp of modernity cannot yield a critical angle on either the West, its present moment and consciousness, or its relation to the non-West. What it can do is to reinforce a conceptual field wherein the non-West never emerges in its commensurate "coevalness," but as an eager aspirant to a preconstituted ideal: it enables thought to proceed, but is itself neither the occasion nor the referent of the thinking. I also suggested that a will to theory marks many debates about subjectivity, discursive resistance, and agency. This will to theory leads to a situation wherein one routinely encounters appeals to "the particular," but the appeals are pitched at such a level of generality that what is being called for (i.e., "the particular" itself) has little chance of emerging. For this reason, African letters cannot be comprehensively understood within the terms of the debates around postmodernity, nor can it within the rhetoric of much of current discussions of postcoloniality.

This chapter traces a certain pattern in the history of African literary criticism as a way of looking at what we might learn if we leave the realm of abstract-universal theory and try to concentrate on what specific historical contexts might teach us about such issues as cultural-political struggle, the way human communities create discourses (academic, literary, as well as popular) to understand and represent their world—in other words, discursive agency. My intention is to demonstrate that at this conjuncture in (literary-critical) knowledge production and dissemination, a productive approach to African literature has much to learn from some attention to the history of its criticism prior to the multiculturalist moment, and before the economic disorder (and mismanagement) that has brought African nations to their knees, begging for the mercy of international finance bodies. What we learn, I want to argue, has crucial implications for further study of African cultures and literatures, as well as the study of literature as such. Viewed this way, a proper critical account of the story of African letters has a crucial place in a genuinely international or, in current parlance, cosmopolitan, cultural criticism.

Disalienation and Modernization

The history to which I refer would begin somewhere in the middle of the past century, when black African countries began winning their juridical independence from the imperial powers—Britain, France and, later, Portugal. In black Africa as in most third world societies, the struggle for political independence was, from the beginning, accompanied by the realization that political independence can live up to its promise only if it goes hand in hand with a corresponding epistemological decolonization, only if the concrete-political is supplemented with the theoretical-discursive. Since the late 1950s when the ex-colonies began to adjust to their new status as sovereign nations, the policies and research/funding priorities of state apparatuses have clearly been determined by this realization. Consequently, the overarching impulse has been that of transcending colonial underdevelopment, that of catching up with modernity. Current work in academic philosophy and the social sciences has shown that such an understanding of political independence undercomplicates the predicament of modernity. So much is this the case that its presuppositions cannot adequately account for Western modernity itself, still less the postcolonial problematic within it. More immediately, however, we are here interested in the way the Africanist appropriation of the ideology of modernity, that is to say, the impulse to catch up, is replicated in African critical thought.

If the hard sciences are sponsored by the often unexamined lure of what is called *technology transfer,* the soft sciences operate on the strength of a corresponding passion. That passion aims to set in place a conducive theoretical-discursive atmosphere, the idea being that the desired concrete-political march towards technologization and the other promises and markers of modernity require an appropriate backcloth in the humanities and social sciences. In accordance with this logic, the project of epistemological decolonization is most often framed in terms of constructing a "decolonized" discourse to (i) counteract the epistemic violence of colonialism, and (ii) reveal an authentic African reality and self. Doing this, it is assumed, will facilitate collective psychic reconstruction, thereby preparing the ground for material (economic-technical) advancement. The work of activists, writers, and other cultural workers contains this rather Hegelian structure: the colonial event acquires the status of a dialectic moment, one that discursive mediation purports to transcend. Seen this way, African letters presupposes a state, contingent on the labor of thinkers, creative writers and critics, of adequate rehabilitation of the African subject. It assumes, in other words, the possibility of an adequate self-construction that remedies the distortions of colonialist discourse.

And further, it assumes the possibility of a discursive space *outside* of the Western (read: colonial) way of knowing.

It might be objected that this account of Africanist discourse is so generalized as to be reductive and simplified; that no discourse, or configuration of discourses, can be so monolithic. It needs to be stressed, therefore, that the configuration of discourses I designate under the category of African letters does indeed reveal divergent and often mutually conflicting positions. Nonetheless, a basic opposition to what is seen as the Eurocentric attitude to knowledge and to other peoples and values, as well as an impulse to rectify its distortions: these seem to me to be their common characteristic.[2] Thus in African literary criticism, although the methods proposed, and the understanding of how methods can be harnessed to generate a desired end may conflict, the desired end remains a common point of agreement, namely, to catch up with cultural modernity by having a discursive tradition centered on Africa and its problems.

This commitment is as old as when black peoples learned to read and write. We do not need to recite the figures of ex-slaves who wrote specifically to advance the cause of "the race" (Gates, *Figures*, 3–28). Nor do we need to recall the ferment of the mid-nineteenth century, when freed slaves from the diaspora took on the burden of Christianizing (understood as civilizing) "heathen" blacks on the African continent (Appiah, *House*, 3–27; Curtin; Echeruo; Mudimbe, *Invention*, 98–134; Zachernuk, 19–46). The rhetorics of these currents differ; by the turn of the twentieth century, however, a specific kind of rhetoric had started to emerge that is closer to the current with which we are concerned. On April 5, 1906, a young South African student named Isaka Seme stood before an audience at Columbia University. He was there to deliver the "Curtis Medal" oration, which he entitled "The Regeneration of Africa." In the following excerpt from his oration, the effusive prose is probably due to youth and a sense of epochal achievement; but what I wish to underline is the rhetoric of a new beginning, a regeneration, that gives Isaka Seme's lines their charm:

> Oh, for that historian who, with the open pen of truth, will bring to Africa's claim the strength of written proof. He will tell of a race whose onward tide was often swelled with tears, but in whose heart bondage has not quenched the fire of former years. He will write that in these later days when Earth's noble ones are named, she has a roll [sic] of honor too, of whom she is not ashamed. The giant is awakening ! From the four corners of the earth Africa's sons, who have been proved through fire and sword, are marching to the future's golden door bearing the records of deeds of valour done. ("Regeneration," 53)

In these lines, Africa is mother ("she"), and the military metaphor places the sons on a march toward the future. Seme's focus on writing—the "open pen of truth," or "the strength of written proof"—also articulates a certain insecurity, one that he hopes will be transcended in part through Africa's rehabilitation in discourse.[3] As we shall see in the next two chapters, the fact that Africa does not have an established indigenous tradition of writing constitutes a particular locus of concern in modern African literature. In this one passage, Isaka Seme encompasses a good deal of the passion and internal stresses of African letters.

About fifty years later, in the era of full-fledged nationalism and decolonization, an African politician and intellectual revisits Seme's oration and endorses its vision. At the first congress of Africanists held in Accra, Ghana, in December 1962, Kwame Nkrumah opens the conference with the claim that the meeting is "a reflection of Africa's recovery and re-awakening. It is also a recognition of the new spirit which now animates the spirit of this great continent" (Nkrumah, 6). Like Seme, Nkrumah's rhetoric follows the logic of catching up quite intimately. His metaphor of recuperation after a period of incapacitation implies that Africa has been asleep in discourse, and the awakening is now (i.e., in 1962) beginning. It also suggests that Africanist discourse, and the knowledge it seeks to disseminate, is *contingent* on the colonial encounter; that, in essence, the event to which the Africanist project responds is the colonial event. Nkrumah therefore locates whatever transpired in 1962 in Accra squarely within the ferment of a politics of reconstruction after the injury of colonialism, after the epistemic violence of that fateful encounter. He gives voice to the commonality I referred to above by announcing, in words quoted directly from Isaka Seme's oration: "The African people, although not a strictly homogeneous race, possess a common fundamental sentiment which is everywhere manifest, crystallizing itself into one common controlling idea" (Nkrumah, 14; Seme, 55).

By the time Nkrumah stands before a congress of academics and replicates Isaka Seme's poetry, a crucial new dimension has emerged. Most African politicians of the decolonization era, some of whom became presidents when their countries were granted Independence, also saw themselves as "men of culture" whose writings acquire what Foucault would call "author function."[4] Their writings are not restricted to explicitly political tracts or ruminations on state administration. Randomly, we may mention writings in philosophy (Kwame Nkrumah, Leopold Senghor), nativist or revolutionary poetry (Senghor, Augustino Neto), ethnography of "tribal" life (Jomo Kenyatta), or translations of Shakespeare into African languages (John Nyerere, Sol T. Plaatje). Not only is Nkrumah's speech delivered before an audience in Ghana, the first black African country to win its political independence, his speech is also that of a "statesman" *performing* (in the sense that speech-act theory gives the term) the concrete opening of an academic event, a venture.

One of the papers delivered at this conference is Alioune Diop's "The Spirit of *Présence Africaine*." *Présence Africaine* is the name of the journal devoted to academic study of Africa within various disciplines, ranging from philosophy to literature and the social sciences.[5] Diop traces the history of this journal from its beginnings in Paris from 1941 to 1946, and its founding in Paris in 1947. Diop uses this historical excursion to reflect on the tasks of the African intellectual in the project of reclaiming the African heritage. According to him,

> Men of culture have [a] . . . clear responsibility. African historians must do more than just dig down beneath the surface of Africa, which apparently has some rather pleasant surprises in store. As persons destined to educate our people, they must provide a structural pattern for the national consciousness, as well as the consciousness of Africa as a whole. This is a function that can hardly be fulfilled by foreigners, a task that no one should question, any more than one would question the right of African linguists to associate politicians, historians, thinkers, theologians, etc., with their work, or doubt the possibility that, through the rigorous discipline of scholarship, they may experience more fully than others the throbbing flesh and soul of African genius. (Diop, 48–49)

The notion of "men of culture" owes much to the Western liberal-humanist tradition. However, Diop narrows the purview of his expectation to the "throbbing flesh and soul of the African genius." Diop's formulation casts the African intellectual as a "man of culture," without qualification. But he yet narrows that grand masculinist universalism into an African particularity. In this sense, he does not quite want the African intellectual to be a universal "man of culture" through disinterested pursuit of knowledge; rather, he is to set his gaze on the African particularity. Participating in the cosmopolitan game of culture, Diop's man comes aboard with a particular mission, that of capturing the rhythm of negritude, of experiencing "more fully than others the throbbing flesh and soul of African genius."

What Diop's rhetoric exemplifies is a logic whereby one participates in modernity but not fully within its preconstituted terms. The controversial Anglophone poet and essayist, Chinweizu, exemplifies a kind of activist perspective (as against a conventionally academic one) that adds another dimension to the dynamic we are sketching. In the essay, "Towards a Liberated African Culture," Chinweizu writes: "Given the psychic and ideological foundation of our subjugation, of both the colonial subjugation from which we thought we had escaped and the neo-colonial form that has manacled us, any spirited drive for genuine freedom must begin with a thorough critique of the bourgeois culture that has made us captives; of the process and content of the modernization that has lured us into captivity; and of the relation, if any, between technological modernization and the Christian bourgeois culture" (416). Later on in the essay, Chinweizu insists that he "is not against modernization. What I ask is that we examine and choose between alternative contents and forms of modernization" (417). Here, we see another level of what I put forth earlier as the fundamental commonality inherent to African letters. Even Chinweizu, a figure who is most notorious for what might be called his Anglophone negritude (that is, his nativist ontologization of Africa and African-ness) endorses in principle the ideal of modernization. He only wants some care exercised in the choice of *which* path to take toward modernization. He thus demonstrates the extent to which the ideology of modernity saturates African letters, even with a die-hard Afrocentricist like Chinweizu.

If Chinweizu asks for differentiations between various forms of modernization, differentiations that he does not really elaborate, Marxism offers one path to modernization that is an alternative to the free market model. In the Marxist versions of the African predicament, the element of catching up remains intact, albeit with the important qualification that what is being caught up with is not capitalist modernity but, putatively, a socialist one. Consequently, some versions of African Marxism proffer the notion of a precolonial African communalism that needs to be remodeled in the direction of a modern socialist state. As V. Y. Mudimbe has argued in *The Invention of Africa,* "since most African leaders and thinkers have received a Western education, their thought is at the crossroads of Western epistemological filiation and African ethnocentrism. Moreover, many concepts and categories underpinning this ethnocentrism are inventions of the West. When prominent leaders such as Senghor and Nyerere propose to synthesize liberalism and socialism, idealism and materialism, they know that they are transplanting Western intellectual manicheism" (185). Very concretely posed therefore, African letters can be said to rest on a simple and salutary agenda. But the simplicity of this agenda should not be read to mean simplistic. Very much to the contrary, the simplicity testifies to the intense sense of purpose and commitment that, from at least the turn of the twentieth century, powered the discourse of the human sciences in black Africa. It is a historic intensity, made sharper by its concreteness of vision and singleness of purpose.

Because the aim of this chapter is to tease out a fundamental blindspot in the criticism of African literature, it is important to stress this historic existential impetus. This involves giving it due epistemological weight without, however, giving up on the need for dialectical critique. At the center of the examples we have been considering is an object of knowledge, Africa. The single word operates at once as signifier and referent; it designates a geographical domain, a cultural identity, and a subjective state brought on by a specifiable history. As the totality of these things, it carries a lot of weight and therefore requires—to have any real use—a presumption of self-evidence. In a poststructuralist climate, this assumption of self-evidence is fully vulnerable to a charge of nativism and essentialism. As indicated in the previous chapter, the reception of African letters in Anglo-American theory generally zeroes in on this blindspot.

And yet, the rejection of essentialism is not entirely unprecedented in the history of African letters. Debates in academic philosophy, in particular, have shown the sense in which an unselfconscious appropriation of Africa as a self-evident and ontological object of knowledge is conceptually flawed. It is crucial to keep this point in mind because the critique of nativist or nationalist discourses in current theory is too often mounted on terms that do not make adequately visible the historicity of these discourses. We hear a lot about negritude and what is wrong with it, but we also know that Frantz Fanon precedes us in this recognition and Fanon is only one of many. Meanwhile, we do not hear enough about attacks on negritude that predated Anglo-American critiques of essentialism. An illustration of this is the current trend whereby anthologies of postcolonial studies and theory include selections from Senghor, Fanon, or Cabral, next to essays by contemporary theorists of postcoloniality like Said, Spivak, or Bhabha. The effect is that a temporal devolution is constructed such that negritude emerges as one phase in a teleological chain that culminates in poststructuralist, postcolonial theory. Quite apart from the problem with such a teleological framing of knowledge and its objects, to pay adequate attention to the particularity of African letters is to recognize that the problematic of Senghor is not seamlessly continuous with that of Said. This is in no way to suggest that these two cannot be thought of together. Rather, it is to say that before they can be thought of together in really interesting ways, the specificity of each needs to be thematized in a manner that goes deeper than perfunctory claims about the importance of historical specificity. Before moving on to the specific instance of African literary criticism, then, let us touch on two exemplary cases of the critique of what has come to be known as ethnophilosophy.

In Africanist circles, perhaps the most well-known example of such critiques is that mounted by Paulin Hountondji, in his book *Sur La Philosophie Africaine*. This book, which first appeared in 1976, was published in English translation in 1983. Hountondji's notoriety rests on his attack on what he called a "unanimist" tradition of African and Western scholars who attempt to reduce the continent's disparate systems of thought into a single "African Philosophy."[6] According to him, this tendency amounts to a culturalism. "The characteristic of culturalism in this sense," he writes,

> is to distort the political and economic problems, neatly side-stepping them in favour of exclusively cultural problems. Worse still, these cultural problems are themselves strangely simplified as culture is reduced to folklore, its most obvious and superficial aspect. Its deeper life and internal contradictions, the fruitful tensions by which it is animated are all neglected, along with its history, development and revolutions. Culture is petrified in a synchronic picture, flat and strangely simple and univocal, and is then contrasted with other cultures which are also trimmed and schematized for the sake of the comparison. (160)

Hountondji rejects culturalism thus defined because it replicates a Eurocentric mode of apprehending culture. Against culturalism, Hountondji poses a cluster of Althusserian themes: the domain of culture is autonomous and at the same time overdetermined; to unravel this overdetermination then becomes the unique province of philosophy. In a later essay, he provides the motivation for his critique: "There was need, in order to deal with the complexity of our history, to bring back the scene of that history to its original simplicity; in order to deal with the richness of African traditions, there was need to *impoverish* resolutely the concept of Africa, to *free* it from all connotations, ethical, religious, philosophical, political, etc., loaded on it by a long anthropological tradition, the most evident of which was to close the horizon, to close history prematurely" (qtd. in *African Philosophy*, xii). A similar impulse to "impoverish" the concept of Africa as a way of freeing it from ideological encrustations imposed by a long tradition of anthropological writing governs V. Y. Mudimbe's *The Invention of Africa*. In this book, Mudimbe undertakes a Foucaultian archaeology of the concept of Africa, as a way of unraveling its constitution. He tries to show, not only the way in which an epistemological category called *Africa* was invented in and by the discourse of the West, but also how that invention is inseparably bound up with the history of the West; that is, the questions the West has posed to itself, and has sought to answer in various ways.

At the beginning of the book, Mudimbe provides a reading of the 1508 painting, entitled "Exotic Tribe," by Hans Burgkmair. That year, Hans Burgkmair was called upon to illustrate a travel diary compiled by Bartoloaus Springer, who had just completed a series of travels overseas. Faced with this painting, Mudimbe identifies in the painter's commitment a tension whose product—a delicately realized work of art—is yet a sign:

> Let us imagine the painter at work. He has just read Springer's description of his voyage, and possibly on the basis of some sketches, he is trying to create an image of blacks in "Gennea." Perhaps he has decided to use a model, presumably white but strongly built. The painter is staring at the pale body, imagining schemes to transform it into a black entity. The model has become a mirror through which the painter evaluates how the norms of similitude and his own creativity would impart both a human identity and a racial difference to his canvas. Perhaps the artist is already at work. Yet he has to stop regularly, walk around the model, leave the luminous space before the window, and retire into a discreet corner. His gaze addresses a point which is a question: how to superimpose the African characteristics described in Springer's narrative onto the norms of the Italian *contrapposto?* (7)

Mudimbe's imaging of Burgkmair at the scene of artistic creation recalls Foucault's account, at the beginning of *The Order of Things,* to the enchanted scene where Velázquez struggled to give form to *Las Meninas.*

This invocation of the remarkable opening paragraphs of Foucault's book is a stylistic as well as thematic move, for Mudimbe's reading casts Burgkmair's representational truth as a sign that yields its own conditions of possibility in the full Foucaultian sense. By proceeding in this way, Mudimbe is able to demonstrate a process of invention—in this case, one that works as a process of othering and of establishing same-ness. A master at his craft, Burgkmair sincerely wants to make his image of primitives "authentic." But this he could only do within the norms of a classic form of structural representation. In Mudimbe's reading, then, the *contrapposto* functions as a condition of possibility for Burgkmair's painting. The point, I think, is clear: Burgkmair inherits an ancient form, and his realization of the primitives of "Gennea" could only emerge within the norms of his inheritance.

And so, "[t]he structure of the figures, as well as the meaning of the nude bodies, proclaim the virtues of resemblances: in order to designate Springer's blacks, the painter has represented blackened whites" (8). What emerges is an ambiguity Burgkmair cannot escape, for the same painting celebrates difference even as it functions as a testimony to the logic of the Same: "in Burgkmair's painting there are two representational activities: on the one hand, signs of an epistemological order which, silently but imperatively, indicate the processes of integrating and differentiating figures within the normative sameness; on the other hand, the excellence of an exotic picture that creates a cultural distance, thanks to an accumulation of accidental differences, namely, nakedness, blackness, curly hair, bracelets, and strings of pearls" (9). Mudimbe is thus urging that we keep two things in constant focus: (i) the status of the signifier "Africa" as a discursive object of knowledge, and (ii) the self-authenticating assumptions contained in the disciplinary apparatus that nurtures the will to knowledge, and whose historicity and parameters constitute the absolute condition of possibility of the expert's undertaking. To fail to foreground the double dimensionality of this project may lead to a situation where, in an attempt to dispel the West's epistemic violence, the critic reinscribes an inversion of the same epistemological order—merely blackening the received (white) details. The language is Foucaultian, but, on the discussion of ideology vis-à-vis science that we conducted in Chapter 1, the problematic is anticipated in Althusser.

And yet, Mudimbe presses on. If academic critical thought is inescapably bound up with the "ambiguous passion of knowledge"; if the cultural critic is ultimately a rebelling but nonetheless legitimate offspring of the West, is she therefore helpless before the Eurocentrism of her patrimony? As we saw in chapter 1, according to Satya P. Mohanty, the problem with poststructuralist cultural criticism is that it does not thematize this question adequately, and so cannot offer perspectives that are of real value. Despite his Foucaultian vocabulary, however, Mudimbe confronts the question explicitly. For him, inventions—willful habitation of the treacherous climates of ideology—are not only inevitable, they are also indispensable and should be theorized as such. The subject *is,* only by being in ideology. The crucial condition is that an awareness of the invented status of discourse, a paradigmatic sense of its own conditions of possibility, can positively inform the critical enterprise.

In this direction, Mudimbe introduces the agency of the subject. We shall quote him at length:

> The masterful demonstrations by Lévi-Strauss and Foucault do not convince me that the subject in the discourse of the Same or on the Other should be a mere illusion or a simple shadow of an episteme. What they teach me is different; namely, that *we lack a theory* that

could solve the dialectic tension between creative discourses and
the epistemological field which makes them possible, on the one
hand, and Lévi-Strauss' unconscious that sustains discourses and
accounts for their organization, on the other. In fact, there is an
obvious way out of this problem by means of the subject, who
directly or indirectly, consciously or unconsciously, participates in
the modification or the constitution of an epistemological order.
(35, emphasis added)

In this passage, we should note a swerve away from Foucault, as well as
the claim that "we lack a theory" that can resolve once and for all the
"tension" between knowledge as discourse encodes it, and the knower
who is himself determined by discourse. Mudimbe raises to the surface
the very question poststructuralists are accused of evading, namely, how
the decentered subject still manages to function, to *know*, precisely
within the maelstrom of discursive impingement or ideological interpellation. What is relevant for our concerns is that Mudimbe (i) privileges,
against Foucault or Lévi-Strauss, the subject without essentializing it
and, (ii) identifies agency as a dynamic that is not yet theorized: "*we
lack a theory* that could solve the dialectic tension between creative discourses and the epistemological field which makes them possible, on the
one hand, and Lévi-Strauss' unconscious that sustains discourses and
accounts for their organization, on the other" (35). It will be inaccurate
to say that Mudimbe in this passage raises the question only to avoid it.
To the contrary, his achievement is that he displaces the question so as
to refocus it on the meandering of the subject in history, on the adventures of that overdetermined capsule of desires who, "directly or indirectly, consciously or unconsciously, participates in the modification or
the constitution of an epistemological order" (35).

Following our conclusions from the analysis of Althusser's theory
in the first chapter and postcolonial theory in the second, we may push
Mudimbe's circumspection about theories of the decentered subject with
regard to human agency further. As we saw in Chapter 1, the achievement of Laclau and Mouffe is that they move within Althusser's
premises to arrive at an apprehension of agency that is ultimately formal, *not* substantive. On these terms, agency cannot be theorized outside of the relational context, the conjuncture, wherein agents are constituted and circumscribed. It is not simply that we lack a theory that
can once and for all resolve the "dialectic tension" between discursive
interpellation and the subject's agency in modernity; rather, such a theory cannot be posed as a substantive proposition because we are still in
modernity. That is, we cannot resolve the issue *in theory* because we are
ourselves its products. For this reason, we may with profit direct atten-

tion to what particular subjects have done or are doing, rather than what is the "right" thing to do—insofar as rightness is framed outside of the context of the doing itself. Our foray into African literary criticism will reveal conceptual limitations that turn out to be the condition of possibility of its institutionalization as an academic venture. In this sense, African literary criticism from the late 1950s grounds our argument that discursive agency is best apprehended in action, not in hermetic theoretical contemplation.

THE INHERITED MANDATE IN AFRICAN LITERARY CRITICISM

In this segment, the history I construct is partial and strategic: partial because I focus only on a particular conjuncture in the adventure of Anglophone African literary criticism, strategic because my construction is driven by a metacritical purpose. My account is not an institutional history of African literary criticism, neither does it claim to exhaust its diverse strands and ideological positions. Rather, my analysis is intended to be illustrative of a sociopolitical and intellectual problematic that can roughly be dated from the late 1950s to the early 1980s. What I want to do is to isolate two principal literary-critical approaches that enabled the struggle for self-representation and self-understanding in Anglophone Africa, namely, "intrinsic" criticism and its "extrinsic" antithesis. Moving backwards, I review these two approaches and the clash they enacted as each sought to claim methodological priority. I then conclude by resituating the conflict within the current situation in postcolonial theory and criticism. My specific claim is twofold. First, in its commitment to facilitating epistemological and socioeconomic decolonization (two domains whose conflation demands unpacking), African literary criticism took a crucial leap at the outset: it gave inadequate scrutiny to categories inherited from European letters. Yet, it is in this leap that the agency of African letters can be located.

In Anglophone African literature, Chinua Achebe is generally credited with inaugurating black Africa's self-representation in fiction. Less than a decade after *Things Fall Apart* (1958), the novel that launched a thousand ships if ever one did, Achebe is already called upon to reflect on his role and his readership. In an essay entitled "The Novelist as Teacher," first published in 1965, Achebe begins with characteristic clear-sightedness: "Writing of the kind I do is relatively new in my part of the world and it is too soon to try and describe in detail the complex of relationships between us and our readers" (40). At the high point of this essay, Achebe writes: "I would be quite satisfied if my novels (especially the ones I set in the past) did no more than teach my readers that their past—with all its imperfections—was not one long night of savagery from which the first Europeans acting on God's behalf delivered them" (45). Somber, almost brooding, this essay has come to be seen as Achebe's artistic manifesto. Let us note the deliberate modesty inherent to Achebe's formulation, the self-circumscription evoked by the phrases "quite satisfied" and "no more than." A little, Achebe is very pointedly announcing, goes a long way. And yet, that modesty is accompanied by some defiance. For in the next sentence after the one just quoted, Achebe adds the following rider: "perhaps what I write is applied art as distinct from pure. But who cares" (45).

This circumscription of purview and defiance towards the conventional definition of "pure art" raises an issue of theoretical interest. What Achebe demonstrates here is at once an acceptance of a modern Western apprehension of the role of literature in society, and a rejection of part of it. Achebe reveals a traditional (reflectionist) attitude to literary representation even as he rejects another traditional (aestheticist, "art-for-art's sake") view. The presupposition underwriting the reflectionist view of literature is that adequate representation of an idea, an object, or a constellation of values is possible. Related to this is the assumption that literary texts encode, or can be made so to do, the reality of cultures or peoples. If this view characterizes some versions of traditional Eurocentric criticism, the anti-utilitarian view is not entirely compatible. If indeed the literary "artifact" rewards us purely in our contemplation of its formal beauty, it really does not matter what literature encodes. In fact, to encode anything other than its own intrinsic-formal worth might detract from its purity as aesthetic achievement. What Achebe does is to claim that his novels reflect the "real Africa" and therefore, cannot be "pure art." In this way, he opens up an immanent tension between two equally conventional attitudes to the interaction of form and content in literature.

In Achebe's essay we see a writer thinking through his craft. But what about the academic critic(s) contemplating what writers do? It is often said that Anglophone African fiction emerged in the late 1950s and 1960s, precisely at the point of the publication of Achebe's *Things Fall Apart*. According to this view, Achebe's novel demonstrates sophisticated literary craftsmanship and portrays precolonial Ibo society and the colonial encounter adequately. By contrast, African writing in the first half of the twentieth century is said to be important but immature, almost subliterary, because (i) the writers lacked the sophisticated craftsmanship associated with "great" literature, and (ii) their vision bought into Western ideology and is therefore not sufficiently decolonized.

Eustace Palmer opens his *The Growth of African Literature* by identifying the moment at which he is writing in these terms: "A quarter of a century after the publication of the first African novels worth the name a substantial body of criticism has emerged which in its range and erudition indisputably matches the volume and importance of the new literature" (*Growth*, 1). And Albert Gérard's *European-Language Writing in Sub-Saharan Africa* attributes the importance of *Things Fall Apart* to the fact that it came to fill a literary vacuum: "the mediocre poetry of Osadebey had attracted little attention and did not deserve more; although the originality of Tutuola was recognized everywhere, his *Palmwine Drinkard* was regarded as a freak of the literary imagination and became for that reason the object of a heated controversy; Ekwensi's *People of the City* had awakened considerable interest, but chiefly as a social document and a sample of popular writing devoid of any high aesthetic ambition or value" (689). Talk of novels "worth the name," of a novel being "devoid of high aesthetic ambition or value" because the interest it arouses is "chiefly as a social document," should recall Matthew Arnold, T. S. Eliot and F. R. Leavis. For them, as for the New Critical regime they inspired, criticism has a crucial job to do (in the face, need we add, of a deadening of sensibility occasioned by the real world of guns and industrial smoke). That job involves demarcating a realm of "great" art, a tradition, that would capture and radiate the spirit of a milieu, thereby disseminating cultural value.

We may cite Eliot's early essay, "Tradition and the Individual Talent," which famously defines literary tradition as an overarching repertoire of literary production generated by and in a given culture. Of course, Eliot has in mind the literary productions that have come out (and will come out) of Europe, and he states this explicitly, characterizing it as "our civilization." In his reading of the so-called metaphysical poets in an essay of the same title, Eliot endorses the "recondite" poetry of the metaphysicals, historicizing it as a testimony to the nature of sixteenth-century English civilization in contrast to that of the Victorians. For Eliot, the difference between Herbert's poetry and Tennyson's "is not a simple difference of degree between poets. It is something which had happened to the mind of England between the time of Donne or Lord Herbert of Cherbury and the time of Tennyson and Browning; it is the difference between the intellectual poet and the reflective poet" (307). This difference resides in the "dissociation of sensibility" which, according to Eliot, occurs in the seventeenth century. Due to this dissociation, poets became "reflective," rather than "intellectual." Thus, earlier poets like Donne could "feel their thought as immediately as the odour of a rose" (307). They could amalgamate disparate experiences, assume an analytical posture in relation to these experiences, and then synthesize them into new wholes, new wholes that thereafter acquire their objective correlative in poetic rendition.

The assumption in this account is that the poem has an internal dynamic that connotes its value as an artistic achievement and a carrier of the temper of its milieu. Value is taken as self-evident, and the burden of Eliot's analysis is to identify the divergent exemplifications of that value in the metaphysicals on the one hand, and on the other, from the mid-seventeenth century onwards. Eliot can then read the poetry of both periods to be symbolic—documentary—of the difference between the mind of England in the sixteenth century, and the mind of England by the nineteenth century. Contemporary cultural criticism has shown that the passion of figures like Eliot or Leavis is impelled by a sense of past cultural plenitude that needs to be rescued from a "contaminating" present. The transposition of this to the United States in the form of the New Criticism inherits this logic and reinforces it with the aspiration to "objectivity."

I bring up the old story of Leavisite criticism and new-critical "objectivity" because the criticism of African literature in Anglophone Africa owes much to both. We need not spend time on the demystification of new-critical orthodoxy that has effectively been accomplished with the emergence of theory and cultural studies.[7] In the New Criticism, there is a basic contradiction whereby texts are said to represent "our tradition" while at the same time representing the best of pure art, pure because it refers most powerfully to its own form and beauty. Despite its constitutive Eurocentric underlay, the New Criticism found an attentive audience in Anglophone Africa, and it is crucial to see why. In "Literature and History in Africa," Landeg White complains about what he perceived in the criticism of African Literature as inadequate attention to the material conditions of the literary work. As a result of this tendency, he argues, "critics [of African literature] set themselves no larger task than simple exposition—a mixture of plot summary and praise" (539). "Part of the trouble," he observes, "seems to lie in the state of literary criticism in England and America in the late fifties when studies of African Literature began to proliferate. The emphasis of the 'new criticism,' of the 'well wrought urn' and 'the verbal icon,' when critics like Ransom and Empson and Wimsatt stressed the benefits of close study of the text as artefact, led too easily to the assumption that there was some special virtue in isolating the text from its social and historical setting" (539). White has legitimate grounds for his observations, but I think he overstates his case. He identifies the surface contours of the critical scene that infuriates him, but he does not adequately identify its structural determinations. Discussing the prevailing tendencies in critical analyses of African Literature, he writes:

It became part of critical strategy to apologise for the assumed anthropological orientation of African novels of the 1950s and 1960s, and to set up such status claiming parallels as that Soyinka uses language like Joyce, that Laye is Kafkaesque, that Armah shares Swift's "excremental vision," that Tutuola's novels are, like *Wuthering Heights,* a "kind of sport." Forced by the very nature of the literature to look a little further, critics have been content to take their image of Africa from the literature itself and then praise the literature for its "truth," operating within such simple concepts as the "traditional African way of life," the clash between African and Western culture, and the corruption following independence—concepts which must seem strangely innocent to the historian or to the social or political scientist. Only recently, with the emphasis on stylistic analysis or on commitment have there been attempts to transcend a criticism based on personal impressions backed up by appeals to a Leavis-type "tradition." (539)

The diagnosis that African literature was ever isolated from its historical setting by critics seems to me inaccurate. I suggest, in fact, that the reverse is the case. From its beginnings, African literature has always been seen as a function of the history of colonialism. The writer's vocation has always been formulated as that of enabling the decolonization of Africa, and authors have been evaluated on the basis of how well they achieve this task. However, although the criticism has always been centrally activated by a political awareness (and prescriptiveness) of the tasks of African literature, critics part ways on the question of method. The divergence in critical method (or, in White's terms, the "improvement" from formalist-aestheticist to "committed" ways of reading) is not a temporal—i.e., "recent"—phenomenon but one that has always accompanied Africanist literary criticism. In this vein, the temporal dichotomy White installs between formalist and so-called committed critical strategies is flawed. Both formalists and nonformalist have always been "committed": committed to the project of contesting the distortions of colonial representations.

Nonetheless, White touches on an important point in remarking a derivativeness in the criticism of African literature, a dependence on Euro-American categories that makes critics fall back on "status claiming parallels" between Soyinka and Joyce, or Laye and Kafka. How then can he be right and not-quite-right at the same time? To answer this question, one needs to historicize both the formalist and nonformalist positions that governed the critical landscape in Anglophone Africa. On the one hand, you have critics for whom the concern with decolonization is expressed via an exclusively aestheticist conception of literature, an aestheticism inherited from Leavis and the New Criticism. But this aestheticism is then appropriated, not simply as a means to the refinement and acculturation of the reader, but rather as a strategic tool for the political cause of decolonization. For example, Abiola Irele suggests in "Studying African Literature" that, although Leavisite criticism is "really not 'sociological' in any methodological or technical sense, [it] implies a strong awareness of the social implications of literature" (*Ideology*, 23). Indeed, argues Irele, Leavis's work "is based on a strongly articulated social theory—of an élite in touch through the best literature with a vital current of feeling and of values, and having responsibility for maintaining, in the practice of criticism, the moral health of the society" (23). Irele finds this pastoralist element "highly questionable"; but, "the basic idea is to my thinking, not: it is a position which has the eminent merit of making us take literature seriously enough to commit one's total intelligence to making explicit what in it takes the forms of nuance and symbol, in other words, of applying its insights to the actual business of living" (23).

In a similar way, Chidi Maduka undertakes a reconciliation of the New Criticism with the political impetus of African literary criticism. He rejects three assumptions he associates with the New Criticism: (i) the idea of "self-containment" in the literary text, (ii) the tendency to "turn literature into a discipline of extreme specialization for *competent readers*," and (iii) the claim of "uniqueness" in true works of art. But he yet maintains that the new-critical rubric "can help in sharpening the critic's sensitivity to the mechanics of language (and structure)." "Consequently," he concludes, "if modified to recognize the importance of seeing form as an instrument of revealing meaning, it [formalism] can contribute to the current search for the essence of African aesthetics" (198–99).

The Africanist formalists inherited their categories from the literary-critical tradition of the Anglo-Saxon world in the middle of the twentieth century, but with the political awareness that these categories have historically been used to ground Western claims of cultural superiority. They therefore took key new-critical categories (e.g., value as an intrinsic quality that gives great art its greatness, and value as an ethical/cultural category that art encodes, and that the critic's objective labor recovers and disseminates), with some unease at its high-cultural leanings, but with a basic adoption of its substantive premises. Their project was to bring these categories to bear on African writing. They simply did for African literature what Leavis sought to do for English literature. In so doing, the Africanist formalists bring their Leavisite/new-critical inheritance down to earth by concretely (that is, in their use of it) deconstructing its self-reification.

A journal like *African Literature Today* served as a launching pad for the institutionalization of African literature. The journal was significant to the reproduction of a new-critical and academicist ideology. The editorial statement of the first issue is an interesting document. Its second paragraph reads in part: "Publishers publish what they decide to publish for a variety of reasons, not least among them the reason that they are in business to make money. Readers also read books with a variety of expectations, not the least being their wish to be entertained. It is the critic's business to read discerningly and demonstrate the qualities of a work and thus (a) to make it accessible to a larger readership than the absence of criticism might have opened to it, and (b) by an accumulation of such examinations to help establish literary standards."[8] What is worth noting in this passage is its recognition of the logics of exchange value in academic scholarship and publishing, a recognition that is immediately followed by a more conventional invocation of aesthetic pleasure and putatively objective establishment of "standards."

There were those who rejected an exclusive concern with the intrinsic dimensions of literature. These critics, who generally tend to be more strongly nationalist than the aestheticists, stress the extrinsic dimensions of literature, claiming that only a sociological approach can ensure effective mobilization of African literature toward the ideal of decolonization. One can delineate within this group the Marxist critics, as against non-Marxist, but patently nationalist ones. The latter operate with a nationalist commitment that may take various forms. *Toward the Decolonization of African Literature,* authored by three Nigerian critics—Chinweizu, Onwuchekwa Jemie, and Ihechukwu Madubuike—is a highly polemical instance of this kind of reflectionist and nativist criticism. Kwame Anthony Appiah has demonstrated that even as the book rejects so-called Eurocentric literary styles and critical tools, its rhetoric is couched in the frame of intra-European nationalism that goes back to the nineteenth century.[9]

Marxist criticism of African literature represents a conceptual antidote to the nativism of Chinweizu, Ihechukwu Madubuike, and Onwuchekwa Jemie. Yet, this is not to say that Marxist African criticism is free of instructive problems of its own. In "Wole Soyinka, T. M. Aluko and the Satiric Voice," the most influential exponent of Marxism in Africanist literary criticism, Ngugi wa Thiong'o, takes up the works of the Nigerian writers Wole Soyinka and T. M. Aluko. He applauds both writers' critique of modern Nigeria, and finds Soyinka's representation of Africa's postcolonial reality "adequate" and politically salutary. It is what he finds lacking that should interest us:

Although Soyinka exposes his society in depth, the picture he draws
is static, for he fails to see the present in the historical perspective of
conflict and struggle. It is not enough for the African artist, standing aloof, to view society and highlight its weaknesses. He must try
to go beyond this, to seek out the sources, the causes and the trends
of a revolutionary struggle which has already destroyed the traditional power-map drawn up by the colonialist nations. And Africa
is not alone. All over the world the exploited majority, from the
Americas, across Africa and the Middle East, to the outer edges of
Asia, is claiming its own. The artist in his writings is not outside the
battle. By diving into its sources, he can give moral direction to a
struggle which, though suffering temporary reaction, is continuous
and is changing the face of the twentieth century. (Thiong'o,
"Voice," 65–66)

For Ngugi, the most exquisitely realized literary work is useless
unless it lends a committed voice to the political struggle of the
"exploited majority." A similar approach informs Omafume Onoge's
account of the contributions of Marxist analyses of African literature.
Arguing for the superiority of Marxist analyses over formalism, Onoge
insists that the Marxist concern with characterization in literary works
is deeper, more robustly nuanced, that what formalism can ever offer.
"Marxist critics," he writes, "have not seen the imagined characters simply as free-floating individuals. On the contrary, the characters who
populate a writer's fictional universe also belong to social classes. And it
was a Marxist oriented critic, Ngugi, who first drew attention to the fact
that one of the problems of Soyinka's literature, was the unreal faceless-
ness of his working-class characters. Since Marxists hold that the working masses are the true makers of history, the images of the masses contained in literature are crucial signals of a writer's political standpoint"
(Onoge, 61). At this point, we might notice a common strain in the
nativism of someone like Chinweizu and the Marxism of Ngugi and
Onoge. All share a utilitarian and reflectionist perspective on literature,
and this leads them to prescribe what the ideal literary text, that which
carries true "value," should look like. But where Chinweizu seeks in literature an authentic *Africanity*, Ngugi and Onoge seek a reflection of the
struggles of the proletariat, a positive representation of the authentic
laboring masses. Two authenticities, it seems, are vying for primacy: on
the one hand a unanimist African authenticity, and on the other, an
equally unanimist class authenticity.

One problem with the Marxism exemplified by Ngugi and Onoge
can be located at this level. They mobilize an inherited notion of class as
a fixed analytical category and empirical social location. This is then

allied with a reflectionist view of literature, such that texts are assessed on the basis of the class consciousness they reflect and the fidelity of their representation of class struggle. Where formalists took after the New Criticism, Marxist criticism of African literature appropriated Georg Lukács's analysis of reification and class struggle, an analysis that is then brought into contact with the controversial reflection theory.[10] Approaching its analyses of African literature with a prioritization of class, tied to a tendentiously Lukácsean understanding of realism and reflection, Marxist-Africanist criticism is limited on two counts. First, it inherits from Western Marxism a problem defined by Ernesto Laclau as a "hypostatization of the abstract." By this Laclau means a procedure whereby "[a] set of features allowing the comparison of very different social realities are abstracted from the latter and transformed into an actually existent entity with its own laws of movement" (Laclau, *Reflections*, 13). Second, it undercomplicates the place of mediation in literary representation. The moment "class" is hypostasized and textual representation is posited as a mechanical representation of the contents of the objective world, mediation is no longer an active principle in literary production. To reflect the objects of reality on this model is simply to freeze a transparent world in a mirror whose outlines are known before the moment of the mirroring.[11]

An illustration of the conceptual cost that a reflectionist grasp of literature exerts can be found in the familiar debate surrounding the use of indigenous languages as against those of colonial imposition. Ngugi wa Thiong'o is currently the most influential critic of the centrality of the colonial languages in the epistemological indentureship of postindependence African cultures. Ngugi's novels constitute one of the most rewarding and perspicacious by any African writer. But the way he justifies his position on the issue of language and the politics proper to it has important problems. In numerous essays, he urges current and fledgling African writers to turn to their native languages in order to break the spell of the European languages as well as to contribute to (i) the development of a literary tradition in the indigenous languages, and (ii) the ongoing struggle for Africa's emancipation from the ravages of transnational capitalism. The intensity of Ngugi's commitment to the recuperation of indigenous African languages is most clearly to be seen in the fact that he has himself switched to writing in his native Gikuyu.

The opening chapter of the greatly influential *Decolonizing the Mind* traces the manner in which, according to Ngugi, colonialist ideology used language as a means of fostering the colonial project. Ngugi distinguishes two functions of language: (i) language as communication, and (ii), language as carrier of culture. Both levels are of course inseparable, but his distinction is meant to serve a heuristic purpose. According to Ngugi, language functions as carrier of culture because culture subsists in and through its transmission in language. Thus defined as the product of a community's interactions—interactions within the same community or with others—language is that construct in which the history of a collective, its conflicts and ruptures, are manifested. The individual's location in society, the sense of who one is and can be, the sense of one's relation to society in particular, and to the world in general: all these are for Ngugi bound up with the communicative cultural basis of language. In his words: "Language as culture is . . . mediating between me and my own self; between my own self and other selves; between me and nature. Language is mediating in my very being" (*Decolonising*, 15).

It is here that the colonial situation reveals itself to Ngugi as a structured aberration. The language that the colonizer imposes on the colonized cannot "carry" the full measure of the reality of the colonized. This is because the imposed language is necessarily the product of another—i.e., the colonizer's—history: "a specific culture is not transmitted through language in its universality but in its particularity as the language of a specific community with a specific history " (15). For Ngugi, then, the forced acquisition of the colonizer's language that the colonized endures is an instance of indoctrination. Imposing his language is the colonizer's means of ideological enslavement. For the imposition disrupts the healthy constellation of images (cultural and thus identity-forming images) contained in the indigenous linguistic world of the colonized.

On these terms, the colonial child who acquires English at school acquires by definition a language whose images are in disjunction with those of his or her native language and universe. For Ngugi, the child cannot but encounter a confusing maze because the order posited in the acquired language does not, and cannot, reflect the order of the native culture and language:

> There was often not the slightest relationship between the child's written world, which was also the language of his schooling, and the world of his immediate environment in the family and the community. For a colonial child, the harmony existing between the three aspects of language was irrevocably broken. . . . Since culture does not just reflect the world in images but actually, through those very images, conditions a child to see that world in a certain way, the colonial child was made to see the world and where he stands in it as seen and defined by or reflected in the culture of the language of imposition. (17)

Indeed, what the colonizer's language gives the impressionable child is a negative self-image. For in, say, French, English, or Portuguese, the child's very humanity is negated. In French, English, or Portuguese, the child sees him- or herself as object rather than as subject: naturally inferior, always-already excluded, if you will, from the movement of the Hegelian spirit.

To this account, we may pose a number of questions. On Ngugi's own terms, language as culture reflects the history of a people, their interaction with others, and so forth. If we grant this much, it would seem to follow that the colonialist venture into the space and history of colonized societies constitutes, in all its military brutality and economic exploitation, part of the history and thus, culture, of the colonized world. Pursuing a similar logic, if language testifies to the ruptures and contingent syntheses of concrete history, will this not imply that the indigenous language and the colonial one will not—at least, not on the turf of the colonized—remain as they were before the violence of the confrontation? The obviousness of my rhetorical question testifies to a certain reductiveness at the heart of Ngugi's narrative of the acquisition of language under colonialism. Granting the entanglement of history with culture, consciousness with representation, he nonetheless reifies all four categories in a fully organicist relay where each "reflects" the others with more or less one-dimensional precision.

To be sure, one cannot dismiss Ngugi's position as one of nativist autarchy. Because for him the struggle of classes and nations over resources is ultimately international in scope, he is in fact opposed to definitions of struggle in purely ethnic, rather than economic, terms. His account of language and the colonial child takes the organicist form because narratives of prelapsarian plenitude are effective as a discursive strategy. After Eliot and Leavis, there is a discursive context where such a story cannot but be meaningful and powerful. Ngugi is led to this organicism, this reification of culture, because his narrative of the African child in relation to language amounts to a version of T. S. Eliot's narrative of the "dissociation of sensibility" in English letters after the metaphysical poets. The culturalist shadow of Eliot, Leavis and the so-called southern agrarians who codified the New Criticism thus inflects Ngugi's account of language and material culture.[12]

The theory of language we find in *Decolonizing the Mind* enables Ngugi to rationalize a cultural and intellectual project that is altogether not just abstract-theoretical. As I have already noted, this project is the establishment of a tradition of letters in indigenous languages, in his own case, Gikuyu. In this sense, I suggest that Ngugi's flawed account of language and the colonial child constitutes an instance of agency in motion. But as we recognize this, we would also do well to indicate why a thoroughgoing materialist interpretation of African literatures cannot benefit from an organicist understanding of traditional Africa. In Ngugi's account, the concrete rupture and reconfigurations that necessarily result from cultural contact (even political subordination) stand, not as permanent dimensions of human sociality, but as aftermaths of aberrations. To approach modern African writing within the parameters of his account is to proceed with an overly schematic frame: in literatures written in the colonial languages is to be encountered a (more or less) alienated vision—what he calls the marker of "Afro-European" subjectivity—while in those written in the indigenous languages is to be found a resilient and subversive authenticity. What needs to be underlined for our present discussion is the reflectionist schematism that accompanies his rejection of European languages and valorization of indigenous ones. Added to the simplification of traditional culture, this schematism can obscure much that is instructive in literary representation.

Whether it is approached as a question of mimesis or as one of aesthetic autonomy, the issue of how literary structures relate to social structures (that is, what exactly literature "reflects," and how) is old and large. Our concern here is not with the details of the question, either in literary criticism generally or Western Marxism in particular. What I wish to bring to our attention is that Marxist criticism of African literature took over a cluster of analytical categories and applied them to African literary texts without thematizing the historicity of those categories. In doing this, they replicated what the formalists did when they appropriated new-critical categories. Because Marxist categories attempt to understand "real" societies and concrete history, however, the conceptual leap is all the more striking and instructive. That is, where the formalists' blindness to the historicity of their categories is in a sense consistent with the desire for ahistorical objectivity associated with formalism, the logic of Marxism as a way of thinking, should suggest that Marxist-Africanists cannot overlook the historicity of their tools. The fact that Marxist-Africanists replicated the same kind of maneuver (that is, ahistorical and unselfconsious use of analytical categories) is therefore all the more interesting.

The last claim demands some elaboration. Marxism as an explanation of social processes and an epistemology logically requires that its conceptual categories cannot be assumed, a priori, to be adequate to the African situation and the literary structures it underpins. Anne Phillips has identified what she calls the "enigma" of British colonialism in West Africa, namely, that on the one hand, its policies served to push subsistence farmers into becoming growers of cash crops like cocoa. Yet, on the other, British policy (as much because of sheer disorganization as a desire to guard the interests of European industrial concerns) worked by various means to prevent the full proletarianization of these farmers, that is, their meaningful consolidation into a peasantry. Mahmood Mamdani has investigated the ways in which the constitution of social identity in modern African societies is played out in two mutually exclusive spheres: that of customary laws governed by putatively precolonial social arrangements, and that of the nation-state—in principle the domain of civil society as it is envisioned in the industrialized West. Whatever the merits or problems of these studies, they at least point to the possibility that class as a category is not universal, that the penetration of capitalism into African society has a unique inflection.[13] This is but another way of saying that it generates unprecedented social contradictions, and thereby calls for conceptual handles not necessarily anticipated in Western Marxism. In this sense, categories developed to understand the nineteenth-century novel or the historical avant-guard cannot adequately illuminate postcolonial African texts, if for no other reason than that postcoloniality is an extension and complication of the socioeconomic history that bred the realist novel or the avant-guard. At the least, the story of the social current that gave birth to Paul's father in D. H. Lawrence's *Sons and Lovers* does not fully exhaust (not even by analogy) that of Azaro's father in Ben Okri's *The Famished Road*. In overlooking this point, Marxist-Africanist criticism reveals the sense in which it is implicated, as much as the formalists, in the epistemological predicament of African literary criticism in particular, and African letters in general.

As a general theoretical position, our preference is for a materialist orientation to discourses. It should not be surprising, then, that I find the Marxist perspective to African literature more promising than the narrowly formalist. But then, it would be a Marxism that sees its own passion and analytical procedures as being part of a broader discursive conjuncture, a problematic. On this view, Marxism cannot simply oppose itself undialectically to something called "non-Marxist" criticism—new-critical or otherwise. As Fredric Jameson's *The Political Unconscious* famously argues, a fully materialist reading does not necessarily eschew form. Rather, it enfolds the formal aspects of texts, working right through them to emerge on the material terrain. If the strongest materialist/political reading (as against one derived from reflection theory) is invariably stronger than the strongest formalist one, it is because a "strong" reading is construed as one that teaches us more about the meanings, contexts, and passions of the text in question.

Lawrence's modernism gives his text a formal structure that clearly dif-
ferentiates it from Okri's, but there is a shared modernity that links them
both, even as its trauma leaves traces on them in different ways. A materialist reading can thus get to this shared modernity by way of, and yet
beyond, formal distinctions between something called "modernism" and
something else called "postmodernism" (or magical realism, as Okri is
sometimes categorized). From this perspective, an "intrinsic" interpretation is not necessarily antithetical to the "extrinsic." Indeed, the basis of
the opposition disappears.

THE PATIENCE OF THE MATERIAL

We have so far isolated and dissolved a polarization in African literary
criticism between formalists-aestheticists, on the one hand, and those
who see themselves as sociological critics, on the other. Where the former espouse Arnoldian assumptions regarding literary value, the latter
operate with reflectionist notions about the role of literature in culture,
the correspondence between authorial intention and textual performance, or the correspondence between these two and the "real world"
outside. It is as though, in an uncanny replication of the real world outside, Africanist literary criticism constituted its own version of the cold
war: aestheticists opted for Anglo-American formalism while sociological critics generated reflectionist readings that insisted on a particular
social vision and particular representational forms. Wole Soyinka, one
of whose plays we shall discuss in chapter 5, saw fit to dismiss Marxist
readings of his plays as "Zhdanovian," after Stalin's minister of culture.

    And yet, common to the formalists and the Marxists is a certain
perspective of language in which adequate, "authentic" literary representation is taken to be possible. By extension, the ideal literary text is
taken to be that which captures the postcolonial condition adequately
and, for the sociological critics, offers what is deemed a revolutionary
political vision. This commonality-in-difference is what Landeg White
overlooks. Ultimately, the two camps we have been tracing differ only
on the question of how to interpret literary texts to fully bring out their
decolonizing efficacy. The theoretical implications of the term "African"
in African Literature, or the question of what cultural decolonization
might entail: these rarely enter the field of interrogation.

    Biodun Jeyifo offers a similar characterization in his "The Nature
of Things: Arrested Decolonization and Critical Theory." The burden
of his argument is to map out a common space where the performance,
if not the claims, of both groups intersects. He suggests that "In the

deafening silence on the techniques and the positions of entrenched power and privilege (or lack of them) from which any scholar or critic evaluates and theorizes, only feminist critics, and to a lesser extent, Marxists, have systematically drawn attention to the political grounding or *situatedness* of critical discourse" (45). The observation that the criticism of African literature has, "with few exceptions" tended to evade the situatedness of critical discourse is an interesting one. But Jeyifo's next move is to fall back on what he calls an "aporia," generated by the mere fact of a critic's institutional location: "This overdetermination [i.e., of African literary criticism] defines . . . the aporia under which we all, singly or collectively, work today. Whatever genuine "truths" our studies and readings generate, there is the uncomfortable, compromising "falsehood" of its displacement from its true center of gravity on the African continent, there is always the harrowing "falsehood" involved in the production and reproduction of Africa's marginalization from the centers of economic and discursive power in an inequitable capitalist world system" (45–46). I do not think that the methodological issue with which we are here concerned can be settled simply by the fact of where the critic plies her trade. This is one instance of situational relativism that is neither convincing nor helpful as to how we might read Africanist writing in the current intellectual and global economic conjuncture.

How, then, proceed? One obvious implication of Jeyifo's contribution is that, at this point in history—some thirty years after the visionary days of the immediate postindependence era—African and postcolonial literary criticism needs to reassess its inherited mandate and tools, to rediscover its loaded historicity. It would be helpful to revisit, not just the issue of literature's relationship to society, but also the question of knowledge *as such* in society—whether knowledge is taken here to mean knowledge about literature or, indeed, about society itself. This implies that one needs to pose the very idea of "African literature" as a theoretical problem. Since African literary texts (like third world postcolonial texts written in the European languages) emerge from a history, a cluster of social contradictions, that particularizes and problematizes them in unique ways, their place in global modernity stands to enrich our understanding of cultural discourses and the processes they enact and to which they witness.

We are therefore brought back to the context of Anglo-American literary theory and cultural studies. On the analyses conducted so far (of theories of postcoloniality in Chapter 2 and African literary criticism in this chapter), the way we read African literature or theorize about postcolonial cultures may, in different ways, betray an avoidance

of the sort of hard question put before us by the reality that Jeyifo characterizes as "arrested decolonization." We have seen that the assumptions by means of which Anglophone African Literature was institu-
tionalized and explicated derive from the center (for example, the New
Criticism, and reflection theory). Consequently, the status of the category "African" rarely entered the field of analysis. And neither did the
possibility that the lessons of literature at its best cannot truly be made
manifest or rewarding, so long as one remains tied to the intrinsic-
extrinsic polarity. It is necesssary, then, to question two premises: first,
that Africa is a self-evident signifier, always-already in epistemological
antithesis to the West; and second, that novels and poems reflect reality via a one to one correspondence.

The poststructuralist theories of postcoloniality that we examined
in Chapter 2 are useful in that they foreground the constructedness of
identity and our categories of thought and cognition. In the work of
Bhabha and Spivak, we recovered two important achievements. First, by
focussing on the discursive inconsistencies internal to modernity as
philosophical discourse, Spivak and Bhabha show up the error of the
Enlightenment dream, a dream which, at one level, gave logic to the
West's colonizing mission. To the extent that this dream continues to ratify global political economy by postulating the integration of the peripheral states within the logic of centralized capital, to that extent should
modernity as theoretical discourse remind us of modernity as economic-
political objectification. The challenge for criticism, then, should be that
of keeping both levels (the theoretical and the material) in focus, without, however, conflating them. Second, under the influence of poststructuralist postcolonial theory, deterministic literary criticism does not
compel much respect, neither does any critical procedure that conflates
discursive constructions with ontological substance. But as we also saw
in chapter 2, these achievements of poststructuralist postcolonial theory
come with their own problems. Under the poststructuralist regime, it
may become easy to dismiss earlier anticolonial work as cultural nationalism while (paradoxically) celebrating non-Western literatures as sub-
versions of Eurocentrism. Under a new grid that claims for itself an
unprecedented approximation to the truth of things, a rhetoric of otherness may get smuggled in through the back door: the rhetoric of difference and subversion. Abstract debates about agency and subversion can
work to this effect. As I argued in that chapter, the very terms of the
debate presuppose a view of cultural contestation that can only yield circular theorizing, for or against subversion. As long as this will to theory
governs postcolonial criticism, we cannot adequately understand the
particularity and agency of African letters.

To go beyond this will to theory, the first knot to be untied resides in the following trivial observation: though the ruling regime of the day, poststructuralism and the postcolonial theory that draws on it originate from "the center." If the New Criticism has given way to poststructuralism, it may reasonably be argued that in the final instance, one inheritance has only given way to another. This is principally a historical, not polemical, claim, and the epistemological implication of its historical dimension is what I am aiming for, namely, that the three critical procedures we have examined—formalism, extrinsic criticism, and poststructuralism—are all attempts by human minds to come to grips with a human reality by deploying the analytical tools at their disposal. All are, in this sense, genealogically in the same disposition as Mudimbe's Hans Burgkmair: earnestly posing in discourse the other, yet bound to do so, under the formal governance of the *contrapposto*. This immediately implies that the usual critique of nativism or reflectionist criticism (that it simply rehearses the preconstituted terms of the Western discourses it seeks to overcome) is actually not as devastating as it may otherwise seem. On this view, the alternative is not simply to shift from a metaphysics of presence (such as characterizes nativist discourses or traditional literary criticism), to abstract and general questionings of "presence," "identity," and so on (such as characterizes a good deal of current postcolonial criticism). This is why our analysis has tried to go beyond simple dismissal or rejection of nativism and traditional criticism as it reveals itself in African letters. We have instead tried to disentangle the ideological roots of African literary criticism in order to specify the problematic of African letters as a discursive formation. In so doing, my aim is to draw out its latent epistemological import and the agency this implies.

In concluding this chapter, let us retrace our steps so far. As argued in chapter 2, current postcolonial theory allows us to see the limitations of reflectionist views of literary representation. My contention, however, is that to identify these limitations is to tell half the story. For although the derivativeness of reflectionist African criticism is conceptually limited, it also comes with an indirect profit. First, it enabled Africanist cultural workers to put "Africa" at the center of an adventure of human minds; that is to say, as the occasion and subject (rather than incidental backcloth or object) of human minds contemplating human affairs. Second and at a deeper level, it exhibits conceptual problems inherent to traditional Anglo-Saxon literary criticism. In resembling an original, the copy shows up the full detail of that original—what it would like to flaunt, what to hide. At one level, Homi Bhabha's notion of mimicry allows us to come to this conclusion. But at another level, it is impossible to draw out the full epistemological import of this conclusion within the terms of Bhabha's theorizing; this, because he also rejects cultural nationalism in principle, thereby assuming that agency can be theorized on an abstract, a priori model. By contrast, the burden of this chapter has been to demonstrate that the blindnesses of African letters carry an insight that, as Althusser might say, were misrecognized at the material juncture of the immediate postindependence era. To the extent, then, that those blindnesses enabled a discursive and material practice at a particular historical moment, African letters offers an example of discursive agency in motion. The epistemological import here is the following: beyond and in spite of what current literary theory and cultural criticism can prescribe as the viable constituents of agency and/or "subversion," the agency of African literary criticism resides in the Althusserian drama of misrecognition that we have sketched. By extension, the concept of discursive agency is best approached through the dialectical labor of a backward glance—a concern with what did happen, rather than what should happen. Here, hermetic theory, searching for a priori parameters, has to reckon with the evidence of concrete reality itself. To borrow a formulation from Theodor Adorno, "If truth has in fact a temporal core, then the full historical content becomes an integral moment in it; the a posteriori becomes the a priori concretely and not merely in general."[14]

It should be clear by now, why the metacritical reconstruction undertaken in this chapter has crucial implications if Anglo-American literary theory is to have a productive dialogue with Africanist criticism. But there remains a possible objection that I need to address. The objection involves the weight my account of African letters has given to its historicity and specificity. The objection might rest on the idea that my argument makes it impossible to develop normative grounds for thinking about as well as assessing sociopolitical or discursive agency. On this view, to buy my argument is to descend into a relativistic abyss, one where discursive or political currents cannot be judged (positively or negatively) simply because they are responses to real historical pressures. We might as well argue, so the objection might go, that a right-wing stalwart is on respectable epistemological grounds when he seeks to limit the rights of immigrants simply because he did lose his job to one such immigrant.

However, if our discussion so far has achieved its purposes, it should be obvious that this objection misses the heart of my argument: it deploys one abstract notion of normativity to object to an argument mounted specifically against abstract notions of normativity. Put differently, a blanket rejection of relativism does not make much sense because a so-called relativist position may be valid in some contexts and invalid in another. In this hypothetical context, I happen to think that the right-wing stalwart is on respectable epistemological grounds if we identify his position as the consequence of his subjectification, his insertion into the productive process as a patriotic citizen threatened by hordes of immigrants intent on grabbing his job. It is in seeking to show our right-wing stalwart that there are other ways in which he can understand himself and his concrete location, other ways in which his subjectivity can take shape, that politics happens. And it is in our success in this project, or failing that, our success in making it institutionally difficult for him to curtail the rights of others, that resistance and the test of agency lie. There are no guarantees here: what happens will happen, not to the extent that our theory prescribes or "gets it right," but to the extent that we succeed in persuading antagonists or, alternately, outmaneuvering them in the trenches where others might be persuaded and votes cast.

If this much is granted, a stronger way of formulating the objection would be to come closer to earth and frame the objection with specific reference to the case of African letters. By restricting myself to the task of drawing out what I call the epistemological lesson of African letters, my account does shift the focus away from normative assessment to genealogical reconstruction. Quite legitimately, then, my account might be accused of providing a veiled excuse, a rationalization, for, say, nativism as a critical or political phenomenon. The potential problem in my account will then be that it glosses over the conceptual limitations (or political dangers) of nativism. And yet, even here the crucial issue should be the context in which the glossing over (such as it is) has been perpetrated. I should think that what I have been doing is not neutral, but critical, genealogical reconstruction. My argument is that current postcolonial criticism is not yet adequately equipped to appreciate the strengths and limitations of African letters *because* of the way notions like "politics," "agency," or "resistance" are often framed. This framing is inadequate because of the tendency to conflate coherence and self-consistency in theory with assumed effects in the real world. Against this theoretical purism and voluntarism, I believe that African literary criticism, such as I've analyzed here, offers an example of cultural representation that was blind to its irreducible conceptual conditions. And yet, whatever future direction the study of African letters takes depends on that initial beginning, the conceptual efforts and textual remnants of the 1960s and 1970s. Consequently, although I have been drawing attention to the problems in nativism and other strands of African literary criticism, my main concern is to stress, not just the limitations, but also their broader implications for theory. My concern, that is, has been to preserve and cancel, to sublate the object of my analysis in order to develop an insight that simple negation cannot generate. The agency of African literary criticism in the immediate postindependence era is indissociable from the context that made it possible and thereby circumscribed it. This of course speaks to its performative, as against constative, dimension as discourse. For meaningful things to get done, the doer does have to be purposive, but the fullness of his or her agency is not reducible to the purposiveness or self-consistency of the intentional act. Meaning can, and often does, go beyond the subject's originating intention.

This brings us to creative literature by African writers as another component of African letters. Perhaps more than the academic criticism we have been exploring, creative literature is well suited as a site for seeking out agency in motion. For what literary texts give us are structures wherein subjects are imagined in the performance of various strivings and conflicts—that is to say, in the performance of (or failure of) agency. Chapters 4 and 5 proceed on the conviction that in a number of texts that have emerged as influential in African literature, the logic of African letters that we have been indicating is dramatized and instantiated. At its farthest reaches, the implication of this dramatization extends beyond African letters and is pertinent to ongoing discussions of agency in postcolonial criticism. In the next two chapters, then, I demonstrate that the understanding of agency I have been developing is coded into some well-known literary texts by D. O. Fagunwa, Amos Tutuola, Wole Soyinka, and Chinua Achebe. In reading these writers, I draw out ways in which acts of will, and acts of language, turn out to be simultaneously productive and limited, purposive and yet uncontainable by the agent's originating intention. In this way, the creative writers turn out to have all along been theorists of agency.

CHAPTER FOUR

D. O. Fagunwa as Compound of Spells

In this chapter and the next, we move from critical-theoretical claims about literature, society, and human agency, to a consideration of African literature as itself a mode of theory. Specifically, our concern now is to consider D. O. Fagunwa and Wole Soyinka as theorists—via their by now "canonical" creative writing—of the consequences of Europe's march into black Africa. As I have suggested in earlier chapters, there is a tendency in Anglo-American postcolonial criticism to elevate theoretical discourse, in and for itself, over creative-literary discourses. In its most innocuous form, this tendency establishes an unproductive binarism and hierarchy of value. By considering creative literary texts by African authors as theoretical explorations of pressing realities—in other words, as sources for and elaborations of theory—our purpose is to dissolve and transcend this binarism. Although the modalities of enunciation have of necessity to be different, theory and criticism are themselves pieces of texts; they are therefore elaborations of investments that intersect, or become isomorphic with, those of literary-creative texts.

A good way of setting us on our way is to revisit Fredric Jameson's controversial essay "Third-World Literature in the Era of Multinational Capitalism." In this essay, Jameson makes the claim that so-called third world texts are best read as national allegories because unlike in first world literature, third world writers are compelled by the social circumstances of their works to address the communal dimensions of social existence. While the "great" modernisms of a Proust or a Joyce can allow themselves to be read in terms of interior psychic dramas or what Jameson calls private libidinal investments, third world writers are compelled to go beyond (or jettison) such hermetic interiorization of conflict. On

Jameson's reading, by what comes across as a social logic that implacably translates into an aesthetic, third world writings gesture decisively toward the communal domain. As is well known, Aijaz Ahmad has contested Jameson's characterization. It is easy to agree with Ahmad that the very category "third-world literature" does not have any theoretical content, and cannot thereby secure a rich account of the diverse texts so characterized: the category acquires meaning primarily within Western ("first world") literary-critical institutions.

But after granting this much, Jameson's categorization yet retains a kernel of interest. Placed within the relational context of the institution of Anglo-American literary and cultural criticism—the context out of which it derives—the polemical thrust of Jameson's account carries some theoretical pertinence. To be sure, a nonsuperficial examination of some of the most influential texts in the "canon" of modern African literature should reveal that they are not always and only concerned with a "public" domain over and against a "private" sphere. Feminist work on African literature has in fact shown that, to the extent that the creative literature lends itself to the "private/public" polarity, it is because those texts are male-authored, their preoccupations eminently gendered (Andrade, Ogunyemi, Stratton). It is also the case, as Ahmad argues, that so-called first world writings can themselves, with the labor of political interpretation, be read as national allegories. Nonetheless, the fact remains that canonical modernist texts have acquired a complex critical construction by means of which they impose themselves (or are imposed) on us in terms that essentially parallel Jameson's. This construction is what gives meaning to Jameson's account. Viewed this way, his "Third-World Literature" is an invention put to work primarily as a counterconstruction.

One problem with Jameson's counterconstruction, however, is that its rhetoric crystallizes on two registers that are not necessarily compatible. There is first a register of social determinism, where third world literature is marked by an intrinsic, hard-wired logic. The driving force of this determinism is Jameson's commitment to the good old Marxian model of a teleological succession of modes of production. Ahmad's critique is most forceful and persuasive when he teases out and rejects this determinism. The second register is most accurately described as one of motivated critical choice. Here, what we have is a situated and polemical register, an up-front prescription for a specific interpretive direction. At this second level, we are dealing with Jameson's elaboration of the sort of reading he feels best captures the contemporary force of third world writing, the kernel of what the latter may be made to say to traditional, Eurocentric, criticism. To the extent that all readings are situated and motivated, Jameson's tendentious prescription is defensible. His account is serviceable, not as the truth of something called third world writing, but as an operable interpretative handle on one incarnation of the writings so labeled.

There is also a nonpolemical sense in which the notion of national allegory is promising. If the analysis conducted in chapter 3 has been persuasive, it should be evident that the story of African literary criticism, as a specific instance in a wider current of African letters, cannot be fully told without taking in the story of the independence movements and the institutional and ideological maneuvers it set in motion. Similarly, going strictly by the claims and self-understandings of many African writers themselves, Jameson's notion of national allegory cannot validly be said to be an imposition of Western theory on non-Western material. A useful question to ask is this: why is it that first world literature has somehow managed to invite the construction of apolitical inwardness, even as the critical establishment seeks (however tenuously) to sustain such a construction? And why is it that, by contrast, African writers and critics have tended to stress the need for outwardness and political commitment—precisely the sort of critical commonsense that authorizes (however tenuously) the construction Ahmad finds unacceptable in Jameson's theory? The answer is that first world literature can take for granted both its national community ("English," "German," "American"), and social-epistemic status within that community. This taking for granted can then, perhaps, allow writers and critics to conceive of their work primarily in terms of narrow interior exploration. As Kwame Anthony Appiah suggests, African writers have not done this because their work is in part an attempt to constitute precisely the sociocultural and epistemological space that the Western world can take for granted (see Appiah, House, esp. 74–76).

In this sense, the theoretical and institutional politics that animates Jameson's theory has a reasonable conceptual payoff wherever it enables a framing of so-called third world texts as sites of discursive agency, loci of the gains and restraints of the modern will to truth. Jameson gets at this point early in his essay when he defends his account by granting the precariousness of the category "third world" while also pointing to the payoff in the problematic naming. "It would be presumptuous," he writes, "to offer some general theory of what is often called third-world literature, given the enormous variety both of national cultures in the third world and of specific historical trajectories in each of those areas" (68). Beyond this, however, Jameson insists that we may grant this variety and still look for ways in which strong readings of so-called third world literature may generate "a new view of ourselves, from the outside, insofar as we ourselves are (perhaps without fully knowing it) constitutive forces powerfully at work on the remains of older cultures in our general world capitalist system" (68). Jameson clarifies the "we" and the "us" of the foregoing formulation as "people formed by the values and stereotypes of a first-world culture" (68). From our reconstruction of the conceptual and historical conditions of African literary criticism in chapter 3, it is valid to say that the "us" in Jameson's formulation has to be conceived as a discursive-community, a socioeconomic and epistemological location, rather than a racial, ethnic, or geographical constituency. We have seen in chapter 3 the construction of a critical and discursive community as part of the construction of knowledge about Africa in the field of academic literary criticism. In this chapter and the next, we will be exploring similar and contemporaneous attempts in the realms of fiction and drama.

This chapter is devoted to the creative work of the Nigerian writer, Daniel Olorunfemi Fagunwa (1903–63). He is generally regarded as an ancestor figure to the later generation of writers who are today the canonical figures of the institutional category we call African literature. In what follows, my contention is that Fagunwa's fiction can indeed be read as an allegory of the Nigerian nation-state. But in this allegory, the discourse of nation is simultaneously, but covertly, a discourse of a particular class and the self-representation of that class in fictional narrative. In this allegory, too, the "public" is not separable from the "private" realm. Whatever else it can be shown to be, the Nigerian nation-state is also the consequence of the self-definition of the educated elite. That is, it is the consequence of a historical predicament faced by a specific generation of the educated elite, the psychic conflicts occasioned by that predicament, and the contingencies and agential choices that constitute its aftermath. In the language of fiction, then, Fagunwa's fiction bears out Jameson's powerfully tendentious theory, while also complicating and revising it *avant la lettre*. In narrating and reflecting upon a sociohistorical moment of which it is a part, Fagunwa's novel cannot but contemplate its own self. In this sense, the novel theorizes itself, carrying at once a principle of interpretation and a vision of history and agency.

I am not arguing that this way of approaching Fagunwa is necessarily applicable to every writer or text of African literature. Neither am I suggesting that Fagunwa in this chapter, or Soyinka and Achebe in the next, consciously intended what my reading unpacks. They may or may not, but the dynamics of authorial intention—useful as these can be in their own way—is not the thrust of my own discussion here. My concern is altogether on a different pitch, and might be formulated in the

following way: to the extent that the thinking mind is located in twenti-
eth- (or twenty-first) century modernity, to the extent that "written
African literature" (an instructive tautology, by the way) is a product of
that modernity, and to the extent that Fagunwa is an acute thinker and
observer, his fiction cannot but encode the issues that occupy the theorists and critics we have been exploring in the previous chapters.[1]

Of Hunters and Writers

D. O. Fagunwa is most famous for his first novel Ògbójú Qde Nínú
Igbó Irúnmalè (literally "The brave hunter in the forest of four hundred
deities"). The novel was written for a writing competition organized in
1936 by Gladys Plummer, who was then a superintendent of the education ministry in Nigeria. The manuscript was subsequently published
by The Church Missionary Society in 1938 (Bamgbose Novels 3). So
favorable was its reception in colonial Western Nigeria that Thomas
Nelson Press took over its publishing in 1950. As the 1986 reprint
informs us, Ògbójú Qde Nínú Igbó Irúnmalè (henceforth referred to as
Ògbójú Qde) has since been reprinted twenty-four times. Translated
into English by Wole Soyinka, Nelson also originally published the
translation in 1968, under the title The Forest of a Thousand Daemons:
A Hunter's Saga (henceforth referred to as Forest).[2] Let us note the
orthographic invention "daemons," which Soyinka chooses in his
translation. In the translator's note to Forest, Soyinka explains his decision to fashion this spelling. According to him, "the spelling is important. These beings who inhabit Fagunwa's world demand at all costs
and by every conceivable translator's trick to be preserved from the
common or misleading associations which substitutes such as demons,
devils or gods necessarily invoke in the reader's mind. At the same time,
it is necessary that they transmit the reality of their existence with the
same unquestioning impact and vitality which is conveyed by Fagunwa
in the original" ("Translator's Note," Forest). Soyinka's insistence on
the uniqueness of Fagunwa's metaphysical entities to the so-called
Yoruba worldview, as it emerges in Forest, is ideologically motivated. I
suggest, in fact, that what we witness in the translator's casting of his
object is less the truth of the object than the specific ideological investment of Soyinka himself.

Abiola Irele has suggested that Soyinka's translation is best understood as an imaginative reconstruction, rather than a simple literal
transfer, of Fagunwa's text into English. We shall return to this point
later in this chapter, when we come to consider Fagunwa in relation to

Amos Tutuola and Wole Soyinka. For now, suffice it to say that the very title of Fagunwa's first novel foregrounds spiritual beings whose proper universe—in a conventional Western apprehension—is mythology, if not superstition and devil worship. Soyinka's translation and prefatory statement insists on stressing the former association (i.e., mythology) because he wants to rescue it from demotion to such stereotypes as "superstition" or "devil worship." To ask what Fagunwa's text itself might have to say on the matter is to take the first step towards unraveling the specificity of his contribution, the agency of his text.

Fagunwa was born in Òkè-Igbó in Western Nigeria in 1903. His parents were converted Christians. From 1926–29 he was trained as a schoolteacher at St Andrew's College, also in Western Nigeria. After his training, he taught at a primary school from 1930–39; Ògbójú Ọdẹ thus appears to have been written during the novelist's ten-year tenure immediately following his certification as schoolteacher. In addition to Ògbójú Ọdẹ, he published four other novels: Igbó Olódùmarè (The Forest of God), Ìrìnkèrindò Nínú Igbó Elégbèje (Wanderings in the Forest of a Thousand and Four Hundred), Ìrèké Oníbùdó (The Sweet One with a Secure Home Ground), and Àdììtú Olódùmarè (God's Conundrum). He also edited a collection of short stories, Àṣànyàn Ìtàn (Selected Stories).[3] He spent 1948–50 in England on a British Council scholarship. His experiences during the sea travel to England, and his impressions of London, designated as "His Majesty's city" (ìlú ọba) form the subject of a travel memoir in two parts (Part I, 1949; Part II, 1951). Each of these texts is explicitly addressed to youngsters, and all the novels incorporate a section devoted to exercises in Yoruba grammar as well as translation (Yoruba-English and vice versa). We are dealing, then, with a writer whose immediate audience is the school child and whose writing is motivated and concretely supported by the colonial education apparatus.

His texts continue to be used following Nigeria's independence. Fagunwa lived into the first three years of Nigeria's independence in 1960. He served as Education Officer with the Publications Branch of the Western Nigeria Education Ministry from 1955 to 1959, and as the Nigeria representative of Heinemann Education Books Ltd. The first novel and his subsequent writings carry a strong didactic impulse that is explained by the author's biographical and professional status as elementary schoolteacher. His publications have offered a fertile ground for experimentation in, and refinement of, Yoruba orthography, and for the development of the academic study of the language in secondary and tertiary education in Nigeria. If for Isaka Seme an important project for the African intelligentsia at the turn of the twentieth century was that of bringing "the strength of written proof" to Africans' claims for a civilization that preceded European colonization, Fagunwa's creative energies are devoted to a similar cause.

The first novel has been adapted into a television drama series in Yoruba, as has *Ìrèké Oníbùdó*. During the Festival of Arts and Culture (FESTAC) in 1977 in Nigeria, Nigeria's entry for drama was a play entitled *Langbodo* (1979) by the Nigerian playwright Wale Ogunyemi.[4] Written in English, *Langbodo* is an adaptation of the third part of *Forest*. What these adaptations of Fagunwa, into the popular medium of television and stage, imply is that his work is by now part of the collective cultural fabric of modern Western Nigeria. Consequently, in modern African literature, Fagunwa is legitimately considered an important pioneering figure. In terms of its place in the intellectual formation of generations of Nigerian school children, as well as its influence on other writers of Yoruba ancestry, his literary career offers an interesting instance of what I have been calling agency in motion. Furthermore, the rhetorical motions intrinsic to his fiction reveal a contemplative overlay that comments on the idea of agency itself.

Of course, since Fagunwa wrote in his native language, the availability of his texts to a wider and transethnic readership depends on translations. The most famous of these is Wole Soyinka's "free translation" mentioned earlier, entitled *The Forest of a Thousand Daemons*. *Igbó Olódùmarè* has also been translated, but the translations currently exist as unpublished doctoral dissertations: Pamela J. Smith's dissertation for the University of Washington, and Gabriel O. Ajiboye's for Bell State University. In 1987, *Ìrìnkèrindò Nínú Igbó Elégbèje* was translated as *Expedition to the Mount of Thought* by Dapo Adeniyi. Fagunwa himself attempted a translation of his last novel *Àdììtú Olódùmarè* (God's Conundrum). This unpublished manuscript, which Fagunwa literally translates as "The Mysterious Plan of the Almighty," is located in the archives of the School of Oriental and African Studies in London.[5] The issue of translation from one language to another, especially when the source language is so much less powerful than the target language, takes us directly to issues of agency and the way it plays out in relation to writers' choice of language. As we saw in chapter 3, Ngugi wa Thiong'o has responded to this situation by writing creative literature in Gikuyu and theorizing his choice as part of a systematic project of mental and linguistic decolonization. The way questions of translation and the cross-pollination of indigenous and colonial languages figure in Fagunwa's work takes us, directly, to the issue of agency.

All of Fagunwa's novels come in the picaresque tradition. The plot is usually simple: for one reason or another, the protagonist ends up in an alien forest teeming with monsters and other supernatural forces. He undergoes many trials but triumphs over them as a result of sheer resourcefulness. Along the way, the narrative voice interjects explicit didactic themes, often in the form of direct address to the reader, and specifically to schoolchildren. The immense success of *Ògbójú Ọdẹ* on its first publication motivated Fagunwa's publishers, and the education ministry for which he worked, to encourage him to do more in that mode. For this reason, the plot and overall artistic profile, which in *Ògbójú Ọdẹ* was new and exciting to the average Yoruba reader, becomes in the later novels studiously formulaic. The novel could not have succeeded if it had been written in English, since it would there encounter the precedence of a long tradition of the picaresque adventure tale. Set alongside *Pilgrim's Progress, Robinson Crusoe,* or the less exalted fantasies of Rider Haggard, Fagunwa's adventure tales will be obviously derivative. In this vein, the immense success and ongoing significance of *Ògbójú Ọdẹ* for its immediate Yoruba audience suggests that the narrative came at a moment when it had an audience waiting for it. As act of language, it acquires its full significance at the point at which it interpellates its readers even as those readers conscript it by appropriating (i.e., by "reading") it as the crystallization of a moment, a subjective state. What in this short narrative makes it touch such a strong cord in its contemporary readers as well as later generations of Yoruba readers? A comprehensive answer to this question opens up some lessons on human agency in a context of African postcolonial modernity. Let us turn, then, to a closer analysis of *Forest* as an act of language, intended for entertainment and instruction.

In Fagunwa's novels, there are two rhetorical currents or levels. First, there is a moralistic-didactic rhetoric about universal "man" confronting adversity, of perseverance being repaid by spiritual and material prosperity. Certainly, this rhetoric has a strong Christian influence, and this is intensified by the missionary educational apparatus that Fagunwa's professional status as teacher obliged him to perpetuate. At a second level, Fagunwa's rhetoric becomes a cultural-nationalist one. At this level, the ideal of collective self-actualization is espoused from the conceptual standpoint of secular modernity. Here, the immediate impulse is presented, not simply as the pious will to do God's will in order to attain divine reward in the afterlife, but as that of improving the lot of black people. This cultural nationalism celebrates the difference of black peoples everywhere, even as it focalizes that black collectivity in the Nigerian reader, the well-mannered schoolchild, or anyone in the "secular world [lode aiye sa] who can read Yoruba well [ti o mọ ede Yoruba ika dada]" (*Ìrìnkèrindò*, v). If at one level the subject is the Bunyanesque universal Christian, in the second it is "we black people" (àwa ènìà dúdú) in the first half of the twentieth century. Oscillating between these two rhetorical modes, Fagunwa draws on two modes of seeing that are not necessarily compatible: a materialistic confidence in capitalism as a structure rooted in secular instrumental reason, and a fully Christian suspicion of the profane world and consequent celebration of suffering and self-abnegation.

Fagunwa's fictional works present allegorical explorations in, and enactments of, these two rhetorical currents. In his writings, the African forests that are consistently his setting are not jungles of darkness or antitheses of civilization. Rather, his protagonists' outward adventures become inward journeys into material or spiritual stations of the self. The outward progress of the protagonist as he ventures further into the forest becomes simultaneously a retreat into the inner self that fears and doubts. In this way, where the outward journey shows the protagonist in his resourceful glory, the inner questing shows the same protagonist in a more vulnerable guise. And where the outward journey often succeeds, the inner journey thematizes the uncomfortable possibility that what comes to count as success may in fact be a matter for interpretation. At this level of Fagunwa's fictional writing, human beings are doomed not to succeed; or, more appropriately, every particular success is the external face of a fundamental destiny of failure that is our existential lot. I should like to demonstrate that by oscillating between these various rhetorical levels, Fagunwa is commenting upon his own project. In this way, the text's contemplative rigor allows it to theorize itself through its own immanent motions. Our discussion in what follows centers upon *Forest* because it is the signature text, so to speak, that inspired the others in Fagunwa's corpus, and because, thanks to Soyinka's translation, it is the most well-known in discussions of Anglophone African literature.

STATIONS AND THE SELF

The modernity that Fagunwa engages in his fiction may be formulated as a chain of ideational inheritances. The first is the notion of nationhood, the obligation of the patriotic citizen to that putative communal, that is to say, national, self-understanding and advancement. The second is the elevation of print literacy over orality as purveyor of a relatively more secure knowledge of things. The third concerns the ideological consequences of science as a process of secularization, a moment of mastery over nature, and a horizon of practical efficiency and social progress. All three are of course fundamentally related, converging ultimately around modes of seeing and doing.

As already indicated, *The Forest of a Thousand Daemons* is a picaresque novel. The protagonist is a hunter named Àkàrà Oògùn, spelled in Soyinka's translation as "Akara-ogun." The name is an adjectival phrase that appears to be Fagunwa's coinage. "Àkàrà" is a common delicacy made out of ground beans fried with a variety of spices. "Oògùn" could designate a number of things. At a purely material level, the word might simply mean medicinal herb. At a spiritual level, it implies metaphysical resourcefulness: to have or acquire "Oògùn" is at this level to acquire some sort of metaphysical power. Etymologically, then, Akara-ogun translates into something like "bundle of medicinal powers" on both material and metaphysical levels. Bestowing on this particular bundle a metaphor of deep seasoning and delectability, Fagunwa already indicates his narrative sympathy with the protagonist. By extension, the reader is discreetly manipulated to adopt a similar moral disposition to the novel's hero: as the literal "Àkàrà Oògùn" is delectable and enigmatic, so is the character Akara-ogun supposed to be. In this sense, the naming performs a crucial role in the overall narrative. Wole Soyinka's choice to translate the name as "compound of spells" is thus both rhetorically effective and thematically well-inspired.

As the story progresses, we come to realize that the hunter is indeed a compound of spells. He is sufficiently rounded and resourceful to confront and triumph over the stresses of earthly yearning. Akara-ogun verbally relates his ordeals in Igbo Irunmale to another character who remains nameless but whose literacy allows the transmission of the tale in written form. Divided into three main sections, the plot moves from individual self-realization to collective uplift. The protagonist sets out in the first section on a hunting expedition to the Forest of a Thousand Daemons. After many ordeals, he returns home safely but then takes off again for a "second adventure in this most terrible forest" (67). The second trip proves very profitable for Akara-ogun; as he informs us, "the things I brought back with me that second time were so numerous that, when I had sold them, I was the wealthiest man up or down the entire kingdom" (67).

Upon his return, he is requested by the King to go on another trip, this time to a place called Mount Langbodo, "a certain city which is approached by the same route as leads to the Forest of a Thousand Daemons" (71). The King wants him to visit Langbodo for a specific reason: "the King of this place [Langbodo] had a singular object which he presented to hunters who visited him there. He never mentioned the object by name but he did say that, if this *thing* came into the hand of any king, the king's domain would win an abundance of peace and well-being, and its fame would resound to every corner upon earth . . . it gives me great joy to summon you today and beg of you from the very depths of my heart not to fail to snatch a brief glimpse of this same king and bring me this *thing* in his possession" (72). Akara-ogun thereafter recruits a number of fellow hunters to accompany him on the expedition. Only on account of the perseverance and collective resources of this band of questers are they able to reach Mount Langbodo, returning with a letter of advice from the King of Langbodo, an achievement which, we presume, ensures the perpetual prosperity of the hunters' native land.

The claim implicit in the narrative seems to be that individual self-realization is to be valued, but the self-sufficient achiever needs thereafter to put his abilities at the service of the collective. The gendered pronoun in this formulation is deliberate, and we shall soon see why. Meanwhile, Akara-ogun "masters" the "forest of a thousand daemons"; he returns home wealthy and wise, whereupon he puts that experience to use in the service of his society. In this respect, the text's individuation of the survivors of Langbodo is instructive. Of the many hunters who undertake the expedition, the text singles out six as "the most intrepid and the most experienced" (78). Of the six, only two make it back home—three, if we include Akara-ogun himself. The two who make it back are Imodoye and Olohun-Iyo. Imodoye is figured as a happy coincidence of intuition and cultivation, discipline and focus: "When he was only ten he was snatched away by the Whirlwind and he lived for seven years with him. In all those seven years he lived on a single alligator pepper every day. He was well versed in charms, wise and very knowledgeable, he was also a highly titled hunter. These qualities earned him the name of Imodoye, that is, knowledge fuses with understanding" (78–79). Where Imodoye is the ascetic intellectual, Olohun-iyo embodies the artistic principle, for his name means the salted voice or "Voice of Flavours," as Soyinka translates it. Of Olohun-iyo we are told: "he was the most handsome of all men on earth, the finest singer and the best drummer. When he drummed smoke rose in the air, and when he sang flames danced out of his mouth; his favourite music was the music of incantations" (79). In the three who ventured to Langbodo and came back to tell of it, we have what Fagunwa seems to posit as a winning combination in the moment of modernity: Imodoye the disciplined intellectual, Olohun-iyo the philosophical aesthete—his music was the music of incantations *(orin ògèdè)*—and Akara-ogun, who takes in these qualities as his own combined essence. Struggling under the shadow of Science and Culture, Fagunwa inscribes these monuments of modern rationality onto the very personalities of his patriots.

Forest begins with what initially appears to be direct authorial address: "My friends all, like the sonorous proverb do we drum the *agidigbo;* it is the wise who dance to it, and the learned who understand its language" (7). The word that Soyinka transforms into *àgídìgbo* is actually `*ogìdìgbó* in the original. As Soyinka indicates in the glossary of Yoruba words appended to his published translation, the word *agidigbo* in his translation refers to "Yoruba leisurely music played mostly at social occasions." By contrast, the word `*ogìdìgbó* in Fagunwa's text refers to a ceremonial drum associated with important communal festivals. The drum, then, connotes ritual and royalty (see Abraham, 454). Soyinka's translation appears to be based on a misconstrual of Fagunwa's intended reference. But the misconstrual is minor, and does not much diminish the implication of the original metaphor. The import of the metaphor is that the textual performance to follow is a communal dance generated out of a serious impulse. In its very design, it merits nothing less than a correspondingly sober reception: "The story which follows is a veritable *agidigbo;* it is I who will drum it, and you the wise heads who will interpret it" (7). If this invitation could all too easily be understood to accommodate pure aesthetic contemplation, the narrative voice seems eager to locate the expected text-reader intercourse in a more explicit material terrain—to socialize the aesthetic, as it were. What the novel calls for in the reader is, very precisely, not the pure reading sensibility contemplating in solitude a textual performance human in its provenance and tensions, but at a distance from lived reality. Rather, Fagunwa's narrator insists on an intimate materiality of the writing and the reading. He casts this materialist presupposition as an imperative, required for the textual performance to reach its addressee: "if you want this dance to be a success, here are two things I must request of you. Firstly, whenever a character in my story speaks in his own person, you must put yourselves in his place and speak as if you are that very man. And when the other replies, you must relate the story to yourselves as if you, sitting down, had been addressed and now respond to the first speaker" (7). There is an ideology of reading inherent here that asks for total identification on the part of the reader. Fagunwa's socialization of the reading experience insists that the world of reader and text become one. The reading encounter should unfold as a total surrender of the reader's self. If the dance initiated by Fagunwa's text is to be successful, the reader should attain a complete identification with the world to which the fiction alludes. But although the reader becomes itself a participant in the narrative action, the participation is not one-dimensional. The passage requests that the reader attain a mode of reading whereby he/she inhabits the moral and experiential universe of every character in the fiction, every word of dialogue and interlocution that transpires in the narrative.

In *The Implied Reader,* Wolfgang Iser suggests that one of the consequences of reading is that the literary text allows the reader to "formulate the unformulated" (294). For Iser, every productive reading experience depends on a fusion of horizon between the text and the reader. And yet, the reading event reorders or nudges the reader's horizon one step forward, such that the process of deciphering the meaning of a literary text "gives us the chance to formulate our own deciphering capacity—i.e., we bring to the fore an element of our being of which we are not directly conscious" (294).[6] For Fagunwa, the text-reader intercourse he expects requires a correspondence of horizons between text and reader. But the total correspondence Fagunwa demands (and the possibility of which he thereby assumes) cannot enable the sort of phenomenological complication that Iser identifies in the reading process. Looked at this way, Fagunwa's text is an explicit document of ideology. The interpellation of reader casually indexed in the passage quoted earlier is posited as a righteous necessity. By figuring the dynamic of interpellation being played out in the image of a communal dance, and by invoking a hallowed, preconstituted cultural symbol and ritual—the ogidigbo drum—the text's opening pages reveal the narrative's ideological work as one of unabashed culturalism.

The novel initially comes through a narrative voice that we take to be the authorial voice. Soon enough, however, we realize that the "author" of the hunter's story is in fact not the voice that initially addresses us. After setting forth some conditions for the ideal reception, the erstwhile narrator informs us of a chance encounter with an old man. The old man exchanges pleasantries with our narrator, sighs deeply, and proceeds with the following instructions: "Take up your pen and paper and write down the story which I will now tell. Do not delay it till another day lest the benefit of it pass you over. I would not myself have come to you today, but I am concerned about the future and there is this fear that I may die unexpectedly and my story die with me. But if I pass it on to you now and you take it down diligently, even when the day comes that I must meet my Maker, the world will not forget me" (8). This passage initiates the novel's staging of a familiar assumption regarding oral cultures in the midst of cultural transformations occasioned by literacy. In his particular staging of this familiar trope, Fagunwa's text reveals one aspect of his vision and plays out a tension at the heart of that vision. In revealing aspects of its epistemological grounding, Fagunwa's text also meditates upon them. For now, let us simply note that what the old man establishes is a privileging of print over the transience of orality. The claim is that to write down an experience is to ensure the permanence of that experience and the knowledge

it yields for posterity. To keep it within the oral medium is to endanger
its permanence: the bearer dies with the tale. Stepping up to modernity,
therefore, requires that the oral becomes written.[7]

That the project of transposing oral knowledge and viewpoints
into the medium of print is dear to Fagunwa's heart (not just to his imagined character-narrator), is illustrated in the peroration that concludes
his travel memoir, *Ìrìnàjò Apá Kíní* (Travel Part 1). In the pamphlet's
closing paragraphs, Fagunwa writes:

> Bí ènìà bá jòkó sí ìlú rè̩ tí kò mo̩ ibòmíràn àbò̩ è̩kó̩ ni olúwarè̩ ní,
> bè̩ni o̩mo̩ ika o̩wó̩ wa kò dógba, kì í̩se gbogbo ènìà l'ó lè rí owó àti
> ma fi rìn kiri, nítorínà l'ó sì fi jé̩ ohun è̩tó̩ wípé kí enití ó bá lo̩ sí
> ibòmíràn ma so̩ ohun tí òn bá rí níbè̩ han enití kò lo̩. Púpò̩ nínú ìtàn
> pàtàkì tí àwo̩n baba nlá wa ti mò̩ l'ó ti so̩nù pátápátá nítorí nwo̩n
> kò ko̩ àwo̩n ìtàn wo̩nnì sílè̩, ìgbàtí nwó̩n sì kú, ìtàn ńà kú pè̩lú wo̩n.
> (*Ìrìnàjò Apá Kíní*, 35)
>
> [If a person remains in his/her native land and is ignorant of other
> places, that person's education is incomplete; and yet, because our
> fingers are differently sized not everyone has the financial resources
> to travel extensively. This is why it is right that the person who has
> traveled elsewhere make known what he/she saw there for the ben-
> efit of those who cannot so travel. Many of the significant stories
> our grandfathers knew are now completely lost because they did not
> write those stories down; when they then pass away, those stories
> die with them.]

The old man of *Forest* is thus expressing a sentiment that coincides with
Fagunwa's. Like Fagunwa's autobiographical voice in the passage above,
the old man of *Forest* privileges literacy over orality. As a way of immor-
talizing the past, the old man offers his experiences to literature. "My
name is Akara-ogun, Compound of Spells," he announces, "one of the
formidable hunters of a bygone age. My own father was a hunter, he
was also a great one for medicines and spells" (9).

What we have in Fagunwa's novel, then, is an (auto)biographical
tale, verbally narrated by the old man, but transmitted to us in written
form by a scribe who we get to know rather familiarly by the end of the
story, but who remains nameless all the way. This scribe is Fagunwa's
alter ego; that is, in him, we meet an "author" who disavows an originating agency, allocating this, instead, to a construct from a "bygone
age" *(ayé àtijó̩)*. If we ask how bygone an age could be when a "formidable hunter" from that age still lives to inform us of it, we shall be asking a question the text cannot raise. It is noteworthy that the letter
Akara Ogun and his fellow hunters receive from the King of Mount

Langbodo is dated "The Twenty Second Day of the Seventh Month in the Year Nineteen Hundred and Thirty Three after the death of Our Lord" (137). Locating Akara Ogun in a "bygone age," that age turns out to be contemporaneous with Fagunwa's own moment of writing. Wholly committed to an unambiguous contextualization of his narrative labor and the ideal reception he expects, the demand of temporal coherence is not a priority for Fagunwa. It is as though, in the political and cultural moment of its address, Fagunwa's novel needs a past to launch an address to the *present*, but also needs an authoritative eye to narrativize that past. "My comrades all," reminisces the narrator/old man, "I have beheld the ocean and have known the sea, water holds no further terror for me!" (70). What better narrative authority than that of a raconteur detailing first-hand experience?

In this sense, the mediation is held up as irreducible. Akara-ogun mediates a bygone age by means of his autobiographical recall, but his own mediation only reaches us by means of the scribe's literate skill. Fagunwa, in other words, locates his quester in the past which, as we have just seen, is also the present, and does so in the service of a discursive pressure to address a present challenge. In exploring and surviving the "forest of a thousand daemons," the formidable hunter allegorizes the black African subject, the precarious but compelling imperative of nation-building, and the overarching epistemological and sociopolitical summons of modernity. The very final line of the novel pronounces a wish and toasts that wish with three cheers: "the world shall become you, your nation will wax in wisdom and in strength, and we black people will never *again* be left behind in the world. Muso! Muso! Muso!" (140, my emphasis). With a precision the overall text seems less fastidious about—for in Fagunwa can also be found a self-righteous existential fatalism—this line recognizes a dual priority central to the moment of modernity: knowledge and power. Toasting to more knowledge and power in the collective future of "your nation" in particular, and "we black people" [àwa ènìà dúdú] in general, Fagunwa's alter ego poses these ideals as prerequisite for the "progress" of an erstwhile benighted and backward collectivity.

Another explicit indication of the cultural-nationalism of *Forest* can be found in the section entitled "The First Day With Iragbeje In The House With Seven Wings." On reaching Langbodo, the hunters who had set out to receive what amounts to the key to prosperous nationhood in modernity spend seven days with an old sage named Iragbeje. Each day, Iragbeje instructs them on a different theme. On the first day, his sermon, so to speak, is centered on parental responsibility in the upbringing of their offspring. Iragbeje's address thematizes patriotism and the importance of cultivating in youths the ideal of achievement in Western terms. Yet, it is an achievement that should bring the modern achiever closer to his or her "African-ness": "Even if you are educated, even when you become a doctor twelve times over, a lawyer sixteen times over; when you become thirteen types of Bishop and wear twenty clerical stoles at once, never condemn your father" (105). In this passage, "Father" metaphorizes nation. As if to prevent even the possibility that the association may be lost on the addressee, Iragbeje proposes the connection in the clearest of terms: "Observe several sons of the black races who are brilliant in their scholarship, who have studied in the white man's cities but who adopt the entire land of the Yoruba as the parent who gave them birth, who love their land with a great love so that many wear the clothes of their land, *agbada* and *buba,* love to be photographed in the clothes of their grandfathers; while others wear the outfit of Ogboni to show that they submit themselves to the country of Nigeria which is the great ancestor who gave them life, and show themselves humble to those who are their elders" (105). Let us note the slippage that occurs here between categories of tribal ethnicity, national identity, and continental or racial identity. The subjects being addressed are "sons of the black races," their "great ancestor" is "the country of Nigeria," and the symbol of their racial and national pride is located in a domain that is much narrower than the national or the racial-continental, namely, a Yoruba tribal-ethnic dress code. Likewise, identitarian self-assertion is specifically posed on the terrain of dressing as a symbolic practice.

The explicit socialization of textual performance and ideal reception that we indicated earlier is thus a formal and ideological scaffold that Fagunwa's text fills out with a story of collective beatitude at the far side of the moment's striving. This "sonorous proverb," the text's very form and rhetoric suggests, occupies a human present, and its didactic seriousness should not be missed. Otherwise, the hermeneutic circle appropriate to it will remain incomplete: "as men of discerning—and this is the second task you must perform—you will yourselves extract various wisdoms from the story as you follow its progress" (7).

The term that Soyinka translates as "men of discerning" is *òmòràn*—a fully ungendered collocation. Unlike in Soyinka's rendering, *òmòràn* is a compound noun more literally translated in the plural form it takes here as "those who know." This points up yet another moment of mediation: a gender-neutral concept becomes gendered in its transformation to English. But if Soyinka's translation confers on *òmòràn*— and the term, we should remember, designates the implied audience of the narrative performance itself—a sexual coding not inherent to the

original, the fact remains that the gender system presupposed and reca-
pitulated in the novel justifies that genderization. In transforming "those
who know" into "men of discerning" in his translation, Soyinka is being
faithful to the inner logic of the novel as a whole.

It is important to press this last point. The rhetoric of the novel
orients its didacticism to an audience figured as male. While not explicitly presuming an objectively male audience—by the third day of narration, "the entire populace" (68) constitutes Akara-ogun's audience—
the implied reader is textualized within a masculinist frame. In
describing how his mother—"a deep seasoned witch from the caul-
drons of hell" (9)—died at the hands of his father, Akara-ogun cautions
his friend, the scribe:

> Look on me, my friend, and if you are not yet married I implore you
> to consider the matter well before you do. True, your wife ought to
> be beautiful lest you tire of each other quickly; and a lack of brains
> is not to be recommended since you must needs hold converse with
> each other, but this is not the heart of the matter. The important req-
> uisite is that your wife should not be prone to evil, for it is your wife
> who gives you meat and gives you drink and is admitted most to
> your secrets. God has created them such close creatures that there
> hardly exists any manner in which they cannot come at a man; and
> when I tell you what my father suffered at the hands of this wife of
> his, you will be truly terrified. (11)

Woman here is the Other, and Akara-ogun enlists a rhetoric of the self
which opposes that self to those whom "God has created . . . such close
creatures." It is a self that accommodates both his father and his listener,
and against the sanctity of that self, his mother can only be invoked in
the third person: "my father suffered at the hands of this wife of his."

The gender system put into play in *Forest* points to a logic of Othering inherent to a broader ideology of mastery. Posed differently, the
demonization of woman and genderization of implied reader in this passage expose the lineaments of an ideological ensemble that sponsors
Fagunwa's text, driving it beyond itself. As feminist work has demonstrated, the path to such ideals as nationhood and modernity is often
cast rhetorically in gendered terms: that is to say, in the dualism of a
male subject in confrontation with nature or the forces of anarchy. If
man is brain and brawn—the qualities it takes to "master" nature, itself
conceived as female—woman embodies emotion and potential treach-
ery; she is an Other from whom the male subject needs to protect itself.
Forest instances this notion most resonantly at the beginning of the third
part, where Akara-ogun goes to recruit an old friend and fellow hunter

named Kako to join him on the expedition to Langbodo. He arrives on Kako's wedding day, whereupon Kako packs his hunting gear and prepares to leave. But his newly wedded wife protests: "she wrapped herself tightly round Kako saying, 'You are going nowhere, not until you find some way to dispose of me'" (77). The text continues: "Our delay grew longer with the woman's desperate hold and Kako grew truly angry. His face was transformed and he pulled out his matchet, saying, 'Woman of death, mother of witchery seeking to obstruct my path of duty, know you not that before earth destroys the evil-doer, much good has already suffered ruin ! Before God adjudges me guilty I shall pass sentence on your guilt.' And, having spoken, he slashed her midriffs, and it lacked only a little for the woman to be cloven clean in two; she fell on earth twitching in the final throes of death crying the name of Kako, crying his name to the other world. Great indeed was my terror!" (77). Kako's violence claims for justification the danger posed by three "attributes" of woman, attributes which make her a threat to the destiny of the questing subject: death-dealing *(oníkúpani obìnrin)*, witchery *(àjẹ́ obìnrin)*, and the tendency to derail "Man" from the path of duty. In thus killing her—the text figures it as a terrifying but pragmatic immolation—Kako is rendered as the rash but committed patriot who places the call of duty above the sentiment of love and attachment. Self-realization and self-subordination to the cause of nation-building are figured as urgent imperatives that require mobility and the "manliness" to plod through an immense vastness. In *Forest,* it seems, the inevitable burden of modern existence is that the stasis associated with domesticity needs to be expunged, however violently.

A parallel dynamic is coded into what may be called Akara-ogun's coming-of-age story. Here, it is his mother who needs to be subordinated to the imperative of male achievement. As a result of a disagreement between Akara-ogun's mother and father, his mother "became so ruthless in her witching, that, before the year was out, eight of my father's children were dead and three of his wives had gone the same way. Thus was I left the only child and my mother the only wife" (9). At risk now of succumbing to the fate of the other children who had been undone by his mother's witchcraft, the latter has to die. For the quester to assume his mandate, his path needs to be free of woman's complication: "I returned to the house just as my father was opening the door to my mother's room, and when he had opened the door and we entered, that moment when I caught sight of my mother, it was all I could do not to take flight. From her head down to her shoulders was human enough, but the rest of her was wholly antelope. She was all covered in blood and swarms of flies. My father touched her; she was dead and had begun to rot" (13). Indeed, this clearing of the decks extends to Akara Ogun's father too; by the end of the first chapter, both his parents are dead. Interestingly, though, it is the father who kills the mother. Returning home at night, the father shoots and fatally wounds a creature he took to be an antelope. But, says our narrator, "she [the mother] was the antelope stealing out at night to feast in the field of okro" (13). If filial identification needs to be removed so that the son can come to his own in modernity, it is the father who initiates the rite, who sets the process in motion. By the end of the first chapter, the father has played his part and the complication of Woman has been transcended: the formidable quester is ready to venture forth. Consequently, the opening chapter ends with a suggestion of the autonomy of the subject—the Father's son—in modernity. With proud ceremony, Akara Ogun authorizes the commencement of his own biography, the trajectory of his self-consciousness: "so did my mother die, and hardly was a month over when my father also followed her. From that day was I orphaned, fatherless and motherless. And thus ends the story of my parents and comes the turn of my own" (13).

INTERROGATING MODERNITY

The preceding section has attempted to set out the ways in which form and content in Fagunwa's novel inextricably combine to impress on the ọmọ̀ràn, the reader that knows, a full measure of the writer's intent. Several critics have pointed to the writer's sheer delight in the well-turned phrase (Bamgbose, Irele, Ogundipe-Leslie, Smith). The novel's rhetorical virtuosity goes a long way in explaining its initial and durable appeal to its primary Yoruba speaking audience. However, the ideological basis and possible consequence of the novel's rhetorical exuberance might repay some clarification. We may pose the issue as a question: if the overall effect of *Forest* owes much to the writer's attention to language itself as a distinct asset, in good hands a lever of form, why might Fagunwa have been so relentless in, as it were, basking in the sheer figurative resources of Yoruba language? And what consequence might this generate here and now?

To the first question, the obvious response would be that Fagunwa is a skillful storyteller. One might also say that the oral background from which his text derives typically revels in the play of language. Both responses are correct, although they do not tell us much: all great storytellers labor to use language well, and all human cultures delight in the well-spoken word. A reason more specific to Fagunwa's colonial situation might be that pushing the aesthetic capacity of Yoruba to the ultimate extent of his talent enables him to compensate—via fiction—for a mission that remains daunting in historical reality. That is, showing Yoruba in the glory he deems appropriate to it serves his cultural nationalist pride, calms the harsh edges of a colonial present and an uncertain future. Although this speculation does not require that Fagunwa have any awareness of any such motivation, or even that we prove it by argument, we do have autobiographical evidence of Fagunwa's race consciousness in the second installment of his travel memoir. On a visit to the British Museum, he records his reaction to artifacts of African origin in language that reveals his cultural nationalism:

> inú mi dún púpò nígbàtí mo rí ǹkan tí ó ti Áfríkà wá; ǹkan fífi owó ṣe ni àwon ǹkan nà. Ère kan báyì tí nwón gbé láti ibití nwón ńpè ní Àngólà ní Áfríkà dára púpò, bẹ nà ṣi ni àwon ará Kóngò gbé ère tí ó dára. Sùgbón èyítí ó wú mi lórí ju gbogbo àwon ǹkan Áfríkà tí ó wà níbè ni orí kan tí wón fi irin ṣe ti nwón wú jáde láti inú ilè ní Modákéké, nwón ṣe orí nà dára tóbè tí ó jẹ pé kò re èhìn bí a bá fi wé ǹkan míràn nínú ilé ńà tí àwon Òyìnbó fi owó ṣe. Ojó ére ńà ti pé ó sì fi han ni pé àwon bàbá nlá àwon Yòrùbá ti bá àwon òlàjú pàdé ní apá Ìlà Òrùn kí ó tó di pé nwón wá sí ibití a wà lóńí (*Ìrìnàjò Apá Kejì*, 33–34)

> [I was very happy when I saw the artifacts that come from Africa; they were all hand-crafted. A particular sculpture from Angola in Africa is very beautiful, and the sculptures from Congo were exquisite. But of all the African artifacts there, the one that most powerfully made my head swell with pride was a bronze bust of a human head that was excavated from Modakeke [in Western Nigeria]; this sculpture is as beautiful as any in the museum made by Europeans. The sculpture is quite old and thus illustrates that the ancestors of Yoruba people had interacted with civilized and enlightened cultures *(òlàjú)* in the Middle East before they came to settle where we presently are.]

This response to a bronze head from Modakeke reveals Fagunwa's racial pride while also recapitulating an influential account of Yoruba ethnogenesis. As in the slippage between racial-continental, national, and ethnic-tribal identities that we encountered earlier with regard to Fagunwa's articulation of his intended audience, this passage conflates all three. Fagunwa is happy that Africa (Angola, Congo) is well represented among the artifacts he sees at the British museum. But he is most especially proud that the Yoruba people are well represented, via the artifact from Modakeke. What we witness here is an instance of rhetorical suturing, a construction that is productive to the extent that it enables Fagunwa's culturalist ideology.

Whether or not Fagunwa consciously sought to displace intractable sociocultural and epistemological tensions with the seductive grace of rhetoric and literary form, we as readers may end up doing so, wittingly or not. A possible way of not doing so is to face very squarely the issue of what might get subsumed in Fagunwa, banished by the sensation of pleasure and fulfillment that his language has to offer. To face this issue is to approach the level of *Forest* that I attributed earlier to its contemplative underbelly. At this level, it is possible to witness Fagunwa's text meditating on its own constative claims and narrative progress, right alongside the overt rhetorical zeal, and against the grain of its overarching assurances. For example, in using the quest motif to allegorize the subject's potential in modernity, *Forest* also shows up a contradiction built into the logic of the modern. This contradiction may be formulated in something like these terms: society opens up to the subject the promise of unhindered self-realization, even as a crucial condition of that realization is the subject's subjection to the order of civil society. The tension here resides in the irresolvable double discourse that valorizes the forlorn, industrious subject, yet retains the necessity of a collective ethos and the subject's answerability to that ethos.

Fagunwa's fiction meditates on this social issue in a number of ways. At the beginning of his second trip to the forest, Akara-ogun makes a ritual offering to his gun and inquires about the omen awaiting him on his trip. In doing this, Akara-ogun may be read as yielding to convention—that is to say, the wisdom of a collective. He casts kolanut pieces in order to read the fate in store for him. But the ritual does not communicate to him the good omen he desires: "when I cast the pieces, the result was inauspicious. For if it spoke good, would two pieces not face down and the other two up ? Alas it was not so for me, sometimes three pieces faced down and one up, and at other times all four faced down—the matter of this kola nut was simply beyond my comprehension. So when I had cast them many times without good augury, with my own hands I turned two up and faced two down saying, 'With his own two hands does a man mend his fortune; if you kola pieces will not predict good, I will predict that good for you.' After I was done I picked up my gun and proceeded to the forest of game" (37). In this passage, Akara-ogun is compelled—by his own willfulness—to choose between individual will on the one hand, and self-submission to a collective ethos, on the other; that is to say, he negates one (the latter) to affirm the other. By communal and culturally sanctioned practice, the positioning of the kolanut pieces after he casts them is to be read by him as a metaphysical pronouncement, an edict. In his willful disregard of the "inauspicious" omen communicated to him by means of the kolanuts' metaphysical self-arrangement, the quester rejects collective ethos. Or, at the least, he shows a readiness to mend his own fortune by the labor of "his own two hands." He manually rearranges the kolanut pieces, coercing his will out of a metaphysical system that guards the unknown, the mystery of possibilities. He thus asserts an autonomous consciousness and instrumentality: "After I was done I picked up my gun and proceeded to the forest of game."

Soon after Akara-ogun declares that "with his own two hands does a man mend his fortune," he runs into trouble. He is captured by a creature who "had two arms, two legs, and two eyes like a human being, but he had a small tail at his posterior and his eyes were enormous; each one was six times the normal size and red as palm kernels" (38). His treatment at the hands of this creature registers a violent reversal of the self-authorizing ideology of mastery: "Sometimes he [the creature] would ask me to neigh like a horse and when my voice did not simulate a horse's satisfactorily he would blast my ears with several slaps. Sometimes he demanded that I toss him up and down like a horse, and there was no remedy but to obey him; if I did not he would thrash the very breath out of me" (39). After enduring this treatment, where the erstwhile sufficient self becomes a beast of burden for the Other, Akara-ogun seems to recognize that the subject is not after all in total control of instrumentality. "What made the situation so dismal," he concedes, "was that he had seized my gun from the moment of my capture and when he arrived home he took it into the cave; he even took my hunting-bag" (41).

This passage is significant for two reasons. First, it instances a dissociation of mortal Akara-ogun from the constructed accoutrements that enable him to negotiate the terrors of an opaque forest. Divested of his gun and hunting-bag, Akara-ogun is forced to confront the rude reality of his limitations as mortal being. He is also made to realize the centrality of his constructs—gun and bag—in his self-image and pragmatic imaginary. A couple of lines later, however, *Forest* takes back the rigorous materialism I just indicated. The text seems to double back on itself, situating the lesson of Akara-ogun's predicament in a heightened awareness of a cosmic order presided over by the Christian God. In the protagonist's words, "much later . . . I began to undertand where I had erred. I realised that I indulged in magical arts but had failed to reckon with God. I forgot that He created the leaf and created the bark of the tree. Before daylight broke on my third day I cried to God and prayed" (41). Resolving the lesson of Akara-ogun's predicament this way, *Forest* interrogates the self-assurance of secular mastery that simultaneously looms large within it. In doing so, the text also reconstitutes an ontological topology sponsored by Christian theology.

This dynamic haunts all of Fagunwa's novels. One illustration can be found in *Igbó Olódùmarè*, where Akara-ogun returns to narrate his father's experience to the same scribe we meet in *Forest*. There is a scene where Olówó-ayé (the protagonist, Akara-ogun's father) confronts a ferocious demon named Èṣù-Kékeré-Òde. In this scene, Olówó-ayé claims an ordained transcendence that authorizes humanity's supremacy over nature. Addressing the demon, Olówó-ayé says: "Take care, you daemons, that none of you show defiance towards me, lest he spend his days wandering without rest through the spheres. Daemons of the forest of Olodumare, hear this today from a man, that when the creator created everything in the universe, He placed man as master over all" (*Igbó Olódùmarè*, 12; Irele, *Ideology*, 180–81).[8] Abiola Irele reads this scene as both an affirmation of humanity's privileged position in the universe and a testimony to what amounts to a traditional African version of instrumental reason. In Irele's words, "Contrary to the theories that anthropologists have peddled, depicting the traditional African as so saddled with the weight of his existence as to be crushed by it and therefore inclined to a passive attitude to the universe, the cosmologies of the different African cultures reveal an intelligence of the world centred upon the privileged position of man, an imaginative and symbolic organization of the world not simply in human terms, but in a comprehensive relation to man" (Irele, *Ideology*, 181). Irele then goes on to suggest that "we are dealing here not with an influence from an outside source—that Fagunwa's humanism is not Western or Christian" (181). In the fight that follows Olówó-ayé's declaration of hegemony, however, he tires out while Esu-kekere-ode remains ready for more. In this scene, the quester's "two hands" prove inadequate to the challenge offered by Esu-kekere-ode. Olówó-ayé resolves this realization by recounting on his flute the Creator's grand design and final sovereignty over the universe and all within it. The epic tune softens Esu-kekere-ode's heart; the two become friends and go their different ways, physically worse for wear and tear. Here again, Fagunwa shows his much vaunted "man" to be less than fully secure in the instrumentality of "his own two hands."

The deflation of Olówó-ayé's and Akara-ogun's grandiose ontology, a deflation both of them concede at the moment of extreme vulnerability, witnesses to a modernity whose specific contours have an uneasy edge that particularizes it. But the unease gets immediately reabsorbed into the logic of Christian theology. In this sense, Fagunwa's humanism shows itself to be influenced to a significant degree by Christianity. It is precisely because of this "Christian-ness" that *Forest* should be appreci-ated for its immanent critique of the ideology of modernity. In displaying worldly pragmatism side by side with religious fatalism, Fagunwa's fic-tion comes upon a tension inherent to that coupling. It is not clear whether Fagunwa consciously set out to dramatize this tension. The strength of conviction one gets from the homiletic passages of his fiction would seem to suggest that if Fagunwa the man was conscious of the ten-sion, the didactic function that his writings sought to serve leaves little room for ambivalence at the constative level. And yet, the ambivalence shows itself in such passages as we have just analyzed, where a contem-plative voice cautions against unrestrained worldly pragmatism by invok-ing the Creator's grand design.

The ending of *Forest* elevates what I have been calling a tension to the status of a paradox. "My friends," says Akara-ogun to his lis-teners, "herein ends all that I mean to tell the world at this time. I want you to use this story as a mine of wisdom that your lives may be good. And so, fare you well, the native returns to his dwelling" (139). At this point, the scribe takes over the narrative, informing us of what hap-pens *after* the completion of Akara-ogun's autobiography: "Thus did the man end his story and we saw him no more. But we found a little scrap of paper on the floor, and on it were the words 'Akara-ogun, Father of Born Losers'" (139). This moment consummates the novel's meditation on the ideology of mastery as well as its own strained attempt to call the modern state to being in the colonial space. First, a protagonist who requires the services of a scribe to transform his expe-rience into print now "signs" his name, so to speak, as a farewell token to his enraptured listeners. Far from being consolidated, the orality-literacy polarity with which the text commences is serenely—perhaps even unintentionally—questioned, such that an illiterate hunter "from a bygone age" now communicates in print. Alternately, we may say that the note left behind need not have been from Akara-ogun's hand, that what we encounter in this scene is a metaphysical intervention—*deus ex machina*—designed to underscore the protago-nist's equally metaphysical disappearance. In either case, it is reason-able to say that the appearance of a written note testifying to the authenticity of the protagonist is necessitated by the fact that the text needs a memorable finale to consecrate the narrative event just near-ing its end. In the combined impact of Akara-ogun's disappearance and the mystery of an inscription dropping out of nowhere, the text seeks to convince us, even as Akara-ogun convinces his immediate lis-teners, that we have all along been in the presence of a peculiarly resourceful character, a true compound of spells.

If we opt for this second reading, the epithet bestowed on Akara-ogun acquires considerable significance. "Father of born losers" is Soyinka's anglicization of a more subtle phrase: *baba òmúlè-mófo* (*Ògbójú Ọdẹ*, 97). Literally rendered, this phrase translates into "patriarch to those who reach out to grasp the earth, only to grasp a void." The epithet condenses, in equal measure, a faith in the need for earthly yearning with a claim for the ultimate limit to all such yearning. The subject on these terms cannot but reach out to get a handle on the world. And yet, the subject's success in the reaching out will yield a different kind of insight altogether, for the world thus grasped turns out to be a void, one vast emptiness *[òfo]*. In this sense, the world is a void, and all worldly yearnings are emanations of desire circumscribed by a profound, overarching, nothingness. Materiality eludes total mastery, at the very moment that the material agent appears to have succeeded in objectifying desire.

Akara-ogun's epithet therefore indicates both the benefit of his resourcefulness and the ultimate limits of his earthly success. The complex scepticism inherent to the formulation "baba òmúlèmófo" undercuts the claims to transcendence that the novel has established all along. More immediately, it undermines, even as it recognizes and celebrates, the metaphysical resourcefulness that the protagonist's disappearing act seeks to underscore. This scepticism could be read in terms of the residual Christian fatalism we have already encountered in Fagunwa's vision. If on one hand modernity—understood as a secular scientific apprehension of social reality—compels his energy, on the other, the particular Christian theology that sponsors his fatalism towards the profane world collides with its secular antithesis. What the collision yields is a very specific historical paradox: as the product of an educated, black African subject in the first half of the twentieth century, Fagunwa's narrative cannot but be saddled with it.

This last point deserves some elaboration. Several commentators have drawn attention to the Christian missionary dimension of the novel (Bamgbose *Novels,* Ogundipe-Leslie, Olabimtan). There is no question whatsoever that Fagunwa's work is inconceivable outside of the history of Christian missionary work in black Africa. As Ayo Bamgbose and Afolabi Olabimtan have indicated, Fagunwa's Christian faith ran so deep that he changed his given name, Oròwọlé, a name that is connected to Orò—"the bull-roarer," a pagan ancestral icon—to Ọlọrunfẹmi, "God loves me." Fagunwa's hybridized apprehension of self and world is thus enacted here in the very act of self-naming. Discussing this apprehension of self and world, Olabimtan criticizes Fagunwa for being complicit in the spread of Christian indoctrination at the expense of traditional

African religions: "It is not at all preposterous to suggest that the Christian Missionaries, having learnt that story-telling was a traditional way of
inculcating beliefs into the young ones, encouraged the late Fagunwa to
write a story book with traditional background in order to teach Christian ideals, and to suppress such elements of traditional religion as could
be detrimental to the growth of the Christian religion" (Olabimtan, 111).

Historical work on missionary activity among the Yoruba gives
substance to Olabimtan's claim that the idea of reaching the natives in
their own language formed a significant part of the strategy of Christian
missions (Ajayi; Ologunde). To this end, the enterprise of "reducing" the
Yoruba language to print in the early and mid-nineteenth century was
spearheaded by Christian missions and missionaries. It was as a result of
this ferment that the King James Bible, translated by Bishop Samuel
Ajayi Crowther (1806–91) became accessible in the Yoruba language
(Ajayi; Bamgbose, "Studies"; Ologunde). Fagunwa's *Forest* thus enters a
discursive space made possible through a conceptual grid, a mode of
apprehension and representation, fundamentally colored by Christian
theology on the one hand and, on the other, secularist visions of enlightenment and progress.

Africanist historians have done a lot of work on this historical
moment.[9] As many have indicated, the classic text that represents the discursive climate in which Fagunwa's *Forest* takes shape is Reverend
Samuel Johnson's *The History of the Yoruba* (1921). This book offers us
a nonfictional exemplification of the epistemological order that governs
Fagunwa's text. Johnson sets out to record the history of the Yoruba by
means of oral testimonies, occasional archival documentary resource,
and participant recollection, since he himself participated in the events
recorded toward the end of his book. Beyond the patriotic tenderness and
scholarly tentativeness of his labor, Johnson—an Anglican minister—fil-
ters his account through a discourse of the providence of the Christian
God, such that Christianization of the Yoruba nation emerges as a grand
culmination, an altogether beatific telos of the historical narrative.[10]

Johnson's account of Yoruba ethnogenesis makes much of the
Yoruba's Middle Eastern origins and their subsequent migration south
of the Sahara to the general area of their current location in tropical
West Africa. Johnson does so in order to link the Yoruba to the great lit-
erate cultures and world religions that originated from the Middle East,
namely, Islam and Judaeo-Christianity. Similarly, and as we saw earlier,
Fagunwa in his reaction to Modakeke bronze recapitulates this histori-
cal version. As he tells us, the bronze sculpture he looked upon in the
British museum "is quite old and thus illustrates that the ancestors of
Yoruba people had interacted with civilized and enlightened cultures

[ọ̀làjú] in the Middle East before they came to settle where we presently are" (34). In his essay entitled "Olaju: A Yoruba Concept of Development," J. D. Y. Peel has shown that the term "olaju" is central to the way the Yoruba speak about and come to terms with Westernization, Christianization, and secular modernity. By invoking the concept of "olaju" (civilization, Enlightenment) and claiming that the Yoruba acquired it through historical and cultural processes that far antedate their encounter with imperial Britain, Fagunwa demonstrates his cultural and racial pride. But to the extent that it leaves the concept of "olaju" intact, the culturalism of Fagunwa and the generation he represents borrows its hierarchy of value from Eurocentric notions of civilization and Enlightenment.

In this sense, Fagunwa's work fits into a pattern shared by a particular generation in the trajectory of modern African letters, a generation that saw itself as a version of the Du Boisian "Talented Tenth."[11] Being the early generation of educated Africans, they saw themselves and their mission more or less as colonialist discourse educated them to see it. They saw themselves as a privileged few who would speed up the process of black Africa's modernization. They generally accepted the key assumptions of colonial rhetoric, some of which include the idea that Africans should be "refined" and made to demonstrate their latent humanity and readiness for the twentieth century through literacy and Christianization. And so, in the service of this vision, Fagunwa yokes together Western secularism and an influential strand of Christian theology. But the idea of a transcendental Christian God that his narrative elevates over traditional pagan worship shows itself to be fatalistic in the face of a secular will to practical achievement. If Fagunwa the man was aware of a tension here, the letter of his texts registers no preoccupation of a corresponding sort. It is as though the providence of God is precisely what will enable humanity to over-reach itself, to come so close to God that, logically, the idea of godhead becomes unintelligible. Although Afolabi Olabimtan is correct to suggest that Fagunwa's novel serves the onslaught of Christian indoctrination, then, his mildly accusatory tone does not get us to the core of Fagunwa's predicament and agency. I am suggesting that Fagunwa's novel serves a Christian missionary agenda, but does so in a way that immanently deconstructs an "uncorrupted" Christian perspective.

Homi Bhabha has written about the ways in which the acquisition of Christian belief in the Bible among a Hindu population transforms the strict logic of Christianity and subordinates it to the immediate desire of the native.[12] This is in part because the Christian mandate and rhetoric itself subsists on repressed contradictions. If in the metropolitan space those contradictions can remain out of sight, in the colonial space they come fully to the light. In acquiescing to colonial (Christian) ideology, then, the native reveals its contradictions. We can understand this aspect of Fagunwa's novel along these lines. Consequently, overtly assured as he might be of his epochal mission and the coherence of that mission, Fagunwa's narrative gestures in directions that transgress the serenity of his assurance.

In the context of contemporary postcolonial theory and cultural criticism, Fagunwa's novel can be made to serve two agendas that might appear opposed but are in effect complementary. On one hand, the text's clear debt to the European picaresque allegory renders it open to a familiar formalistic normalization, whereby the text is read to bear witness to the universal themes shared by all literary texts regardless of particular histories. Such universalism can be found in an early reaction to the novel by L. Murby, then editor for Nelson Press. In his "Foreword" to Nelson's first publication of Ògbójú Ode Nínú Igbó Irúnmalè, Murby writes: "It is probable that scholars will compare them [i.e., Fagunwa's "'epics' or 'allegories'"] . . . with the great epics that stand at the threshold of European literature . . . in their treatment of character and story, in their use of myth and legend and allegory, and in their proverbial and epigrammatic language they bear definite resemblances to the Odyssey and Beowulf and the early medieval romances on the one hand, and on the other hand to that great cornerstone of the English novel, Bunyan's The Pilgrim's Progress."[13] Murby's well-intentioned universalism leaves out historical and political determinations that are specific to Fagunwa's novel. A politically oriented criticism may shift attention to the novel as the aesthetic achievement of an "African" imagination. This way of relating to the novel rescues authorial agency away from the muffling embrace of an abstract, universal literariness. But it does so by delivering the text to a different kind of muffling embrace, that of an abstract "African tradition" or a generic "postcolonial discourse." Moreover, the fact that it is written in an indigenous African language, the spectacle of magic, of strange spirits and mysterious jungles, these can easily feed a reading that exalts the novel only in the status of the captivating "other"—the native's different mode of seeing, subversive only in its otherness. This political agenda would seem opposed to the former because it claims, or seeks, some specificity that is free of the West's enveloping tentacles. But both agendas actually complement each other. The universalist subsumes Fagunwa's lesson under European literary history masquerading as the universal, while the proponent of alterity reinstates the category "Europe" as a coherent and self-sufficient frame of reference. That is, even as it seeks to escape an alien monster, the agenda of alterity remains locked within the oversight of the monster because alterity always requires its antithesis—the alien monster—to constitute itself.

This leads us to the question of language. In chapter 3, I argued that a conceptual frame that, in the name of decolonization, imputes to indigenous languages an authentic otherness risks flattening out the rigor of the best of African literature by depoliticizing the terrain upon which languages thrive. To be sure, this is counterintuitive, since the imputation is in the first place motivated by a political impulse to salvage indigenous languages from the hegemony of English, French, or Portuguese. Yet, insofar as the realms of culture and politics are by definition muddy and muddying, and insofar as the languages of daily life have a tendency to continue doing their own thing, oblivious to the pronouncements of cultural theorists in books and at conferences, evocations of otherness and authenticity emerge sounding battle-shy, cozily distanced from the reproductive contamination of the concrete world. Against the view that indigenous languages can ever be protected from the consequences of an epistemic and sociocultural drama as epochal as colonialism, *Forest* suggests that the celebration is at once historically reductive and conceptually undialectical.

Fagunwa's achievement, then, cannot adequately be read as a triumphantly "Other" elaboration that escapes by opposing the shadow of the West. But neither can it be leveled out into a lateral formal or ideational reiteration of John Bunyan or Daniel Defoe. As we have seen, Fagunwa complicates the secular with the sacred; in his novel, a pragmatist ideology of mastery is qualified with an existential resignation to the providence of the supreme Being. The complication arises because one arm of the ideology that governs his narrative (secular scientific mastery and the liberal nation-state), collides with another arm, namely, the religious fatalism of his Christian faith. And yet, both arms are traceable to the overarching ideology of modernity that the colonial enterprise forced onto the space, history, and consciousness of twentieth-century Africa. What this means is that, beyond the formal and ideational resonances between Fagunwa and the early modern allegories he knew and respected, beyond even his cultural nationalism, his achievement can be more deeply historicized, richly theorized. If we grant that Fagunwa's text interrogates modernity immanently—that is to say, not by rejecting it or seeking to overcome a putative West, but by internalizing its assurances and enacting its contradictions—we will be better placed to more deeply historicize and appreciate his achievement as story-teller and cultural worker.

What *Forest* indicates is the mud and contamination within which moral agents actually live, and out of which the grounded imagination actually creates. Rather than being a compromising element, the mud and the contamination are historically inevitable, and the writer's achievement therefore lies in the rigor with which the narrative encompasses them. The postindependence African novel may have transcended Fagunwa's Bunyanesque faith in the Bible, but other contradictions immanent to the ideology of modernity are not so easily overcome: contradictions, for instance, between ethnic identity and national identity, or within a masculinist secular individualism that preaches the ethic of a stable "us" while suppressing the evidence of gender and particularity of women. Many commentators have discerned in the failure of many African nation-states an immanent critique of the ideology that sought to call them into being. By extension, narrativizing the contradictions and the failures have in part been the province of modern African literature. In dramatizing the claims of modernity with its contradictions, Fagunwa's text demystifies them precisely because he acts them out. His value, then, derives from the fact that he traveled this province once, tortured by its muffled storms and buried mines.

THE CASE OF AMOS TUTUOLA

Our analysis so far explores Fagunwa's work in terms of the clash of ideas enacted in *Forest*. We sought, too, to locate the writer against a background of his historical moment and discursive conditions. In the rest of this chapter, I should like to consider Fagunwa's place relative to other writers, and relative to the cultural context his work has influenced. That is, if up till now we have been considering Fagunwa's work in terms of what informs and impacts it, it is necessary now to explore what his work informs and impacts.

Abiola Irele and Ato Quayson have plotted a literary history for Nigerian writing, which places Fagunwa in a line that connects him with Amos Tutuola and Wole Soyinka (see Irele, *Ideology*, 174–97; Quayson, 44–64). The story of Tutuola's relationship is pretty straight-forward, and we may briefly indicate it here. In a piece entitled "My Life and Activities," appended to the first printing of his novel *The Palm-wine Drinkard* in the United States, Amos Tutuola provides a number of biographical details that are instructive. He was born in 1920 in Abeokuta, a town sixty-four miles from Lagos in South Western Nigeria, and started school only in 1934—that is, only at the age of fourteen. He attended the Salvation Army School briefly, but because of financial constraints, had to move to another school in Lagos. He finally gave up schooling altogether in 1939. Between 1939 and 1946 he learned blacksmithing and enlisted in the West African Royal Air Force. He was discharged in 1945 and began working as an office messenger in 1946. According to an assessment of Tutuola published in *West Africa* magazine, May 1, 1954, he started writing stories on scrap paper as a way of relieving the boredom of his job as office messenger (see Lindfors, *Perspectives*, 36).

He started writing, then, strictly as a pastime, and had no intention of publishing the things he wrote. The portrait concludes by stressing the element of serendipity in Tutuola's entrance into the world of book publishing and the literary establishment:

> Tutuola might never have changed this intention [of simply writing to relieve boredom] had he not read an advertisement in a local paper, in which the advertisers had set forth a list of their latest publications. A few days before Amos had written *The Palm-wine Drinkard*. This extraordinary book was completed during forty-eight hours' febrile work. He spent the next three months enlarging on the original. When he felt satisfied that he had obeyed all the dictates of his imagination, he laid aside his pencil, wrote a final copy in ink, and trustingly sent it off to the organization whose advertisement he had safely kept (The United Society for Christian Literature). They can be considered the "finders" of an author who wrote as no one with whose works they were familiar had ever before written. . . . Faber and Faber published *The Palm-wine Drinkard* in 1952. It was subsequently published in the U.S.A., and in a French edition. (*Perspectives*, 36)

I have dwelt at this length on Tutuola's biographical background as well as the story of the publication of *The Palm-wine Drinkard* in order to stress the fact that (i) he has barely a Standard VI primary education, and (ii) his first published novel was originally written as a kind of "hobby" and thereafter sent out in the hope that some financial return might come off it. What this implies is that the level of his formal Western education is lower than Fagunwa's, and that unlike him, Tutuola wrote on a "freelance" basis, not under the sponsorship of a missionary educational apparatus.

In the educational system of colonial Nigeria, of course, acquisition of the English language is tied to one's level of education. Because of his level of education, then, Tutuola was not fully proficient in the English language. Although he wrote in English, Tutuola was clearly influenced by the works of Fagunwa.[14] By writing *The Palm-wine Drinkard* in English, Tutuola gives us an example of a text that is written in a language (English) and a genre (fictional narrative) that the author has, by all conventional standards, not fully mastered. As has often been remarked, this is very evident in the awkward structure, as well as the very prose, of the novel. *The Palm-wine Drinkard* generated an instructive controversy when it was first published. The narrative generated an enthusiastic response from Western critics when it appeared (see Lindfors, *Perspectives;* Owomoyela). Western readers noted the awkwardness (or unconventionality) of language and form in the novel, but cast these as stylistic idiosyncracies. Indeed, for them, the stylistic awkwardness comes across as something close to technical novelty. African readers dismissed the book as a severely flawed, even embarrassing, work. For them, the writer had no control over the linguistic as well as narrative idiom he was using. The ghost of anthropology also reared its head in this initial reception, such that it was hailed by the eminent scholar of African religion, Geoffrey Parrinder, as a specifically "African" text. It evinces, so Parrinder claimed in his foreword to Tutuola's *My Life in the Bush of Ghosts* (1954), the still extant beliefs of the "traditional" Yoruba and their worldview.[15]

The initial discrepancy between the reaction of, on one hand, Western readers and, on the other, African readers of Tutuola can be explained in terms of the ideological presuppositions that each brought to *The Palm-wine Drinkard*. In the 1950s when the novel appeared, educated Africans wanted a novel like Chinua Achebe's *Things Fall Apart* or Camara Laye's *L'Enfant Noir*. In this context of cultural nationalism, where literature became a way of showing the glory of one's culture, Tutuola's awkward English and clumsy narration came across as an embarrassment. The ethnographic enthusiasts and their nationalist mirror-images did not approach Tutuola for what he might teach us about the untidy processes of cultural transformation, or of discursive agency within those processes. Rather, they held his text against preconstituted (hegemonic) values and biases: the well-wrought novel on one hand, the exotic African imagination on the other. If one looks instead at the cultural and epistemological dynamics silently at work in Tutuola's discourse, one can locate his legacy elsewhere. What Tutuola offers is not aesthetic virtuosity, for he doesn't speak to, nor is he spoken by, preconstituted norms of Western literary language. What he offers is the occasion to confront those norms in their imperfect approximation. He permits us to see the violation of hegemony at the level of literary form.

The Palm-wine Drinkard is conceived and stylistically executed within a traditional African oral narrative frame, but in terms of ideational profile and sphere of reception, it is primarily a product of writing and the print medium. In this sense, it is, like Fagunwa's corpus, a dramatization of the encounter between (Western) literacy and (traditional African) orality. The text also has elements that are pagan and at the same time Christian. The strange beings who confront the hero are presented, not as generic "supernatural" beings, but as nonhuman entities who nonetheless inhabit the mundane realm just as surely as we do. However, like Fagunwa, Tutuola's conceptual universe is profoundly Christian. When the hero first meets the lady he eventually takes as wife, her beauty is said to be like that of "an angel" (18). When he comes across a monster who makes his victims immobile by staring at them, he "prays to God" to deliver him (54). And later, when he is buried alive by the spirits in the "Unreturnable heaven's town," he attributes the rainfall that enabled him to free himself to God's will (62).

And yet, the Christianity is often tempered with attitudes that are rooted in a secular work ethic. He starts out as a lazy and licentious individual; he ends up as a culture-hero who rescues his community from collective disaster. Along the way, circumstances force him to try his hand at farming and small-scale trading (47).[16] In addition to the sylistic peculiarity of Tutuola's narrative, then, the text reveals a conceptual universe that is neither Western nor simply traditional Yoruba. As the author indicates in the autobiographical document that prefaced the first edition of the novel, the late 1940s in colonial Nigeria were marked by economic uncertainties occasioned by the massive infusion into the labor market of demobilized soldiers returning from World War II (*Drinkard*, 129–30). Against this background, *The Palm-wine Drinkard* is an attempt to come to terms, at the level of fiction, with this social condition. Taken together, the novel's religiosity and celebration of hard work and self-discipline add up to a rhetoric of collective prosperity as the just consequence of work, communal will, and God's providence.

In this sense, what *The Palm-wine Drinkard* represents is in content similar to what we have been exploring in Fagunwa's work. Both speak to and dramatize the epistemological ferment of a moment in the history of Western Nigeria where traditional Yoruba worldviews are undergoing deep transformations as they encounter Christianity and Western secularism. It is these two levels of Western modernity that are revealed in their interaction with the traditional Yoruba worldview. What connects Tutuola to Fagunwa, then, is the sociocultural history they both distill and enact. This condition may be extended to the very language of the novel. Unlike the canonical figures of modern African literature, Tutuola's rudimentary Western education and the way this shows itself in his prose offer us a glimpse of a class of modern African subjects who are neither Westernized, nor yet representatives of some putative authentic Africa. He thus represents and re-presents a culture in motion, and his writing is itself a witness to, and a participant in, that motion.

Tísà Oko: The Village Schoolteacher

If Tutuola represents a class that is a notch below Fagunwa's in terms
of level of Western education, Soyinka represents a later and more formally Western educated class. The next chapter will consider Soyinka's
work in detail. Here I want to indicate his relationship to Fagunwa, a
relationship we can accurately cast as that of a literary patriarch to a
discerning offspring. I want to demonstrate this relationship here by
examining their dramatization in two textual moments drawn from
Soyinka's writing. In the preface to his *Myth, Literature, and the
African World* Soyinka insists that his attempt to reconstruct the
"African psyche" after the interruption of colonial history is a necessary path toward genuine "self-apprehension," as he calls it. Soyinka
struggles in the preface to justify the book's philosophical impetus.
"There is nothing to choose ultimately," he contends, "between the
colonial mentality of an Ajayi Crowther, West Africa's first black
bishop, who grovelled before his white missionary superiors in a plea
for patience and understanding of his 'backward, heathen, brutish'
brothers, and the new black ideologues who are embarrassed by statements of self-apprehension by the new 'ideologically backward'
African. Both suffer from externally induced fantasies of redemptive
transformation in the image of alien masters" (xii). In this passage,
Soyinka illustrates an instructive tension in the reception of the pioneering generation of African intellectuals and "modernizers," exemplified here by Bishop Ajayi Crowther, by the later generation that
would include Soyinka himself—namely, those we associate institutionally with African literature. As he has indicated on many occasions,
Soyinka does not reject modernity. What he rejects and contests in writing is the racialist understanding of culture and modernity upon which
European imperialism rationalized its violence, and to which the likes
of Crowther—as far as Soyinka is concerned—remained enslaved.

It is a suggestive feature of the discursive conditions of African letters that the founding figures of the tradition tend to be burdened by an
embarrassing Eurocentrism or, at the least, a Victorian condescension
towards the uneducated masses whose cause they were writing to cham-
pion.[17] That is, since the figures who produced these texts were more
often than not products of missionary schooling, teachers who worked
for Christian mission schools, or outright proselytizers of the Christian
faith, their outlook tended to buy into certain axiomatic premises of
colonialist representations of pagans. Soyinka thus demonstrates here an
Oedipal relationship to a preceding generation, a relationship of pointed
self-differentiation. The suggestion is that the pioneering generation

bought too readily into Western ideology. Soyinka thereby legitimizes his position in the domain of culture by claiming for it a more decolonized and decolonizing outlook.

For our second example, let us consider Soyinka's representation of a cultural icon in modern Nigeria known as the "tíṣà oko," or village schoolteacher. As I indicated earlier, it is conventional to speak of the educated class that began to crystallize in the late nineteenth century and became larger, more self-assured and nationalistic in the early decades of the twentieth century. But there are crucial differences in the levels of formal education attained by members of this elite group. The tíṣà oko is a less-exalted subclass of this group. As a social location, it refers to those who had just enough formal education to teach in rural mission schools or minister to rural Christian converts. It refers to those whom scarce opportunities limited to the remote hinterlands, the scantily documented protectorates of colonial governance.[18]

One such figure is represented in the character Lakunle in Soyinka's early play, The Lion and the Jewel. As a structural location, his character represents a lower segment of the educated class that sets for itself the project of providing "enlightened" guidance to a rapidly changing black Africa. Lakunle's level of education would be something like a primary school certificate (Tutuola's level of education), or perhaps the teacher training certificate (Fagunwa's when he wrote Forest). In the first half of the twentieth century, the historical moment in which the play is set and during which Fagunwa's works and The Palm-wine Drinkard appeared, this level of education was enough to make anyone who possessed it part of a distinct local elite.[19] Consequently, the primary schoolteacher is, in the world of Soyinka's play, an object of awe for the uneducated rural folk. Today, one evidence of the socio-cultural importance this sub-class held in Nigeria is to be found in the fact that the term "tíṣà oko" is among the Yoruba a term of gentle rebuke, comedy, and some nostalgia. The tíṣà oko persists, then, as a real social location as well as a durable sign in the collective imagination.

In this sense, the tíṣà oko is an index to a moment in Nigerian culture as well as an agent (or progenitor) of cultural production since at least the mid-nineteenth century. And D. O. Fagunwa, we will recall, was a schoolteacher who began his careeer in Oyo province of the Western Nigeria bureaucracy. In different guises, this figure can be found in many of Soyinka's writings. He is not always and only a schoolteacher. He may be a Christian cleric, a semiliterate civil servant whose principal credential is a basic knowledge of the English language, or a semiskilled worker of the artisanal cadre. As the schoolteacher Lakunle in The Lion and the Jewel, he is an object of ridicule. As Erinjobi, the Christian patriarch in

Camwood on the Leaves, he is a churlish but tragic figure. *The Road* and *The Trials of Brother Jero* are set in a later period—urban Nigeria in the 1960s—but we see traces of him in the characterization of Professor and the ambitious Member of Parliament. If we turn to Soyinka's prose writings, the two biographical novels *Ake: The Years of Childhood* and *Isara: A Voyage Around Essay* have a delicate texture that is unique in Soyinka's corpus, and this is in part due to the lyrical tenderness with which "Essay," the teacher figure common to both texts, is evoked. Whether he is a comical figure, an exasperating Christian zealot, or a commanding presence like the "Essay" of *Isara,* the various textual realizations of this figure indicate that he means something important to Soyinka's imagination. The fact that Soyinka's father—the "Essay" of *Isara*—was a schoolteacher gives some clue to Soyinka's tender fascination with the schoolteacher figure, but this biographical explanation is not the site of my interest here. Rather, what I am primarily interested in is the drama of discursive agency that Soyinka's evocation of the patriarchal-ancestral figure of the *tísà oko* makes available to us.

As metonym for the pioneering generation, the *tísà oko* has proven to be great material for dramatic and narrative representation. As Dan Izevbaye has argued, the representation has enabled writers like Soyinka to distance themselves and their cultural mission from the alleged Eurocentrism of the pioneering generation of educated Africans.[20] One result of this distancing is that African writers claim the right to "recover" African traditions and culture in order to counteract colonialist distortions. By extension, literary criticism becomes a way of gauging the extent of the writers' success in this cultural recovery, as we saw in our reconstruction of African literary criticism in chapter 3. As we argued in that chapter, and as critics like Simon Gikandi and Ato Quayson have also suggested, African writers are not recovering any such thing as an African (or Gikuyu or Somali) culture but rather transforming, and thereby recreating, it by means of literary language. Posed this way, modern African literature is neither simply a reflection of African culture nor simply its recovery. Rather, the literature actively participates in the ongoing production of culture by the mere fact of being the imaginative work of a segment of contemporary African (or Nigerian, or Yoruba) reality.

Writing of Soyinka's relationship to Fagunwa's Yoruba language in particular, and African literature in the European languages in general, Dan Izevbaye argues: "The language of this text had its beginnings in nothing—that point of contact between [indigenous and European] languages—and, growing into a marginal discourse, was forced into resistance by its marginalization. It soon developed into a language that, by its accomplishment, has been generating its own discursive power as a new center of attention and the language of a new community" (168). The schoolteacher is a character type that allows Soyinka to define a voice and a self-positioning. We can savor one instance of Soyinka's representation of the teacher-figure by examining the opening scene of *The Lion and the Jewel*. The villagers are in the middle of a mime that re-enacts the arrival and misadventures of a European tourist in the village. The traveler signals the encroachment of modernity, and this encroachment is symbolized by the fascination that the tourist's camera and automobile holds for the indigenes of Ilujinle. After a while, Chief Baroka enters to join the good-natured playacting. The village schoolteacher, Lakunle, has all along been playing the European tourist. Upon the arrival of Baroka, he abandons his role and, in the words of the stage direction, "begins to sneak off" (*Collected Plays*, 16). The line "Akowe. Teacher wa. Misita Lakunle" (16) is Baroka's greeting to the fleeing schoolteacher, meant to draw the latter back into the playacting. Rendered in English, the line means: "The one who writes. Our teacher. Mr Lakunle."

Taken together, the three phrases elaborate a discreet movement that prepares us for the play's overarching argument. "The one who writes" *(Akòwé)* is empty of any specific personalization or embodiment: it refers to a social role, a structural location in the order of life the village is beginning to confront and fitfully welcome, and this new order is what the villagers' mime of the traveler's arrival enacts. "Our teacher" *(Teacher wa)* brings this structural location closer to home, as it were. That is, by calling Lakunle the "teacher" of the Ilujinle collectivity, Baroka designates a relationship between two structural locations: the first is that of the writing subject *(akòwé)*, the second the non-literate collective whom the *akòwé* is employed to serve. "Our teacher" acquires meaning, then, fundamentally in relation to the collectivity from which it is thereby differentiated. Finally, *"Misita Lákúnlé"* specifies the occupant of the structural location thus delineated. The honorific "mister" and the proper noun "Lakunle" combine to name the body that inhabits the abstract location called up by the first appellation.

But there is an uneasy fit between the proper noun and the honorific that qualifies it. Being a Yoruba corruption of an English title, "misita" silently invokes the foreignness of what is being named to the mind and mouth that pronounces the name. Tonally, Misita Lakunle is a triple mid-tone *(misita)*, conjoined with a triple high-tone *(Lákúnlé)*. In this way, the tri-syllabic parallelism established between the two components of the phrase is accompanied by a tonal rise in enunciation. This musical intensification, occasioned by the tonal rise, works to confer on the name "misita Lakunle" an ominous aspect. When, therefore, all the villagers repeat the phrase "Misita Lakunle" in a chorus that joins Baroka's call to the fleeing schoolteacher (*Collected Plays*, 16), the scene locates the entire village on the side of the old man and, as a consequence, places the teacher outside of the choral community thus constituted. Baroka's greeting to the fleeing schoolteacher implicitly captures one dimension of the play's argument. In the sound and syntax of the collective enunciation of the teacher's name (i.e., the proper noun and the phonetically indigenized honorific), Soyinka locates the Ilujinle population on Baroka's side the very first time he appears on stage. And by using as basis for that community the sonorous tension occasioned by a chorus of Yoruba mouths intoning an English honorific the only way they can, the play points us toward a rather large issue of class in culture. I will return to this location of Lakunle *outside* the Ilujinle choral community in a moment.

The progressive intensification of epithets in Baroka's naming of Lakunle signals a crucial dimension of the play's conflict. The plot poses Lakunle and Baroka in competition for the hand of the village beauty Sidi. If Lakunle represents an uncritical acceptance of (half-digested) foreign values and habits, Baroka is the wily pragmatist: he does not reject change, but will embrace it only with an opportunistic eye. On the terms of the play, Baroka offers a model of agency and cultural change that is more nuanced and serviceable than Lakunle's commitment to an abstract, imposed ideal. Baroka is not offered as a perfect alternative; the play gives us enough evidence of his self-serving, self-indulgent tendencies. But it is precisely this quality that makes the scheming old man victorious in the end. Confronted by Lakunle's ascetic tunnel vision, Baroka's wily sensuousness emerges, on the terms of the play, as the more seductive alternative: it is earthy and fathomable to the young Sidi, where Lakunle's pretentions are alienated and shallow. When Sidi chooses to marry the sixty-two-year-old Baroka, we are to understand her choice as her rejection of the sterility and inauthenticity of Lakunle's vision.

And yet, the play carries a hint of unease. When Baroka speaks of the "rich mustiness of age" (27), or of "the gloss/Of ancient leather" (48), we appreciate the comedy of it all, but will do well to wonder if his notion of "strength/Knit close along the grain" (48–49) is indeed a tenable alternative to Lakunle's bungling. It is all the more interesting, therefore, that the play dissipates this unease by means of dance and communal revelry. Here is the stage direction for the play's closing moments: "Festive air, fully pervasive. Oil lamps from the market multiply as traders desert their stalls to join them. A young girl flaunts her buttocks at Lakunle and he rises to the bait. Sadiku gets in his way as he gives chase. Tries to make him dance with her. Lakunle, last seen, having freed himself of Sadiku, clearing a space in the crowd for the young girl" (*Collected Plays*, 57–58). In this way, the play ends on a note of collective jubilation, as all the villagers (including Lakunle, who has just been rejected by Sidi), dance together in celebration of her impending marriage to Baroka. We leave Lakunle as he confronts the sexual taunts of the female revelers and tries to become part of the communal dance by creating a role for himself: "last seen, having freed himself of Sadiku, clearing a space in the crowd for the young girl." It is as though Soyinka's play cannot bring itself to pronounce Baroka "victorious" without also redeeming Lakunle's place within the choral community, where he is neither a total outsider nor a complete insider. One can for this reason argue that a character like Lakunle, and the schoolteacher type he exemplifies, is actually a mask under which Soyinka struggles, in his early work, to come to terms with the inheritance and socioepistemic location of educated Africans. Dan Izevbaye's summation is apposite here: "The fictional consciousness of this community [of African writers] produced a hero who bore a tragic burden that, at first, did not seem to be related to that of its creator. Lakunle and Professor, like characters from Medza to Obi Okonkwo, are held at arms length by the use of various techniques of critical scrutiny, distancing, or rejection: parody, satire, states of absurdity, and pathos. But these characters are the pioneers of a new postcolonial literary community within which African writers, the authors of these characters, confront their decentered condition by creating a language of the reconciliation of both home and exile" (168). Under the guise of ribald playfulness, *The Lion and the Jewel* is in fact about a determinate sociocultural dynamic, one in which Fagunwa's class location stares back at us, indirectly brought to light in the poetry of a successor, who thereby seeks to define a new direction.

We have seen the sense in which one level of Fagunwa's novel celebrates the self-assurances of modernity while a second level forces a qualification of precisely those assurances. Thus, Akara-ogun is presented as an archetypal achiever, an embodiment of the comprehensive agency associated with the modern subject. Yet, Fagunwa is forced to qualify the agency of this subject because of his Christian evangelical formation. In this vein, Fagunwa's text is able to qualify the certitudes of the modern subject because of his interpellation by Christian theology. Viewed this way, if Fagunwa is a victim of Christian ideology, his "victim-hood" makes possible his immanent critique of modernity. His agency as critic of modernity is enabled by his subjection to the colonialist institution represented by Christianity.

This interplay of subjection and agential subjectivity is what Soyinka implicitly recognizes by choosing Fagunwa as a literary precursor. Certainly, in criticizing Samuel Ajayi Crowther's alleged Eurocentrism or lampooning Lakunle's zeal for "progress," Soyinka might as well have been referring to Fagunwa, whose Christian indoctrination made him, at the least, ambivalent towards Yoruba paganism. Our discussion of Fagunwa has demonstrated that his writing qualifies him for the charge of Eurocentrism that Soyinka levels against Crowther. And yet, Soyinka does not identify Fagunwa as a target of his political stricture. He overlooks the arguably Eurocentric dimensions of Fagunwa's text, and emphasizes instead the metaphysical universe that the latter's writing evokes. Soyinka conscripts Fagunwa, then, specifically as a literary ancestor, a figure on whose contribution his own work builds. He enlists, in short, the animating impulse of Fagunwa's literary work. This impulse includes a glorification of Yoruba culture. But Soyinka carries Fagunwa's project in a significant new direction by figuring traditional culture without the reservations that the latter's Christianity forces into his rhetoric. Our concern in the next chapter is to investigate the results and implications of Soyinka's use of Fagunwa's legacy.

CHAPTER FIVE

WOLE SOYINKA AND THE CHALLENGE OF TRANSITION

This chapter explores the sense in which Wole Soyinka's continuation and redirection of D. O. Fagunwa's passion offers us a view of agency considered at the discursive as well as political level. Fagunwa, as we saw, construes modernization to be an ideal that a properly Christian morality can accomplish. In the metafictional, contemplative overlay of his texts, we confront a complex motion of critique, where the teleological accession to modernity that his texts overtly express is subjected to discreet questioning. This questioning has its roots in the fatalism of the same Christianity that otherwise sponsors his exuberance for modernity as an ideal. Soyinka's confrontation with the theme of modernity takes a significantly different direction. Where Fagunwa relied upon and was institutionally enabled by Christian missionary ideology, Soyinka turns pointedly against Christianity or any form of what he would call alien religions. By deploying archetypes and ritual forms derived from traditional Yoruba culture, Soyinka celebrates the pagan belief system that is ambivalently figured in Fagunwa. And where Fagunwa's work forms part of an evangelical apparatus, Soyinka's immediate milieu is neither explicitly invested in any single moral cause, nor particularly populist.

Soyinka's self-definition as an artist and intellectual in the modern, European senses of the word, precludes him from being either morally righteous or populist in quite the same way that Fagunwa was. It turns out, therefore, that the figure who writes in Yoruba lays no claim to a "universal" audience but is ideologically more overtly "Western"—that is, Christian and "pro-modern." By contrast, the one using the English language is more "Yoruba" (that is, pagan and anticolonial), even as he lays claim to membership of a universal republic of letters. To disentangle this seeming contradiction is to get at the specific contours of Soyinka's contribution, and to read another instance of agency in motion.

There is a second layer of seeming contradiction to be found in Soyinka's work. Perhaps more systematically than any other African writer of his generation, he has worked out a personal mythical system for his artistic purposes. Drawing on Yoruba mythology and the rituals that derive from it, he has elicited from ritual a drama of archetypes, developing in the process a vision of history, society, and tragic drama. A range of critical work has shown this vision to be based on a sociocultural passion, even as the writer's corpus constitutes an attempt to work through the passion by means of language and symbol.[1] This understanding of Soyinka gives a sociological accent to his mythopoeic vision and aesthetic. His specific refashioning of traditional Yoruba myths and archetypes emerges as, on the one hand, a theory of historical being and the often brutal adventure of the social, and on the other, of literature as witness to both. However, his use of Yoruba mythology as a way of working out a putatively "African" perspective on tragedy comes close to an "Afrocentric" nativism, and a number of critics have pointed this out (Booth; Appiah, *House,* 73–84). And yet, running through his work is a consistent idea that genuine literature worthy of the name should speak to everyone. This is another way of saying that literary texts pass the test of authenticity and value only if they are "universal." We are already on the fringe of a controversy here, for universalist arguments often derive from Eurocentric assumptions, whereby "Western" or European things become the normative "universal" standard of judgement. But Soyinka, as we saw towards the end of the previous chapter, is also quick to criticize or satirize those he considers Eurocentric. For him, the artist is a universal cultural worker whose primary constituency is dual: the society that is the artist's formative base and consequent nourishment, and the world of art and letters that she wants to join on account of her vocation.[2] This dual conviction— namely, that the African writer should draw on her roots even as her vision should speak to an abstract universal (as against a narrowly national or even racial) condition—is quite precarious. Likewise, Soyinka's tendency to evoke an abstract realm of "art," a domain of creativity that deserves to be sheltered from politicians and "overzealous" literary critics, points to some version of universalism in his thinking. And yet, his personal choices and concrete political engagements indicate that he is far from being apolitical or pacific.

Without claiming that this is the most appropriate way Soyinka should be read, I want to suggest that the combination of universalist and nativist rhetoric in Soyinka, as well as his combination of a civic life of political engagement with a conceptual insistence on the autonomy of art, is an index of the mission he sets for himself as writer and intellectual. It is a mission he shares with other writers of his postindependence generation, a mission that is historically related to, but conceptually distinguishable from, what we saw at the heart of Fagunwa's work as a pre-independence author. If there is one work that goes a long way toward encapsulating many of Soyinka's thematic concerns as well as literary style, that work is *Death and the King's Horseman*. And if there is one work that condenses a good many of his ideas as theorist of culture, it is the collection of essays entitled *Myth, Literature, and the African World*. Our discussion in this chapter will concentrate on these two texts. I begin by briefly laying out the "Africanist-nativist" dimensions of Soyinka's theory of culture and tragic drama; I then go on to show how this theory operates in *Death and the King's Horseman*. My specific claim is that the play yields insights into questions of agency that Soyinka may or may not have intended.

Both texts were substantially written during 1972–73, when Soyinka was a fellow at Churchill College at Cambridge University. The fellowship year at Cambridge seems itself to have been occasioned by Soyinka's voluntary exile after his unjust imprisonment from 1967 to 1969 during the Nigerian civil war, and his subsequent publication of a controversial memoir of his imprisonment, *The Man Died* (1972). Appended to *Myth, Literature, and the African World* is an essay, "The Fourth Stage: Through the Mysteries of Ogun to the Origin of Yoruba Tragedy." This essay was written earlier, and in writing it Soyinka seems to have had as an ideal reader the Shakespearean scholar Wilson Knight, his former teacher at Leeds University. As Soyinka notes in his preface to *Myth, Literature, and the African World*,

> I have long been preoccupied with the process of apprehending my own world in its full complexity, also through its contemporary progression and distortions—evidence of this is present both in my creative work and in one of my earliest essays, "The Fourth Stage," included in this collection as an appendix. The persistent thread in the more recent lectures stems from this earliest effort to encapsulate my understanding of this metaphysical world and its reflection in Yoruba contemporary social psyche. "The Fourth Stage" was in fact published in its first and only draft—I was arrested and became incommunicado soon after I sent it to the editor, requesting him to pass it on to G. Wilson Knight, my former Professor at Leeds, for his comments. (*Myth*, ix)

"The Fourth Stage" has justifiably been seen as Soyinka's most condensed statement of his theory of tragic art and social being. In the essay, Soyinka articulates a conception of the origins and manifestations of tragedy as form and sensibility among the Yoruba. Soyinka articulates his theory in prose that inextricably links it to a theory of social change, disintegration, and renewal. The fact that the essay conjoins cultural theory with a meditation on tragic art speaks to the intimate connection Soyinka sees between literature and social processes.

We may isolate two of the essay's central moves as a way of opening out onto our discussion of *Death and the King's Horseman*. As "The Fourth Stage" clearly shows, central to Soyinka's vision and the metaphysics that underwrites it is a notion of duality and contradiction, understood both in ontological and materialist terms. That there may be significant incompatibilities between thought expressed in terms of ontology and thought expressed in terms of materialism does not appear to worry Soyinka. For him, a crucial difference between the African worldview and the modern (read Western) cast of mind is that traditional African belief systems are not embarrassed by contradiction. Under the governance of positivistic science, the West seeks to transcend contradiction or, failing that, actively repress it by various institutional means and rhetorical management. By contrast, the Yoruba worldview apprehends duality as a cosmic immanence, and contradiction an intrinsic feature of secular social experience. The coexistence of good and evil in the same subject, or creative and destructive principles in phenomena that are no less dynamic and agential as a consequence—these are aspects of the Yoruba mind that mark for Soyinka a mode of seeing signally different from conventional Western modes.

It remains unclear how far Soyinka is prepared to argue the basic antithesis he establishes between the so-called Yoruba mind and the so-called Western mind. One does not have to go far to identify the problem in such binary characterization. Hegelian dialectics, for instance, is rooted in an understanding of the immanence of contradiction in ontological as much as historical realities. And Marx, as is well-known, was later to press the dialectic of mind and matter in a specifically historical direction, thereby secularizing Hegel's idealization of materiality and history. If Hegel and Marx posited contradiction at specific historical moments as being transcendendable and, indeed, destined for transcendence in the implacable movement whereby history fulfills thought as it fulfills itself, contemporary Western theory has done much to reject the rationalistic and teleological kind of thinking exemplified by these figures. The entire debate over the pros and cons of poststructuralism is in part a consequence of the attempts to go beyond Enlightenment rationalism and its ramifications for knowledge of self and Other. In this sense, the capacity to grasp contradiction as a permanent coordinate of sociality and agency cannot validly be posed as a point of essential difference between something called the Yoruba mind and something else called the Western mind.

It is interesting that Soyinka's essay is significantly influenced by Nietzsche's "The Birth of Tragedy." That the ideal reader, so to speak, to whom he first sent a draft of the essay is a Shakespeare scholar would suggest also that the prime interlocutor, the implied audience, is someone who is at the least conversant with the Western literary and philosophic tradition. For my purposes, the sweeping generalization about the Western mind and the Yoruba mind on the matter of logic have their force, not in their accuracy or otherwise, but in the dynamic of thinking it enacts. It allows Soyinka to demarcate a specific, datable terrain of thought and knowledge production, to enter a conversation that preceded his own intervention and will be recognized as such. In other words, the essentialism and binarism that presides over much of "The Fourth Stage" is substantively unsustainable but formally and rhetorically enabling. Like Habermas and the Azande, or Lyotard and the Cashinahua, Soyinka here conjures up a textual "Western mind" to enable his thinking to proceed. It is an essentialism that acquires meaning only in the relational logic of a preconstituted discursive field, in which there is something called the West, and something else called the non-West.

What then does Soyinka do with the essentializations thus rhetorically put in place? According to him, to understand the Yoruba mode of seeing, one is required to delve into its intricacies as encoded in myths and dramatized in festivals and rituals. In his interpretation of the Yoruba myth of origins, Soyinka focuses on what he calls a "primordial rupture" in the human psyche and cosmic order. One way in which the Yoruba apprehend and represent this rupture is in the myth of the fragmentation of godhead occasioned by a primal act of rebellion. According to this myth, all of what now constitutes humanity's faculties were once concentrated in the figure of the deity Obatala, also known as Orisha-nla (arch divinity). A serene essence of creation, Obatala is not itself a principle of dynamic creativity: he superintends creation only if and after an external agency provides the all important creative spark. In this sense, the god Obatala is the embodiment of hegemonic social order, of preconstituted totality. Obatala reigns over this cosmic/social totality and destiny. To serve him in this dispensation is a slave, another mythic figure named Atunda or Atooda. It was this slave who initiated the primal rupture by rolling a huge boulder over Obatala, shattering the godhead into a thousand and one fragments.[3]

The consequence of Atunda's rebellion is that Obatala's lone hegemony over the faculties of existence is broken: among the gods, a division of labor ensued. Posed in different terms, with Obatala's fragmentation results a fragmentation of totality: "the creation of the multiple godhead began a transference of social functions, the division of labour and professions among the deities whose departments they were thereafter to become. The shard of original Oneness appears to have passed into the being of Ogun, who manifests a temperament for artistic creativity matched by technological proficiency. His world is the world of craft, song and poetry" (*Myth*, 28). Ogun, the Yoruba god of iron and metallurgy thus functions in Soyinka's system—which he will of course want us to accept as a felicitous reconstruction of traditional Yoruba worldview—as the very embodiment of agency. The "shard of original Oneness," which passed to Ogun, makes him the one who among the gods undertook the original journey to reunite the faculties of existence shattered by the primordial rupture. This journey of restitution is on Soyinka's account also a way of reuniting mortal human beings with their gods, indeed, with godhead itself. Ogun's journey symbolically promises a reunion of "self" with "essence," what we are in reality, with what we ideally can or should be. The fact that Ogun is the one who is capable of achieving this restitution is due to the fact that he represents the fusion of artistic and technological creativity. The poet, the sculptor, and the nuclear scientist become for Soyinka bed fellows, birds of a feather who no longer flock together because of the alienation of self from essence in the modern world.

On these terms, the ability to effect changes in society, to make decisions or take actions that contribute to the collective good, is for Soyinka as much the province of the poet as it is the scientist's. We recall here Fagunwa's invention of the singer Olohun-iyo and the intellectual Imodoye as indispensable members of the questing subjects of his world. What Soyinka does is to locate in Ogun a happy coincidence of the principles of artistic and scientific instrumental creativity. In the opening chapter of *Myth, Literature, and the African World*, he writes: "Ogun, by incorporating within himself so many seemingly contradictory attributes, represents the closest conception to the original oneness of Orisanla" (31). And in "The Fourth Stage" we are told that "Ogun not only dared to look into transitional essence but triumphantly bridged it with knowledge, with art, with vision and the mystic creativity of science—a total and profound hubristic assertiveness that is beyond any parallel in Yoruba experience" (157).

However, Ogun's creative assertiveness comes with a price. Being a warrior, a lover of palm-wine, and something of an intemperate misanthrope under conditions of stress, Ogun is prone to excesses. So much is this the case that he could turn on his own people in the heat of battle without realizing his mistake (*Myth*, 28–30, 157). In his long poem, *Idanre*, Soyinka captures this duality in the section entitled "The Beginning." There, an extended panegyric to Ogun is elaborated in imagery that connote his contradictory significance as emblem of creativity and destructiveness:

> Ogun is the lascivious god who takes
> Seven gourdlets to war. One for gunpowder,
> One for charms, two for palm wine and three
> Air-sealed in polished bronze make
> Storage for his sperms. (*Idanre*, 72)

On his way to war, Ogun's paraphernalia epitomizes his duality. Gourdlets of "gunpowder" and "charms," emblems of destruction, are accompanied by regenerative vessels of "palm wine" and "sperms." It is no wonder, then, that the hero's shield could just as well be inward-spiked, that the agency of humane philanthrophy could at the same time be one of aggression: "Ogun path-maker, he who goes fore where other gods/Have turned, Shield of orphans, was your shield/In-spiked that day on sheltering lives?" (*Idanre*, 72).

In this sense, Ogun can push humanity toward its ideal, or just as intensively negate the achievement of that ideal. On Soyinka's terms, change in all societies involves recurrent negotiations of this tense dualism, the archetypal passion and process represented in the myth of Ogun. What histories (as against History with a capital "H") offer are instances of the disintegration and reintegration of humanity's inherent and transhistorical ideals (that is, our essence) in cycles of triumph and failure, shame and redemption. In this way, human agency is thoroughly unpredictable; agency cannot be identified outside of specific moments and particulars, outside of the contingent manifestations of Ogun's cycle. This logic of human agency is fully at work in *Death and the King's Horseman*, to which I should like now to turn.

TRAGEDY AND THE "AFRICAN WORLD"

In the twenty-odd years since its first publication, *Death and the King's Horseman* has come to occupy a stable place of prestige in modern African Literature. According to the playwright's "Author's Note," the play's primary plot is based on events that actually happened in Oyo, "ancient Yoruba city of Nigeria, in 1946."[4] It is set in the colonial era, when Oyo was part of British Western Nigeria. The plot revolves around a Yoruba traditional practice whereby, on the death of the King of Oyo (the *Aláàfìn*), the commander of the King's stables—in the play, the Olórí Elésin—has to commit suicide in order to accompany the dead King to the world of the dead.

In the play, the colonial District Officer, Simon Pilkings, intervenes in an effort to put a stop to what he sees as a barbaric custom. He arrests Elesin, preventing him from committing the act. Olunde, Elesin's heir (a medical student in England who has hurriedly returned home to perform the necessary burial ceremony) feels anger at Pilkings's colonialist arrogance and shame at his father's evasion of the one duty for which his entire life had been a preparation. Fearing the cosmic catastrophe that could befall the community on account of this disruption, and in order to restore the family honor dreadfully tarnished by his father's failure, the son commits suicide: "better late than never" seems to be the logic. On learning of his son's superior will, Elesin kills himself in shame, right in front of Pilkings and his guards.

Although based on a true historical event, Soyinka's play changes some of the precise historical details. As his prefatory note informs us: "The changes I have made are in matters of detail, sequence and of course characterisation. The action has also been set back two or three years to while the war [World War II] was still on, for minor reasons of dramaturgy."[5] Not only does he locate the play in the middle of the Second World War, he also changes the social location of the son who commits suicide. In the true story, the son is a trader in Ghana who returns home, whereas Soyinka's character is educated, based in England, and a medical attendant to World War II casualties. In the true story also, the Elesin figure did not commit suicide after his son's death; according to D. S. Izevbaye, he lived on, although we have no way of knowing whether or not his reputation in Oyo suffered irreparable damage as a result of the incident.[6]

The changes Soyinka makes to the historical details are relevant to any discussion of the ideological work the play is designed to do. We shall begin, however, by limiting our analysis to the question of the ideological work the play performs, even before the added factor of the playwright's historical changes is considered. In other words, I want to begin by trying to answer the following question: what might the play look like to a reader who is not familiar with the details of the historical event, a reader who accepts Soyinka's underplaying of the changes he made ostensibly for "minor reasons of dramaturgy"? After providing what is at the least a plausible answer to this question, we shall then complicate it by investigating what the gesture of "artsy" maneuvering and masking enacted by Soyinka might teach us about the question of agency in literary representation.

In seeking to understand the play, we have the playwright's own interpretation as an originary lead, but it is a lead that will show itself to be part of the cultural drama being played out. According to Soyinka's account of Yoruba metaphysics as outlined in the preceding section, what Simon Pilkings sees as feudalistic barbarism is an important mechanism of communal regeneration. The Elesin, at the moment of self-sacrifice, embodies the collective social and psychic aspirations of the Oyo community. He is a ritual scapegoat who mediates the world of the living, the dead, and the unborn. By his willful death at the summons of the community, he accedes the world of the dead on behalf of the living and the unborn. His death thus ensures renewed harmony between the three levels of existence constitutive of traditional Yoruba cosmic order, namely, the dead, the living, and the unborn. Indeed, on Soyinka's terms, "suicide" is a misnomer. That is, Elesin's death does not turn on a brutalization of the corporeal body; rather, it operates via an "act of will" through which his totality of being submits to a monitored dissolution almost anaesthetic in essence. Elesin's calling is hereditory, tied to lineage: his father occupied the social position he currently occupies, and all things being equal, his heir will do likewise, thereby ensuring the continuity of Oyo tradition and social-spiritual harmony.

The crucial role he plays in his society's well-being makes Elesin a highly revered citizen, pampered with collective awe, praise, and whatever else his worldly self desires:

> . . . In all my life
> As Horseman of the King, the juiciest
> Fruit on every tree was mine [. . .]
> The honour of my place, the veneration I
> Received in the eye of man or woman
> Prospered my suit and
> Played havoc with my sleeping hours. (18)

These lines are from Act I of the play. Against it as background, we can see the sense in which Simon Pilkings's intervention affronts the entire Oyo community—and Elesin himself even more severely. However, Soyinka complicates the drama by rendering his Elesin as an eminently worldly figure—a lover of food and wine, and a predator on women. Immediately following the lines above, Elesin adds:

And they tell me my eyes were a hawk
In perpetual hunger. Split an iroko tree
In two, hide a woman's beauty in its heartwood
And seal it up again—Elesin, journeying by
Would make his camp beside that tree
Of all the shades in the forest. (18–19)

It is this love of the flesh that makes Elesin coerce the market women
into allowing his wedding to a virgin (already betrothed to another man)
on the very night he is supposed to die. In a poignant moment of self-
analysis after his failure, Elesin, shackled and confined to a cell, confides
in the Bride: "You were the final gift of the living to their emissary to the
land of the ancestors, and perhaps your warmth and youth brought new
insights of this world to me and turned my feet leaden on this side of the
abyss. For I confess to you, daughter, my weakness came not merely
from the abomination of the whiteman who came violently into my fad-
ing presence, there was also a weight of longing on my earth-held limbs"
(65). The possibility this claim opens up is that his failure to die at the
appointed time is due more to his own human weakness than to the
agency of British colonialism: "I would have shaken [the 'weight of
longing on my earth-held limbs'] off, already my foot had begun to lift
but then, the white ghost entered and all was defiled" (65).

This is the reading the playwright requests—indeed, demands.
"The bane of themes of this genre," writes Soyinka, "is that they are no
sooner employed creatively than they acquire the facile tag of 'clash of
cultures,' a prejudicial label which, quite apart from its frequent misap-
plication, presupposes a potential equality *in every given situation* of the
alien culture and the indigenous, on the actual soil of the latter"
(Author's Note). Against such a "sadly familiar reductionist tendency,"
Soyinka insists that the District Officer should not be cast as a major
player in the tragic event: "No attempt should be made in production to
suggest it. The Colonial Factor is an incident, a catalytic incident merely.
The confrontation in the play is largely metaphysical, contained in the
human vehicle which is Elesin and the universe of the Yoruba mind—the
world of the living, the dead, and the unborn, and the numinous passage
which links all: transition. *Death and the King's Horseman* can be fully
realised only through an evocation of music from the abyss of transition" (Author's Note). According to Soyinka's account of his intentions,
then, the conflict in the play is principally an interior one: the "Yoruba
mind" in confrontation with itself, "man" called to account by his own
universe of values. In the contrast between the Elesin of Act I and that
of Act V (before his failure and after it) Soyinka wants us to see a figure

who is defeated primarily within the matrix of his own culture and self-understanding. Viewed this way, Simon Pilkings merely wanders into a struggle that is both too timeless and too interior to Elesin-as-subject for his narrow colonialist confidence to grasp or single-handedly influence.

The Aristotelian tenor of such a reading is rather obvious, Elesin being the doomed protagonist whose human flaw facilitates an intersection of events towards catastrophe.[7] And yet, Soyinka insists that the play's tragedy—by which I mean its universal meaningfulness, or what he calls its "threnodic essence"—is rooted in traditional Yoruba cosmology and its ritual enactment in festival and music. Further, Soyinka's reading demands that the colonial factor be subordinated to the specificity of the Yoruba worldview. A crucial dimension of the play's theoretical value for postcolonial cultural studies is to be found here; that is, in the playwright's dual insistence (i) that the play's philosophical pedigree lies in the resources of Yoruba metaphysics even as it reminds us of classical Western tragic drama, and (ii) that the colonial intervention is peripheral to the action—"catalytic merely," to the interior dynamic the play claims as its province.

As many commentators have observed, the playwright's emphasis on Elesin as the locus of conflict is consistent with his interpretation of Yoruba myth of origins and theory of tragic art developed in "The Fourth Stage." A number of critics have also argued that Soyinka's reading of his own play is not persuasive. I shall have occasion to return to these issues in a later section of this chapter. For now, suffice it to say that, not only is Soyinka's reading not persuasive, it is entirely consistent with the playwright's discursive politics. Soyinka cannot produce a persuasive reading of the play because the reading is itself part of a discursive struggle, of which the play is but one level. The play is in this sense an ideological document that Soyinka's reading needs to misrecognize in order for play and authorial reading to complement each other. To begin to see how this might be the case, let us consider two characters who might on first thought be taken for mere minor figures in the movement of the tragic action proper: Joseph and Amusa.

CONTEMPLATING MIMICRY

Joseph is househelp to Simon Pilkings and his wife, Jane, while Amusa is a sergeant in the colonial police. They come across as inarticulate, obsequious fools who provide comic relief, and their structural purpose lies in being the dramatist's vehicle for pointing up certain natives' self-submission to the colonial machine. At one level, one can say that they embody the consequences of such a submission, namely, docility and intellectual confusion. In being so unimpressive, they are set up as a mirror against which the lyricism of, say, Iyaloja (literally, mother at the market—the leader of the women traders) or Elesin, acquires full visibility. It would however be reductive to understand both characters in this way. Joseph appears only once—in Act II—while Amusa appears thrice, but very briefly on all three occasions. Despite their limited role, however, both characters call attention to complexities underneath the cultural or metaphysical conflict that bestride the surface of the play. Being "eunuchs" of the white man as the market women see Amusa, and at times frustrating "natives" to the Pilkingses, Amusa and Joseph belong to both camps and to none. This liminality emerges in the text as an immanent cultural critique, so to speak. In their ineptitude, they silently reconfigure the terms of the conflict as the major characters articulate it, and as the play's rhetorical mood might otherwise lure us to understand it.

In Act II, the Pilkingses call in Joseph to inquire about the meaning of the native drums throbbing in the background, and this exchange ensues:

> PILKINGS: Let's ask our native guide. Joseph! [. . .] (Joseph reenters) What's the drumming about ?
>
> JOSEPH: I don't know master.
>
> PILKINGS: What do you mean you don't know ? Its only two years since your conversion. Don't tell me all that holy water nonsense has wiped out all your tribal memory.
>
> JOSEPH (visibly shocked): Master! (30)

Simon's frustrated explosion, and Joseph's shocked reaction, prompts Jane to remark: "It is'nt my preaching you have to worry about, its the preaching of the missionaries who preceded you here. When they make converts they really convert them. Calling holy water nonsense to our Joseph is really like insulting the Virgin Mary before a Roman Catholic. He's going to hand in his resignation tomorrow you mark my word" (31).

Joseph's uncritical acceptance of Christianity witnesses here to something more interesting than the threadbare observation that he has "sold out." By his acquiescence, Joseph stirs up a contradiction built into the colonial enterprise and its discursive explanation of that enterprise. The exchange dramatizes a fissure between Church and State, one originating in the metropolitan center and reenacted here at the colonial frontier. On this reading, Simon represents the colonial bureaucratic apparatus that is intermittently dogged by the "holy water nonsense" of

Christian missionaries in the colonies. Joseph's naiveté thus reveals Simon's secular enstrangement from the religion that, by an influential strand of his culture's self-understanding, individuates him as European. In the spectacle of a native internalizing Christian doctrine so thoroughly that he irritates the "whiteman," *Horseman* distances the European self at play in the real world, from the Self spelt out in its discourses of self-apprehension. It might be argued that this Self is in fact not Christian but secular scientific, in which case the scene becomes a figuration of the secular self (Pilkings) showing disdain for religious mythmaking. But even here, Joseph's immanent critique retains its edge, for in the discourse of colonialism in Africa, what defines "European-ness" is *both* Christianity and secular-scientific sophistication. Where colonial discourse rests precariously on a rhetorical suturing of these two identities, Pilkings's exasperation introduces a disjunction. In this sense, Joseph prompts a fissure between the European self instanced by missionaries, and the self instanced by the colonial, "rationalist" administrator.

The lesson Joseph offers is further elaborated in Amusa's career. He is a dutiful police officer and a devout moslem. Our first glimpse of his predicament comes up when he arrives at the Pilkingses' to make his report about the ritual suicide that was supposed to take place later that night. Here are the stage directions:

> The verandah of the District Officer's bungalow. A tango is playing from an old hand-cranked gramophone and, glimpsed through the wide windows and doors which open onto the forestage verandah are the shapes of SIMON PILKINGS and his wife, JANE, tangoing in and out of shadows in the living room. They are wearing what is immediately apparent as some form of fancy-dress. The dance goes on for some moments and then the figure of a "Native Administration" policeman emerges and climbs up the steps leading onto the verandah. He peeps through and observes the dancing couple, reacting with what is obviously a long-standing bewilderment. He stiffens suddenly, his expression changes to one of disbelief and horror. In his excitement he upsets a flowerpot and attracts the attention of the couple. They stop dancing. (23–24)

The "fancy-dress" that Simon and Jane are wearing is an *egungun* mask that has been confiscated from the natives. It represents, in the traditional scheme of things, the spirit of dead ancestors incarnated.[8] Confronted with his boss and his wife dancing in a costume that signifies the spirit of the dead, Amusa runs into an epistemological conflict: he has come to report an unlawful tribal custom having to do with death (i.e., ritual suicide), and now his boss presents himself costumed as the

embodiment of death. Amusa thus refuses to make the report, so long as
Simon remains in the Egungun costume. As he puts it in his Pidgin English, "Sir, it is a matter of death. How can man talk against death to person in uniform of death ? Is like talking against government to person in
uniform of police. Please sir, I go and come back" (25).

What Amusa reveals here is that his conceptual universe remains,
at the least, deeply tied to traditional Yoruba culture even though the
secular demand of his job requires him not only to repudiate that culture, but also to subject it to the discipline of colonial modernity:

> JANE: Oh Amusa, what is there to be scared of in the costume ? You
> saw it confiscated last month from those *egungun* men who were
> creating trouble in town. You helped arrest the cult leaders your-
> self—if the juju didnt harm you at the time how could it possibly
> harm you now ? And merely by looking at it ?
>
> AMUSA (without looking down): Madam, I arrest the ringleaders
> who make trouble but me I no touch *egungun*. That *egungun* itself,
> I no touch. And I no abuse am. I arrest ringleaders but I treat *egun-
> gun* with respect. (25)

We might say that the demands of economic subsistence compel Amusa
to arrest the *egungun* on the authority of the colonial administrative
apparatus, but the superstructural overlay—the material culture and its
constitutive institutions—metonymically represented by the *egungun*
stands in conflict with the enforced economic dispensation.

Act III gives us a representation of the new superstructural ensemble forcibly getting entangled with the one that remains formative and
resilient in Amusa's "big pagan heart" (24). The scene is the marketplace
and Amusa has come to arrest Elesin, who is at that moment consum-
mating his wedding to the virgin. The trance sequence that closes Act III
is one of the most powerfully realized moments in all of Soyinka. The
evocation of Elesin's movement toward the final assertion of will that
will ease him into the world of the dead is achieved by means of poetry.
In the following excerpt, the mystical interiority of Elesin's undertaking
is given the status of unquestionable social redemptiveness, and the
dramatist's tool is the Praise Singer's lament:

> PRAISE SINGER: How shall I tell what my eyes have seen? The
> Horseman gallops on before the courier, how shall I tell what my
> eyes have seen? He says a dog may be confused by new scents of
> beings he never dreamt of, so he must precede the dog to heaven.
> He says a horse may stumble on strange boulders and be lamed, so
> he races on before the horse to heaven. It is best, he says, to trust no

messenger who may falter at the outer gate; oh how shall I tell what my ears have heard? But do you hear me still Elesin, do you hear your faithful one?

(ELESIN in his motions appears to feel for a direction of sound, subtly, but only sinks deeper into his trance-dance.) (44)

In this passage we see the playwright relying on the sheer capacity of poetry to persuade. By putting before us the spectacle of Elesin's ritual dance, the compassionate enablement of the choral retinue (Iyaloja and the market women) singing a dirge in the background, and the incantatory exhortation of the Praise Singer, Soyinka poses the self-assurance of the native culture against the colonial apparatus where the entire ritual is to be seen as barbarism. And by finessing that moment with some of the most elegant lines to be encountered in his dramatic works, Soyinka invites us to take on a worldview by partaking of it as an aesthetic experience.

Though this moment is designed as the play's pivotal moment, there is yet an ostensibly comical moment that has considerable significance for the kind of reading I am pursuing. The scene involves Amusa, the market women, and the schoolgirls. As Amusa tries to bully his way into the bridal chamber to arrest Elesin, the schoolgirls (daughters of the market women) lose their patience. In a swift change of code, they take on the character of European colonialists at a party. Over the next fifty-two lines, the playacting mounts and approaches such verisimilitude that Amusa is drawn in. By the end of the girls' performance he is so enchanted that, in a reflex action typical of his duties for the colonial regime, he comes to attention at the command of the girls:

[GIRLS]
—Is there racing by golly ?
—Splendid golf course, you'll like it.
—I'm beginning to like it already.
—And a European club, exclusive.
—You've kept the flag flying.
—We do our best for the old country.
—It's a pleasure to serve.
—Another whisky old chap ?
—You are indeed too too kind.
—Not at all sir. Where is that boy ? (With a sudden bellow.)
    Sergeant !
AMUSA (snaps to attention): Yessir !
(The women collapse with laughter.) (38–39)

In my reading of Amusa's earlier altercation with Simon, I suggested that it dramatizes his predicament in a social nexus where a new (colonial) infrastructure collides with the old (native) superstructure. In the altercation with the schoolgirls, the new superstructural ensemble ushered in by colonialism is embodied—albeit in jest and derision—in the new generation of natives. What the schoolgirls enact is the subterranean formation of a resentful but acculturating elite—the educated, "Westernized" native.

Implicit in the schoolgirls' performance is an enactment of class formations and realignments amidst social change. The new native, as embodied in the schoolgirls, constitutes the white man's future adversary. Paradoxically, he is a more formidable adversary because he resembles the white man and speaks his language more securely than Amusa. In the presence of this new native, Amusa can be made to cower exactly as he does in the presence of white men. The mothers put the children's destiny most concisely while expressing wonder at their performance:

> WOMEN: Do they each you all that at school ?
>
> WOMEN: And to think I nearly kept Apinke away from the place.
>
> WOMEN: Did you hear them ? Did you see how they mimicked the white man ?
>
> WOMEN: The voices exactly. Hey there are wonders in this world !
>
> IYALOJA: Well, our elders have said it: Dada may be weak, but he has a younger sibling who is truly fearless.
>
> WOMEN: The next time the white man shows his face in this market I will set Wuraola on his tail. (39–40)

The schoolgirls, then, can be read as a budding avant-garde of sorts, defending the dignity of the community against an alien colonial structure. They are able to do so because they can readily access the cultural patterns of that structure, can on a whim imitate its form. If there is an irony here, it is the irony of mimicry, one that complements and reinforces the versions we've already indicated in the trio of Simon, Joseph, and Amusa.

As we saw in chapter 2, the implication of this spectacle of mimicry has been theorized by Homi Bhabha. The aspect of his theory that is pertinent here is his account of what amounts to the deconstructive implications of the native's collusion in the colonial enterprise. Bhabha's account is useful because it implicates both colonizer and colonized in the dynamic of mimicry. By extension, the texts addressed to, or resulting from, the drama of a colonial encounter can be read by way of the logic of mimicry. Following Bhabha's account, we may legitimately recover in *Horseman* a drama of identity proper to the site of a colonial encounter such as is figured in the play. On these terms, Joseph and Amusa can be read as mimic men: their discursive and institutional "partial fixation" as obliging colonial subjects, to use Bhabha's terms, emerges as a demystification of the fantasy at the core of the colonizer's claim to mastery. We have seen how Joseph serves to reveal the contradiction in Simon's understanding of himself and his position as law enforcer on behalf of imperial Europe. We have also seen how Amusa's comic blundering actually points to an epistemological and social disorientation and reorganization, in the midst of which he is a structural pawn and whipping boy, as well as a liminal figure of unmeditated critique. By means of the three characters, *Horseman* enacts the complications of social identity—colonizer and colonized—amidst the ferment of a structural transition predicated by colonialism. The schoolgirls are as much part of that upheaval and reordering as the white colonialist. In them the play instances the "new natives," the educated Africans who necessarily participate in the structure of colonial modernity by being its product. In the colonial encounter between Africa and the West, *Horseman* seems to say, every social location is touched by contradiction.

Having said this, we should add that in order to arrive at the real intricacy of *Horseman* as a text that theorizes agency, Bhabha's theory needs to be supplemented. As I argued in chapter 2, there is in Bhabha's theory a conflation of the psychic terrain with the sociopolitical, even as his own premises would seem to suggest that such a conflation is conceptually problematical. It is not my intention to reopen the debate as to whether or not psychoanalysis can lay claim to being a theory of society in the specifically political sphere. I broach the question here because it emerges in Bhabha's theory as the index of an unthematized tension, and hence a limitation. One limitation in Bhabha's theory, which *Death and the King's Horseman* reveals, is that the category of the psyche cannot in itself pose the issue of differential social locations. After sorting out the drama of hybridity enacted in the interactions between Joseph-Amusa and the Pilkingses on the one hand, and Amusa and the schoolgirls, on the other, our analysis can yet profit from further specifications that the notion of mimicry cannot yield. One such specification is that a substantive distinction needs to be made between the sociopolitical valence of, say, Amusa's and Joseph's acquiescence, and the schoolgirls' ambivalent acculturation. If it is true that all the characters I have considered enact the paradoxes of identity inherent to a colonial order, it is also true that the differences in their social location can be specified only on the terrain of a materialist consideration. Simon wields an institutional power that his "boys" are concretely subject to, and by the fact of their Western education, the schoolgirls are bound for an institutional authority that Joseph and Amusa, barely literate, can ever hope for. By the same token, the schoolgirls occupy a terrain made more complex by their gender difference from an Olunde.

This appropriately leads us to Olunde, the African character who is already secure in the cultural terrain mimicked by the girls. A medical student in England, his is the voice of the educated African. He is presented as having seen the West on its own grounds, complete in its wartime vulnerability. He attends to soldiers wounded in England's prosecution of World War II and has therefore seen England in the throes of a universal human predicament. He has also mastered the language, so much so that he can argue Jane to a stalemate. As Simon says, "[h]e's picked up the idiom alright. Wouldn't surprise me if he's been mixing with commies and anarchists over there" (66).

On one level, Olunde is Soyinka's vehicle for explicitly criticizing European cultural arrogance. The playwright goes so far as to put direct articulation of Olunde's location in his father's mouth, just as, as we saw earlier, he puts the articulation of the girls' promise in their mothers'. In a cell, and having been denounced by Olunde as "eater of left-overs" (61), Elesin takes consolation in his son's rejection. Addressing Simon, Elesin warns: "You may have stopped me in my duty but I know now that I did give birth to a son. Once I mistrusted him for seeking the companionship of those my spirit knew as enemies of our race. Now I understand. One should seek to obtain the secrets of his enemies. He will avenge my shame, white one. His spirit will destroy you and yours" (63). On another level, however, Olunde's character presents a complication that, at the level of authorial politics, the play as an intentional structure can neither thematize nor successfully repress. If we pose Olunde's "enlightened" confrontation with Europe against Amusa's jittery confoundment within it, we stand to approach this dimension of the play. Two lines after Amusa makes his final exit in Act IV, Olunde comes onstage for the first and only time we see him alive. From Jane we have already been warned that this young man may be "much too sensitive . . . the kind you feel should be a poet munching rose petals in Bloomsbury" (28). We know from Simon, too, that he is a "most intelligent boy," a go-getter who has the courage to defy his father and escape in a boat bound for medical school in the "land of the nameless" (60). And we know from the market women that there runs in his blood an aristocratic destiny: "It is not he who calls himself Elesin Oba, it is his blood that says it. As it called out to his father before him and will to his son after him. And that is in spite of anything [the] white man can do" (35).

When we finally meet him, he comes in looking for Simon Pilkings at the ball where the colonial functionaries have congregated to welcome the visiting English royal party. The stage directions present him in the following way: "A figure emerges from the shadows, a young black man dressed in a sober western *[sic]* suit. He peeps into the hall, trying to make out the figures of the dancers" (49). Soon after, his first line comes with the playwright's strategic irradiation:

> OLUNDE *(emerging into the light):* I didn't mean to startle you madam. I am looking for the District Officer.
>
> JANE: Wait a minute . . . don't I know you ? Yes you are Olunde, the young man who . . . (50, emphasis mine)

Where all along we have only heard others on both sides of the cultural divide talk about him with a sense of readable ontology (the natives) or enigmatic promise (the Pilkingses), his entrance measures up to his reputation. With the stage direction whereby a "young black man dressed in a sober western suit" (49) observes a group of Europeans dancing in strange—"fancy"—costumes, Soyinka invokes and reconfigures Joseph Conrad's Marlow observing half-naked natives doing strange dances. In Soyinka's evocation, the African is neither a dark shadow stomping in the night, nor Marlow's boilerman, "that really fine chap . . . hard at work . . . with an impromptu charm, made of rags, tied to his arm and a piece of polished bone as big as a watch stuck flatways through his lower lip" (Conrad, 38–39). Rather, Soyinka's African is here in a "sober western suit." He is scrutinizing Europeans engaged in a farcical ritual, but is himself positioned away from the countergaze of his hapless objects. In this way, Olunde's entrance reconfigures the entire subject-object infrastructure of colonial discourse. Soyinka gives Olunde a subjective centrality that is only further nourished by the quiet authority with which he speaks. His subsequent argument with Jane, coupled with his final suicide, simply complete the picture.

Critics have said a good deal about the argument between Olunde and Jane in this scene. Cleverly showing Jane that self-sacrifice is an impressive human value—"an affirmative commentary on life" (51)— rather than an aberration peculiar to primitives, Olunde compels Jane's respect, if not agreement. By means of this exercise in cultural comparison, Soyinka positions the educated native and the European in dialogue. For our purposes, what is interesting is not the argument as such, but the fact that Olunde discourses with Jane at all. Amusa, we recall, refuses till the very end to address the Pilkingses in the *egungun* costume. Indeed, he is ultimately punished for his intransigence: Simon relieves

him of his duties (49). By contrast, to Jane's query about whether or not
he is shocked, Olunde's response is a defensive-aggressive "Why should
I be ?" (50). And yet, he immediately goes on the offensive: "No I am
not shocked Mrs Pilkings. You forget that I have now spent four years
among your people. I discovered that you have no respect for what you
do not understand" (50).

For dramaturgical reasons, of course, it is important that Olunde
be sufficiently free of "tribal superstition" as to be able to argue with
Jane about death and suicide. The argument prepares us for his subsequent objection to his father's failure. It is also consistent with his overall characterization, since he is a Westernized African. But we may begin
to understand Olunde and the historical juncture he typifies by remarking the simultaneous defensive-aggressive posture just indicated. Olunde
defensively asserts his secularization only to confront Jane Pilkings with
its roots and consequence. Rhetorically, it is as though he needs to be
secularized on the terms of his Western education, and yet not fully
within those terms. What Jane grasps as his liberation from the mumbo-
jumbo of natives becomes in Olunde's response the condition of his
exasperation at her presumptiveness: "No I am not shocked Mrs Pilkings. You forget that I have now spent four years among your people. I
discovered that you have no respect for what you do not understand."
His altercation with Jane Pilkings becomes even more interesting when
we realize that the *egungun* mask that she is wearing at that moment
operates via a logic of immediate transparency. As Amusa insists, the
mask signifies the spirit of the dead, regardless of who is wearing it.
Amusa is locked into the total transparency of the mask as signifier of
the world of the dead, but Olunde pays attention to the body wearing
the mask. For Olunde, intentionality mediates his reaction to Jane
dressed as *egungun*. Since a white colonial functionary cannot wear the
mask for the same reason that a native wears it, he is able not only to
see Jane as herself, but also to act effortlessly on that knowledge. He
thus disregards her status at that moment as "mask-in-motion"—which
is to say, spirit of the dead in material incarnation.[9]

We can delineate here another instance of immanent critique:
marked by his culture as deserter, Amusa remains closer to the letter, as
it were, of Yoruba worldview as the play has established it. By taking the
masked figure on its pure physicality and the metaphysical status traditional culture confers on such physicality, Amusa is more faithful to the
logic of ancestor-worship as it is encoded in masquerade traditions.[10]
Although Olunde is a more formidable defender of local traditions, his
Westernization comes across here as an effortless secularization. This
secularization allows him to negate, in the process of mediating, the

unadorned logic of Yoruba tradition. But as we have just seen, such mediation is enabling, insofar as Olunde needs it in order to point to Jane's misrecognition. Olunde's Westernization, then, emerges in the play as a constitutive paradox: it is at once a condition of political and institutional enablement as well as what Homi Bhabha calls hybridity. Indeed, the hybridity is the enablement. "Hybridity" here does not mean a condition where two discrete entities coexist or intersect in the same agent while at the same time retaining their distinct self-sufficiency. Rather, it means a situation where the two entities or identities are incommensurable, and can therefore be entangled in the same subject only in the form of mutual deformation and transformation. The subject of hybridity, then, functions precisely and only on the leverage of the deformation and transformation. Consequently, Olunde is alienated from—or can effortlessly alienate—the fetishistic logic of masking, but that very alienation is the condition of possibility of his secular confrontation with Jane.

SOBER WESTERN SUITS

My discussion so far has concentrated on aspects of the characterization of three broad strata within the colonial scenario played out in *Horseman*. Joseph and Amusa occupy the first, Simon Pilkings occupies the second, while Olunde and the schoolgirls inhabit the third. My concern has been to draw attention to the ways in which the play intrinsically details paradoxes of identity and subject position in a context of sociopolitical change. There is a final, overarching dimension attaching to Olunde's positioning, and it is in understanding this dimension that we are brought back to the issue I deferred earlier on, namely, Soyinka's insistence on the *endo-cultural* nature of the play's tragic conflict. We will recall that Soyinka insists that the colonial factor is no more than a catalytic incident as far as the play's "threnodic essence" is concerned. On the basis of what can be called the drama around the drama, that is, Soyinka's preemptory reading of his play, I want now to suggest that the paradox of hybridity coded into Olunde's career allegorizes the play's own materiality—its very being—as a postcolonial cultural artifact in the contemporary global village. By means of the character of Olunde, *Horseman* figures its own condition of existence as an artifact of culture originating from and addressed to the postcolonial conjuncture that is the latter half of the twentieth century.

To develop this last point, let us return to the actual story that Soyinka dramatizes. The play's setting is to some extent anachronistic.

In 1945, when the incident happened, the "Yoruba world" was no longer as "traditional" as the play's rhetoric suggests, neither was the "West" and what it implies such an alien phenomenon. According to J. A. Atanda in his book *The New Oyo Empire: Indirect Rule and Change in Western Nigeria 1894–1934*, the King of Oyo, Alaafin Siyenbola Ladigbolu, whose death set the play's events in motion, reigned for thirty-three years (1911–44) and was legendary for his collusion with British authorities. Although Ladigbolu was not literate, by the time of his death in December, 1944, many Yoruba kings of other towns were literate and fluent in the English language (Atanda, 292). Atanda argues that Ladigbolu was a strong ally of the British colonial system and personal friend of the District Commissioner for Oyo, Captain W. A. Ross. Indeed, Ladigbolu's coronation as King to succeed his father, Alaafin Lawani, was actively pushed by Ross (Atanda, 109). Both Ladigbolu and his father (and predecessor), Alaafin Lawani saw themselves as friends of Captain Ross. Atanda recounts one occasion on which Alaafin Lawani and Captain Ross united to expel an American Baptist missionary who questioned the former's authority, Reverend S. G. Pinnock, in June 1909 (Atanda, 114–15).[11]

By 1945, it was no longer unprecedented for Olokun Esin to refuse to die with the King. Indeed, almost a century earlier, King Atiba had abolished the practice of having the first son (the Àrèmo) die with the King as was also the custom, thereby paving the way for his first son, Adelu, to reign from 1859–1875. Ladigbolu is grandson to King Adelu, and his tenure followed after Adeyemi his uncle, and Lawani his father, in that order. What is important for our purposes is that Ladigbolu ruled in a third line of succession from Adelu, whose rule constituted a well-known instance of the abolition of a traditional practice.[12]

In his "director's notes" to a production of *Death and the King's Horseman*, which he directed in 1979, Wole Soyinka refers to King Atiba's momentous abolition of the crown prince's customary suicide. In this document, to be found in the production files of the play at the Goodman Theater in Chicago, Soyinka writes:

> Like all empires the world had known, it [Oyo Empire] was remarkable both for its sophisticated social organization and for its unspeakable cruelties and excesses. The tradition of ritual suicide (even murder) of principal membership of the King's household especially of the Aremo (eldest prince) therefore had a political rationale, even if we are in no position to identify with absolute certitude its historical origin. One way to totally eradicate the traces (and policies) of a detestable reign was to eliminate all those who had enjoyed the privileges of such a reign since they would, natu-

rally, have a vested interest in perpetuating its policies. Not surprisingly, when society became more stable through the emergence of comparatively progressive kings, such a king would decree a stop to the custom of ritual suicide. An example was King Adelu who ruled from 1859–1876. . . .[13]

What I am getting at is that ritual suicide in the play functions as a metonymic-literary category, not an ethnographic one. As can be seen from the passage above, Soyinka is not blind to the reprehensible aspects of the practice, nor does he shy away from remarking the repressive aspects of the traditional culture. Although the play surrounds the practice with such lyricism and human affect as to constitute its justification, it is less a justification of the practice as such, than an artistic statement of the immanent integrity of a way of life and mode of seeing. A reading of the play that accuses Soyinka of conservatism, on the ground that he is defending a degenerate aristocratic practice, has a point (see Booth). But to fully grasp what Soyinka achieves through his precarious aestheticization of an inegalitarian practice, we will benefit from going beyond ready labels. Conservative it may be in the motif it chooses to explore, but the play thereby confronts Western humanism with an ostensible aberration rendered natural by means of language.

On this question, Kwame Anthony Appiah's study of the play takes us in the right direction (see *House*, 73–84). Against Soyinka's reading, Appiah rightly argues that the colonial factor is actually central to the drama. He finds the playwright's account consistent with the ambition of his well-known project referred to earlier, that of articulating the logic of tragedy within an "African" philosophical framework. By Appiah's account, Soyinka conceals his intention as well as the true conflict set out in the play because his self-appointed mandate as voice of modern Africa is to break free of European categories and discourses. Because imperial Europe sets itself up as the originating agent of Africa's entry into history, any project that wants to reclaim the latter's autonomy is logically pressed to challenge at the same time the very idea of Europe as central agent. And so, argues Appiah, precisely because his play seeks to recuperate "African culture" from colonial denigration, Soyinka is forced to claim for his Africa a historical, psychic, and spiritual dynamism that predates European colonization. Writes Appiah:

> If African writers were to play their social role in creating a new African literature of the 'secular social vision,' drawing on an African metaphysics, then the colonial experience *would* be a 'catalytic incident merely'—it could only be the impetus to uncover this metaphysical solidarity. Furthermore, [Soyinka's] own work,

viewed as an examination of the 'abyss of transition,' serves its ideological purpose just by being a *metaphysical* examination, and
loses this point when reduced to an account of the colonial experience. Paradoxically, its political purpose—in the creation of an
African literary culture, the declaration of independence of the
African mind—is served only by concealing its political interpretation. (*House*, 83)

The significance of Appiah's reading can be located at a number of
levels. The first and most obvious one is his recognition of a dissonance
between what the play shows and what Soyinka says about it. Beyond
this, Appiah also provides a strong account of the reason for the dissonance, namely, that the writer demands an endogenous (or, as it were,
prepolitical) reading of the play's tragic conflict because of a political
design to contest colonialist rhetoric. Appiah also wants to question the
particular direction Soyinka's politics of cultural/racial recuperation
takes, and as a result, he moves too quickly over his own insight.
Because he is concerned with setting forth an alternative direction for
African cultural politics, Appiah uses the play mainly as a stepping-stone
to a postinterpretation thesis. In order to get to his postinterpretative
rejection of Soyinka's account of a unitary African metaphysics, Appiah
does not linger long enough on the play. He is thus unable to tease out
a fuller lesson from the dramatist's struggle.[14]
    What then happens if we linger a bit longer on the dissonance
made visible by Appiah and the predicament that explains it—that is
to say, if we look more closely at the intersection of the Author's Note
and the play itself? Between the Author's Note and the play itself,
what we have is a relationship of dissonance on one level, unity, on
the other. On the one hand, what the play shows contradicts what
Soyinka's Note says about it; however, in that contradiction resides a
meaningful co-extensiveness of play and authorial claim, where both
coalesce into an epistemological and cultural struggle. By insisting
that the play's universal tragic essence can only be grasped if it is
located within the cultural order of the African world, Soyinka makes
the specificity of Yoruba worldview function as collective protagonist. This collective protagonist is a poetic invention, pure text, pure
desire. In the density of its self-understanding, this collective protagonist surreptitiously becomes particular and universal. It is particular
because the playwright says that we respect the tragic action only if
we locate it within the context of "the Yoruba mind." And it is universal because the play's tragic essence is supposed to carry a universal amplitude that transcends history—the history of colonialism, of
"the culture clash."

Soyinka's maneuver recalls that which is always put into play when apologists of a high-canonical legacy insist on the timelessness and universality of the "Great Tradition." In this maneuver, traditionalists argue in the same breath for the particularity and universality of, say, Shakespeare, constituting the specificity of "the Elizabethan world," the "Elizabethan mind," into a naturalized ground of universal tragedy. Tragedy here designates not merely technical form, but also humane sensibility. If we understand this maneuver—whereby European particularity is endowed with the status of the universal—as a case of "Western" literary culturalism, Soyinka is in effect engaging the latter within the parameters of its own *langue,* rather like Olunde engages the Pilkingses on terms that he has come to share with them. Looked at this way, Soyinka is writing back to Europe by seizing a discursive form and filling it with a different content.[15] And in so doing, he acts out a basic self-refutation that culturalists of the canon act out all the time: he plays politics, so to speak, by insisting that we take our minds out of the gutter of politics.

If Soyinka shares with culturalists of the canon this self-cancelling disavowal of politics, and if one can read this self-cancellation as an immanent critique of culturalism as such (that is, culturalism wherever it is to be found, in African letters or in traditional Anglo-American criticism) the sociohistorical condition that Soyinka's play addresses compels it to reveal something the playwright himself may or may not have intended. Olunde's repudiation of colonial arrogance is necessarily enabled by the very colonial structure whose blindnesses he critiques—directly in his argument with Jane, and indirectly in the symbolic logic of his suicide. Moreover, on the terms the play gives us, we are to assume that his self-sacrifice, undertaken because "he could not bear to let honour fly out of doors" (75), cannot in concrete terms save the community from the consequences of Simon's intrusion. At the beginning of Act 5, Elesin assures Simon that the moment when the suicide would have been unquestionably redemptive has already passed (*Horseman,* 62). In other words, Simon's interference has already dealt the community a basic blow that no amount of consequent redress can erase. Furthermore, by dying in place of his father, Olunde disrupts the order of life presumed by all human communities: the child is not supposed to die before the parent. This is at least one way of reading the Praise Singer's lines, spoken in anguished denunciation of Elesin's failure: "Your heir has taken the burden on himself. What the end will be, we are not gods to tell. But this young shoot has poured its sap into the parent stalk, and we know this is not the way of life. Our world is tumbling in the void of strangers, Elesin" (75).

These lines evoke a sense of dissolution, but it is one that above all yields uncertainty. Elesin's failure implies the dissolution of a mode of ordering reality and society, and, like all upheavals, this one leaves in its wake apprehensions about what is to follow: "What the end will be, we are not gods to tell." In a profound sense, then, the social process that Elesin's failure signals is one that Olunde's self-important suicide cannot arrest by a mere gesture of will. For his self-sacrifice is finally symbolic, driven as much by an aristocratic concern for the metaphysical balance of the "Yoruba world" as by the transforming gaze of the colonial eye. By a similar logic, Soyinka contests European cultural arrogance by seeking to deny Europe the status of originating protagonist in his play; yet the very fact of the contestation restores Europe to the status under contestation. For the specific idiom of address—the modern stage, the printed text, and the perceptible influence of classical tragedy—remains at the least of European provenance. Europe, not to belabor the point, remains the occasion and irreducible addressee of the playwright's labor. At the intersection of Soyinka's play and his preemptive interpretation of it, the oblique dynamic at work is one of disavowal.

In "The Fourth Stage," Soyinka identifies tragedy as that genre where the vicissitudes of individual and collective existence are explored by means of the agony of the tragic protagonist at a specific historical conjuncture. In his words,

> On the arena of the living, when man is stripped of excrescences, when disasters and conflicts (the material of drama) have crushed and robbed him of self-consciousness and pretensions, he stands in present reality at the spiritual edge of this gulf, he has nothing left in physical existence which successfully impresses upon his spiritual or psychic perception. It is at such moments that transitional memory takes over and intimations rack him of that intense parallel of his progress through the gulf of transition, of the dissolution of his self and his struggle and triumph over subsumation through the agency of the will. It is this experience that the modern tragic dramatist recreates through the medium of physical contemporary action, reflecting emotions of the first active battle of the will through the abyss of dissolution. (149)

For Soyinka, at times of great stress in the life of a collective, there invariably emerges an Ogun-figure, suffused with hubris, whose burden is to have concentrated in him the full extent of the suffering of the era. But viewed in the long haul, and against the transtemporality of historical unfolding, such suffering is the challenge of transition, a call—for better or worse—to some form of change.[16] The particular moment of trauma is therefore an abyss that dares to be crossed, testing the resources of the suffering collective and the will of its arch-sufferer, the ideal carrier. This scenario is timeless; for it is in the very nature of history to have it enacted over and over again as epochs stand at the edge of the abyss, challenged to witness and suffer the rupture, or, perhaps, commingled rapture, of change. My concern has been to show that *Horseman* condenses a good many of the contradictions entailed in historical change. So comprehensive is the play's condensation of these contradictions that it thematizes its own being, puts before us an allegory of its reality as a product of culture. In this way, the play accounts for Soyinka's own reading by unveiling within its fold the historical and discursive context, as well as purpose, of such a reading. Rendered in another way, the milieu that the play addresses also addresses us through it.

We can go further still: the protagonist of *Horseman* can be read back to the dramatist in particular, and the postcolonial elite (critics and cultural workers included) in general. As we have seen, the one figure who not only takes it upon himself to initiate some kind of redress, but also has the wherewithal to do so, is Olunde. In this sense he is the playwright's alter ego, and the play is the idiom of redress. By allegorizing its own condition of possibility the play figures itself within its field of vision, and thereby implicates its readers by challenging us. Being no politicians in the conventional sense, the challenge is for us a hermeneutic one, and the "us," on this understanding, includes dramatist and critic, African and otherwise. Looked at in this way, *Horseman* points up a discursive struggle more engaged and instructive than claims about "subversion," such as one often gets in contemporary postcolonial theory. The text invites criticism to go beyond either easy celebration or denunciation: it invites us further into itself, and rewards us there.

We may now conclude this section by drawing out more explicitly the lesson of the discursive struggle instanced by Soyinka. As we have seen, *Horseman* deals with the failure of its central character, Elesin, to commit suicide as demanded by his culture. It subsequently takes the son, Olunde, to redress the social threat signaled by his father's failure; this he does by means of a ritual suicide that is belated but still symbolically valuable. At this level, Soyinka's play presents the son as a subject with positive agency. At another level, however, the play also shows that the social trauma that Elesin's failure signals is one that Olunde cannot arrest by the sheer act of symbolic self-assertion. That is, the play locates Olunde's agency in the fact of symbolic self-assertion, and takes care to separate that realm from one of concrete arrest or redirection. In this sense, his gesture redresses the trauma of colonialism specifically by the force of its discursive intervention, not its phenomenal effectivity. Olunde is Soyinka's alter ego, and his gesture of assertion is an allegory of the playwright's artifice of symbolic redress: the play, *Death and the King's Horseman*.

In this sense, the predicament of father and son in Soyinka's play is an allegory of the location of black African sexed subjects within (post)colonial modernity. The relationship between Fagunwa and Soyinka is as well an intertextual allegory of the adventure of African letters up to and since the independence era. This relationship is that of a literary son and patriarch. Because he wrote in the preindependence era, Fagunwa's text is sponsored by Christian ideology. By contrast, Soyinka's milieu is the postindependence era, where Christian theology is no longer a strong intellectual influence—where, indeed, it has come to be seen as a colonial relic to be transcended. Free of the interpellation of Christianity, then, Soyinka is able to celebrate agency with greater single-mindedness. But he does so by stressing the value, in and of itself, of symbolic self-assertion. Where submission to Christian theology enables Fagunwa's critique of modernity, Soyinka's critique in *Horseman* is enabled by his submission to the norms of classical drama.

Consequently, the move from Fagunwa to Soyinka is not a teleological ascent from compromised agency to a more antiseptic, more coherent one. In both writers, an act of will, or act of language, can be at once compromising and enabling. Indeed, agency in both texts happens at the broiling heart of this paradox. *Forest* and *Horseman* are therefore implicit commentaries on African letters in particular, and cultural criticism in general. What distinguishes Soyinka's achievement from Fagunwa's is the stress the former places on the fact of assertion and symbolic redress itself. And so should it be since, unlike Fagunwa, Soyinka belongs in the generation that fashioned "African literature" into an institutional, academic project. African letters is therefore an ideology in the Althusserian sense of the term. It is a practice of symbolization and representation that, though grounded in and oriented toward the material realm, is not reducible to it. And though marked by important conceptual limitations and misrecognition, it is neither simply right or wrong, subversive, or otherwise.

OF FATHERS AND SONS

The thrust of my discussion of *Death and the King's Horseman* has been to show that it is more than an "artsy" mediation on death and the will. It is this; but it is also a document that speaks of, and for, a particular class and the mission the class set for itself. In the idiom of drama, the play theorizes a historical moment and the vagaries and nuances of agency within it. My argument will be complete if I can also demonstrate, through immanent textual reading, that Soyinka shares the discursive struggle that concerns him with others of his generation. We have seen the sense in which his relationship to Fagunwa is that of a literary descendant who transforms a predecessor's passion in the very motion of carrying it forward. Soyinka's relationship to Chinua Achebe is substantively distinguishable from his relationship to Fagunwa: it is a relationship of peers who inhabit a similar epistemological and structural-material location. Soyinka shares the Yoruba language with Fagunwa, but doesn't share the latter's epistemological and structural space. That he shares these with Achebe is at a basic level signaled by the language in which both writers became world renowned. It is helpful, therefore, to locate Soyinka's discursive struggle within a broader national and continental context of creative literature in the English language. I will use Achebe to do this because the latter is the acknowledged "founder" of Anglophone African literature, and because Soyinka has initiated such an encounter by meditating in print on Achebe's work. I have in mind Soyinka's famous reading of *Arrow of God*, set out in the third lecture of *Myth, Literature, and the African World*.

According to Soyinka, Achebe's *Arrow of God* secularizes supernatural phenomena in a way that renders the incursion of Christianity almost logical and inevitable. "The secular nature of *Arrow of God*," writes Soyinka, ". . . is actually poised on a very delicate ambiguity. Considerations of the authenticity of spiritual inspiration, or of manifestations which may be considered supernatural, or at the least, ominous coincidences, are given alternative (secular) explications in the casual reflections of members of his Igbo community (*Myth*, 87). In his analysis, Soyinka suggests that Achebe "over-secularizes" traditional culture, or at the least, that he doesn't give adequate weight to its properly numinous aspects. From our foregoing discussion, it is easy to see why Soyinka might quibble with a perspective on agency and literary representation that (in his view) underplays the ultimate centrality and self-sufficiency of myth in African life. Soyinka's use of archetypes drawn from a traditional Yoruba mythical system is his way of restoring the numinous aspects of traditional African culture to their proper place, a prepolitical, self-contained realm. This is in part what he set out to do in *Death and the King's Horseman*. But as we have seen, the rigor of his dramatization of the conflict over ritual suicide is such that the play restores the secular and the political—as it must, since Soyinka's elevation is itself a political gesture. I want now to take up the secularization that Soyinka perceives in Achebe. I should like to demonstrate that Achebe's secularization of Igbo culture yields precisely the sort of self-allegorization that we saw earlier in Soyinka's *Horseman*.

So far, Achebe has published five novels. The first and most well-known, *Things Fall Apart* (1958), is set in the late nineteenth century and deals with Umuofia's first contact with British colonialism in the form of the arrival of Christian missionaries as well as secular government, both being aspects of the imposition of Western modernity. *No Longer at Ease* (1960) is set in the 1950s, on the eve of achievement of nominal independence for the administrative entity that had by then come to be known as Nigeria. The novel works as a sequel, and concerns the fate of a later generation once removed from the world depicted in *Things Fall Apart*. In *Arrow of God* (1964), Achebe returns to the theme of the disruption of native society by European colonialism.[17] In this sense, *Arrow of God* dramatizes an aspect of, or a moment in, a single story that stretches from the late nineteenth century to just before World War II. *A Man of the People* (1965) and *Anthills of the Savannah* (1987) deal with modern Nigeria after independence.

Taken together, Achebe's novels bear out the interpretation that they trace in fiction the sociocultural trajectory of a part of what today constitutes southeastern Nigeria.[18] *Things Fall Apart* and *Arrow of God* were centrally concerned with rescuing precolonial Igbo culture from the distortions of colonialist representation. In *No Longer at Ease,* Achebe turns his attention to the Westernized Africans who inherited the mantle of civic authority from the colonial order. The world of *No Longer at Ease* is the world of post-World War II colonial Nigeria. It is the world Mahmood Mamdani characterizes as the moment of "deracialization" without democratization, wherein "natives" are entering the colonial bureaucracy and looking forward to political independence and nation-building.[19] *A Man of the People* and *Anthills of the Savannah* concern the failures of those new African nation-states. In both novels, Achebe considers the failures of the Westernized elite and the political leaders. The historical progression in Achebe's novels is accompanied by a remarkable correspondence of theme and vision in all of them. In his creative work can be found a view of culture wherein history is inexorable and yet contingent, activated by human agents, and yet not fully subject to voluntaristic control. This vision enables the novelist to achieve in narrative a complex exploration of issues of social change and realignments in modern Nigeria in particular, and black Africa in general.

As commentators have noted, Achebe originally intended *Things Fall Apart* to be part of an expansive story covering three generations.

Robert M. Wren has suggested that the tragic story of Okonkwo represents a first generation, while *No Longer at Ease* represents a third, dwelling as it does on the tragedy of Obi Okonkwo, grandson to the protagonist of *Things Fall Apart*.[20] Nwoye (Okonkwo's son later baptized Isaac) represents the middle generation, and his story unfolds only as an integral part of his temperamental father's and his college educated son's. Because of the impact of *Things Fall Apart* and the ethnographic aspect of Achebe's novels, he is often read as a novelist who sheds light on "traditional" African life and modes of seeing. But as Simon Gikandi has shown in *Reading Chinua Achebe*, what the novels offer is a critique of the ethnographic simplification whereby cultures are hypostasized to make them legible, or novels hypostasized as documentation of culture. Likewise, Rhonda Cobham has shown that *Things Fall Apart* is a selective and gendered re-presentation of an African culture, not its unmediated documentation.[21] Here, I would like to argue that the critique of ethnographic hypostasization to be found in Achebe is also a discourse of class, gender, and the vagaries of agency in social space.

Like Soyinka in *Horseman*, Achebe started out by engaging the problematic of ritual murder. If *Things Fall Apart* has become a classic of world literature, the protagonist's murder of Ikemefuna is its central narrative event. It is as a consequence of the murder that Nwoye first begins to articulate to himself his growing dissatisfaction with aspects of the Umuofia culture that his father would die defending. His turn to Christianity in the final part of the novel is his way of dealing with Ikemefuna's murder. It is tempting to read this as a statement, by the novelist, that the conflict Nwoye faces can be posed as one between cruel tribal customs and cruel Christianity disguised as emancipatory doctrine. Although such a reading is defensible, it tells only part of the story. In his second novel, *No Longer at Ease*, Achebe revisits Ikemefuna's murder and Nwoye's abandonment of his tribe in favor of Christianity. In this novel, we are about sixty years after the events narrated in *Things Fall Apart*. Nwoye (now baptized, of course, as Isaac) returns as the protagonist's father. Isaac forbids his son Obi Okonkwo from getting married to his fiancée, Clara, because she belongs to the *osu* "untouchable" caste. The situation is thus neatly reversed: where in the first novel (set in the late nineteenth century) he is the son who rejects his father's commitment to an unjust cultural norm, in *No Longer at Ease* (set in the middle of the twentieth century), he is a patriarch trying to convince his educated son to perpetuate another unjust cultural norm.

What we have in the intertextual dialogue between *Things Fall Apart* and *No Longer at Ease* is an enactment of agency that rises to the level of a theory of culture, subjectivity, and agency. In this multivalent theory, coded as narrative, lies a specific interpretation of the path to, and complications of, modernity in Nigeria. As a teenager, Nwoye becomes a Christian in *Things Fall Apart* because he blames his father for the brutal killing of Ikemefuna in the name of a communally sanctioned ritual murder. Although the Ikemefuna episode is not voluntary suicide as in *Horseman,* the theme of a communally sanctioned practice that any modern liberal worth the label would denounce immediately places Soyinka's passion alongside Achebe's. Some sixty years after the events of *Things Fall Apart,* Nwoye returns as Isaac, an aged Anglican catechist who urges his son not to flout tradition by marrying into the *osu* caste. If being a "true son" means helping the patriarchy along in its imagined purity, it turns out that the Okonkwo of *Things Fall Apart* was wrong when he feared that he didn't father a true son. So wrong is Okonkwo that, in his misogynistic anxiety, he misreads the real site of culture's resilience. It takes half a century to be sure, but, thanks to the steady memory of Achebe's craft, we are allowed to see that a rebelling Nwoye can age to become the conservative patriarch, Isaac. The binarism that the typical modern reader may be tempted to set up between an unjust "traditional" system and a disruptive but rational "modernity" is thus displaced, for the character in whom the modern yearning is embodied in *Things Fall Apart* turns around, in *No Longer at Ease,* to uphold another unjust "traditional" practice. In this way, Achebe forces us into a concession: it becomes logically impossible to locate the (so-called) traditional at a pure temporal, phenomenological, or epistemological distance from the modern. The "us" in the last formulation is the first world literary-critical establishment or discursive community, the professional home of that privileged class that is in Fredric Jameson's formulation, "formed by the values and prejudices of a first-world-culture."[22] Through narrative, Achebe forces us to see anew the fluidity of self-understanding as well as class and caste alignments in a living African culture. He thus retrieves Igbo culture from discursive fossilization; and in so doing, his texts constitute an instance of cultural nationalism that intertextually *joins* a discursive community by contesting its simplifications. In contesting the denial of agency to traditional Africa and Africans, Achebe's authorial agency as theorist of culture "happens."

The last point indicates the sense in which the epistemological contestation coded into Achebe's texts may be read as an instance of third world cultural nationalism that articulates itself as an address to (among its many possible audiences) a first world audience. This cultural nationalism can also be read as an allegory of an African community's encounter with modernity as well as the educated class it spawned. The scene where Isaac forbids Obi from marrying Clara is evoked in a manner that repays close attention. To begin with, the scene revisits a trope already made famous in *Things Fall Apart*. In the latter, the figure of a masquerade, "Evil Forest," presides as dispenser of the law. His representation as upholder of communal law first emerges in the first part of the novel (chapter 10), before the arrival of missionaries. In the third part, when things had started to "fall apart," he reemerges in the scene where the nine masked spirits of Umuofia arrive to destroy the Christian church (in chapter 24). Physically setting fire to the church, the masked spirits seek to rid the tribe of the "abomination" brought upon it by the actions of Enoch, the Christians' most zealous convert, who had unmasked one such spirit in public. Where in chapter 10 he is referred to as "Evil Forest," in the scene in front of the Christian church he is referred to in the Igbo word, *Ajofia*. It is helpful to reproduce the passage here at length:

> Ajofia was the leading *egwugwu* of Umuofia. He was the head and spokesman of the nine ancestors who administered justice in the clan. His voice was unmistakable and so he was able to bring immediate peace to the agitated spirits. He then addressed Mr Smith, and as he spoke clouds of smoke rose from his head.
> "The body of the white man, I salute you," he said, using the language in which immortals spoke to men.
> "The body of the white man, do you know me ?" he asked.
> Mr Smith looked at his interpreter, but Okeke, who was a native of distant Umuru, was also at a loss.
> Ajofia laughed in his guttural voice. It was like the laugh of rusty metal. "They are strangers," he said, "and they are ignorant. But let that pass." (189–90)

The name Evil Forest/Ajofia does not appear to have any etymological connection with the other "evil forest" in the novel—the patch of land reserved in every village for burying the rejects of the community: those who die of diseases considered abominations, twins, and the Osu "untouchables." But there is a thematic link, and it lies in the fact that the evil forest (as physical space) was allotted to the Christians when they asked for land upon which to build their church. In the reasoning of the Mbanta community where the offer was given by the tribe and accepted by the Christians, no group in its right mind would joyfully agree to build their "shrine" in the forest. When the Christians happily agree to build on the land, and survived the mad choice, a crucial blow was dealt the traditional belief system. It is as though, as the villagers put it, the Christians must possess strong magical powers to be able to withstand the challenge of the supremely haunted forest. In this sense, the Christians' survival in the evil forest constitutes one demystification of the tribal metaphysical system. It is this elaborate metaphysics that is symbolically invested in the intimidating ancestral mask, Ajofia—here, the masked entity that goes by the name evil forest.

On these terms, as masked spirit or as piece of land, both instances of "evil forest" evoke an elaborate superstructure. As the Christians demystify the evil forest as piece of land, so do they the metaphysical resonance and judicial power of the masked spirit. As a patch of land endowed with metaphysical power, evil forest is demystified, thereby resulting in a sundering of the material-spiritual link it carries for the traditional society. This sundering bespeaks a secularization: henceforth, the land is to be lived on, harnessed materially, rather than burdened with metaphysical, nonscientific, meaning. And as masquerade, a spiritual essence that dominates the traditional civic process, Ajofia/evil forest is also symbolically unmasked, such that a sundering results between religion and secular civil society. That is to say, between a religious, metaphysical superstructure such as accompanied the tribal material foundation, and a secular one being forcibly ushered in by European modernity. In both cases, the tropes of the masked spirit and the evil forest enable Achebe to dramatize a process of Weberian separation of spheres, of rationalization.

And yet, the Western dispensation that unmasks Ajofia and transforms the evil forest into serviceable habitation is here not entirely "secular." As we have seen, the demystification of the piece of land called evil forest is made possible by the superiority of a secular-scientific apprehension of space. But it is achieved in Achebe's novel, not so much in the name of secularization as in that of Christianization. What *Things Fall Apart* makes visible is that the commerce, courts, and schools that the Europeans bring to traditional Igbo society are, at the least, inseparable from the church. If then, for the sake of argument, we say that a unique achievement of Western modernity consists in its separation of the secular from the religious domain in the matter of social governance and collective self-understanding, Achebe's evocation of the incursion of modernity into Igbo society points up its irreducible specificity. Here, black Africa's modernity turns out to be forced secularization complicated by forcible Christianization. In *Things Fall Apart,* in the matter of what to worship, the indigenes of Umuofia are simply asked to trade in the pagan fetish for the Holy Trinity.

Achebe revisits this complication and explores one of its consequences in *No Longer at Ease.* This happens during the argument between Isaac and Obi Okonkwo, when the father asks the son for the name of his fiancée. The following excerpt reproduces this remarkable moment:

"She is the daughter of Okeke, a native of Mbaino.". . .
His father laughed. It was the kind of laughter one sometimes heard
from a masked ancestral spirit. He would salute you by name and
ask you if you knew who he was. You would reply with one hand
humbly touching the ground that you did not, that he was beyond
human knowledge. Then he might laugh as if through a throat of
metal. And the meaning of that laughter was clear: "I did not think
you would know, you miserable human worm!"
Obi's father's laughter vanished as it had come—without warning
and leaving no footprints.
"You cannot marry the girl," he said quite simply. (150)

The terse pronouncement by Isaac prohibiting his son's marriage to
Clara Okeke is a rhetorical echo of the pronouncement that follows
Ajofia's derisive laughter, in *Things Fall Apart,* during the confrontation with Rev. Smith and his assistant also named (significantly, perhaps), Okeke. As we saw earlier, upon saluting Smith and Okeke in
"the language in which immortals spoke to men," both addressees are
"at a loss" because they do not know what to say in response (*Things
Fall Apart,* 190). Consequently, Ajofia's "laugh of rusty metal" under-
scores the "alien-ness" of the two Christians and vocalizes their epistemic subordination at this specific moment in the action of *Things Fall
Apart:* "'They are strangers,'" he said, 'and they are ignorant. But let
that pass'" (190).

The effect of this rhetorical echo is that *No Longer at Ease* rewrites
an easy conclusion that *Things Fall Apart* may otherwise invite. In *No
Longer at Ease* we see that the defeat of tribal metaphysical system
enacted in *Things Fall Apart* is neither total nor totalizable. In this way,
the secularization that the demystification of evil forest signals in the first
novel is in the second one questioned. By imaging Isaac as a latter-day,
"postmetaphysical" masquerade, *No Longer at Ease* suggests that the
traditional system whose weak links are made visible in *Things Fall
Apart,* has only given way to a new dispensation, one that may not after
all be implacably irreconcilable. Dynamic human agent that he is,
Isaac/Nwoye yokes both together and makes them work for him in his
mundane confrontation with his progressive but inevitably alienated son.

Isaac is an Anglican catechist whose son is a civil servant in the
fledgling nation-state that is Nigeria. Both father and son participate in
the new secular dispensation: the father as religious worker, tutor in the
ideological state apparatus of the Christian church, the son as a university educated bureaucrat in the state's civil service. But the father's non-
secularism, his deep Christian faith, is paradoxically what provides conceptual anchor for his perpetuation of a traditional pagan norm. Achebe

signals this by making the figure of the masquerade—which in *Things Fall Apart* connoted the tribal way of life—resurface as trope of patriarchal authority that is now both Christian and tribal. Hence, the Christian father who as youngster rebelled against tradition incarnates that very tradition when he, like an ancestral mask, laughs at the secular idealism of his son. Confronted with a deeply intimate familial decision over whom his son should marry, Isaac/Nwoye behaves exactly as a pagan, non-Christianized native of the world of *Things Fall Apart* might have behaved: "'You cannot marry the girl,' he said quite simply" (*No Longer*, 150).

One does not have to agree with Isaac's prejudice towards the *Osu* caste to note that Achebe is working out the complexity and contradictions of human choices in history. There are many aspects of the tribal way of life that are oppressive, and caste systems, like ritual suicide, are such instances. But if at the end of *Things Fall Apart* the reader concludes that the Western worldview has supplanted the tribal way in a linear trajectory towards secular modernity, Isaac's reappearance as ancestral mask suggests a more complex process of change and choice in culture. Achebe thereby pries open a contradiction that nineteenth-century colonial discourses regarding European identity cover over by the sheer force of rhetoric, namely, that what defines "European-ness" is Christianity and secular-instrumental reason. Kwame Anthony Appiah articulates the point I am making here in the course of his critique of the conventional account of Western modernity as the triumph of secular-instrumental reason. According to him,

> the beginning of postmodern wisdom is to ask whether Weberian rationalization is in fact what has happened. For Weber, charismatic authority . . . is antirational, yet modernity has been dominated by just such charisma. Secularization seems hardly to be proceeding: religions grow in all parts of the world . . . Jimmy Swaggart and Billy Graham have business in Louisiana and California as well as in Costa Rica and Ghana. . . . What we can see in all these cases . . . is not the triumph of Enlightenment capital-R reason . . . but what Weber mistook for that: namely, the incorporation of all areas of the world and all areas of even formerly "private" life into the money economy.[23]

When Isaac/Nwoye and Obi get into an argument over the ethics of the *Osu* caste system, Obi hypocritically invokes the Bible as a way of justifying his decision to reject tradition: "The Bible says that in Christ there are no bond or free" (151). The father then responds by reliving his rebellion in *Things Fall Apart*:

"I was no more than a boy when I left my father's house and went
with the missionaries. . . . When they brought me word that he had
hanged himself I told them that those who live by the sword must
perish by the sword. Mr Braddeley, the white man who was our
teacher, said that it was not the right thing to say and told me to
go home for the burial. I refused to go. Mr Braddeley thought I
spoke about the white man's messenger whom my father killed. He
did not know I spoke about Ikemefuna, with whom I grew up in
my mother's hut until my father killed him with his own hands. . . .
I tell you all this so that you may know what it was in those days
to become a Christian. I left my father's house, and he placed a
curse on me. I went through fire to become a Christian. Because I
suffered I understand Christianity—more than you will ever do."
(*No Longer,* 157)

Father and son are here reading a canonical text, the Bible. Where the
son, a university educated civil servant in the fledgling modern nation,
focuses on the Bible as pure ideational document, the father reads it as
allegory of his own historical experience. More importantly for our purposes, the father does not disguise this mode of reading: for him, he can
relate to the Bible, not necessarily because it holds forth timeless truths,
but because it tells of human suffering, and he as a human being has suffered. He insists on his agency as reader, and subordinates the lesson of
the Christian Bible to his specific existential needs. If this is a case of universalist thinking on narrative, it is one that has been subordinated to
the specificity of a particular passion, namely, Isaac's individual passion
as he understands it. Traditional literary criticism interpellates the reader
in a way that parallels Obi Okonkwo's desperate but opportunistic reading of the Bible during his argument with his father: he reifies narrative
by constituting it into an abstract-universal ethical document. But the
father implicitly contests this sort of universalism by bringing the Bible
down to earth.

Isaac's account also hints at the misrecognition of the European
teacher, who had appropriated his story as evidence of the triumph of
the Christian way understood as an abstract universal. By Isaac's
account, his defection is the result of a private psychic wound: the killing
of Ikemefuna. In this one passage, then, Achebe fleshes out the story of
Nwoye's defection so that we see (i) its specificity outside of the appropriation of a benign European and his own Westernized son; and (ii) the
uniquely interior drama that furnishes evidence of Nwoye's human
agency, his choices as thinking and acting subject. The exchange
between father and son in *No Longer at Ease* reveals the human element
involved in Nwoye/Isaac's defection to Christianity, as well as his

defense of an un-Christian tribal practice in his old age. The exchange thus thematizes the human element in the altercation of ideas between him and his son. The ideational contest is not the sort of abstraction whereby the modern is presented as a process of one-dimensional secularization away from illiberal traditions.

If in *No longer at Ease* Isaac and his son perceive their disagreement in solely personal terms, the link that Achebe makes with the world of *Things Fall Apart* raises that personal issue to the level of a larger sociocultural and political one. For Obi Okonkwo is Achebe's narrative mask for his own generation, even as Olunde is Soyinka's mask. This becomes evident when we realize that in the late 1950s when *No Longer at Ease* is set, Obi is twenty-three years of age, where Achebe (born 1930) would also have been in his twenties. I am not making a simplistic biographical analogy between Achebe the man and the protagonist of *No Longer at Ease*. Rather, I am suggesting that Obi's location is exactly the location of an entire class to which Achebe, as writer and theorist of culture, belongs. It is not at all accidental that Obi plans to write a novel about the predicament of the character Mr. Green, his European boss. Achebe's novel, which shows Green's naiveté on issues of the so-called African personality, turns out to be in part a critique of the colonialist type he represents, just as *Horseman* is in part a critique of Pilkings. In this way, *No Longer at Ease*, like *Horseman*, becomes casually involuted: Achebe has written such a novel as his main character plans to write. Likewise, in representing Obi by distancing him from his father, and in fleshing out the latter's motivation as initiated in *Things Fall Apart*, Achebe is working out the complexity of the historical challenge faced by his class.[24]

This historical challenge surfaces on multiple levels that we may roughly schematize in the following way. First, there is the discursive-intellectual level, where the class seeks to defend the integrity of the tribal way from the distortions of colonial discourse. Second, there is the concrete political level, where the class is invited, and actively undertakes, to lead the way in the construction of the fledgling nation-state. At both levels, there is an assumption of the value of the secular nation-state modeled on Western Europe and the United States. But this secular nation-state rhetorically needs, as its conceptual legitimation, to appeal to a collective identity that is putatively non-Western, "authentically" African. We thus have a situation where the sociopolitical mission is concrete secularization of social norms and structures, while the collective self-identity is supposed to be authentically "African." But logically, "authentic" African identity or society cannot be "secular," because a binary opposition of the secular to the spiritual is not intelligible in a strictly pagan (Pre-colonial "African") worldview.

This contradictory tangle is dramatized by Fagunwa, in whom as we saw earlier, secularization is yoked to Christianization and God's providence. Soyinka and Achebe inherit it and can meditate on it explicitly, where Fagunwa couldn't. Obi's secularized, nationalized, and racialized identity conflicts with his barely educated father's tribalism and Christianity. For the father's sincere Christianity simply finds a sub-terranean but concrete complement in his visceral tribalism. As subject-positions, the tribalism and the Christianity can effectively anchor iden-tities that exert their hold, not at the cerebral level, but in the visceral core of the self. Isaac's Christianity and tribalism sit deep in that site where the abstract logic of secular universalism or cosmopolitan modernity cannot compete. In this sense, Isaac/Nwoye is a version of Soyinka's Amusa, or Joseph, or Lakunle. Though literate, the father's rudimentary Western education is not enough to effect the fine-tuned, Euro-modern interpellation that Obi undergoes in England. And yet, Obi's interpellation is precisely what stands to enable the secularization and detribalization necessary for successful nation-building. In this way, in the interstices of his saga of the Okonkwos, Achebe explores the complicated and contradictory underbelly of modernity and the nation-state called Nigeria.

We are now in a position to specify the nature of the secularization with which Achebe leaves us in *Arrow of God*. At the end of the novel, the people of Umuaro welcome Christianity and, by implication, the modern structural ensemble that comes with it. But in so doing, they effect a powerful misreading of the concept of the Trinity to articulate and ratify their choice. In the novel, the hubristic protagonist Ezeulu refuses to pronounce the day for the festival of the New Yam in order to assert his supremacy as guardian of the community's secular and meta-physical system. The accidental death of Ezeulu's favorite son Obika weakens the position of the chief priest, thereby spurring the people to turn to the Christian church. The Umuaro people see the death of Ezeulu's son as punishment of the arrogant chief priest by the commu-nity's guardian god, Ulu. They therefore feel empowered to turn to a new religion that allows them to proceed with harvesting their crops.

Soyinka is correct to remark the hard-nosed pragmatism that Achebe's narrative ascribes to the people of Umuaro. He is also correct to remark that the effect of this desertion (and Achebe's representation of it) is to make the supernatural subservient to the contingencies of daily life and the choices of thinking human beings. Soyinka articulates Achebe's narrative choice in the following way: "The struggle among the gods has been placed squarely in the province of the political, and although the spir-itual and the mysterious are never absent or invalidated—certainly the affective or responsive in the lives of the community is constantly used to reinforce this dimension of reality—yet the strongest arguments in favor of a divine factor in the life of Umuaro is deliberately subverted by impure associations insinuated through the manipulations of language, contradicting situations, or the preponderant claims of a secular wisdom" (*Myth*, 88–89). Soyinka reads *Arrow of God* in this way because, for him, the representation of the conflict Achebe tackles in the novel is best approached in the language of the sacred and the mythical. But it is possible to read the ending of *Arrow of God,* not as the defeat of Ulu by triumphant "secular wisdom," but as the appropriation and reenchantment of the Christian God on the terms of Igbo traditional paganism. The Umuaro community accepts the Christian God by "reading" him within their traditional hermeneutic frame. The terms in which they understand their defection (their theory of their actions, as it were) is immanent, drawn from their protean pagan epistemology.

We can see this if we look closely at the novel's narration of the conversion. Simon Gikandi has drawn attention to the novel's modulation of narrative point of view (*Reading,* 59). In the final paragraphs of *Arrow of God,* the story comes to us from a distanced point of view— the voice of a nonparticipant in the action. But it is a limited, third-person voice that ventriloquizes the pagan consciousness of the Umuaro community. The novel's final paragraph indicates the swift change that befell Umuaro and accounts for it from the phenomenological standpoint of the community: "To them the issue was simple. *Their god* had taken sides with them against his headstrong and ambitious priest and thus upheld the wisdom of *their* ancestors—that no man however great was greater than his people; that no one ever won judgement against his clan. . . . The Christian harvest which took place a few days after Obika's death saw more people than even Goodcountry [the catechist] could have dreamed. In his extremity many a man sent his son with a yam or two to offer to the new religion and to bring back the promised immunity. Thereafter any yam harvested in his fields was harvested in *the name of the son*" (230, my emphasis). The deity Ulu does not die at the end of *Arrow of God;* very much to the contrary, he fulfills his role as communal guardian by delivering himself to the opportunity for reenchantment offered by Christians. The people turn to Christianity because the church promised that they could harvest their crops without any consequences. In becoming Christians, they are spurred on by brute mundane survival, for the chief priest Ezeulu's intransigence stood as a threat to their material subsistence. In making their choice, however, the people translate the theology of the Trinity into terms that fit their purpose: "In his extremity many a man sent his son with a yam or two to offer to the new religion and to bring back the promised immunity. Thereafter any yam harvested in his fields was harvested in the name of the son." If in Christian theology human beings have the road of salvation open to them because of the sacrifice of "the son" of the Holy Trinity, in their rereading of the theology, they are authorized to harvest their crops if it is done in the name of the son, here reread by them as their literal "son." Achebe's narrativization of the agency of his characters thereby stresses the density and resilience of their self-understanding. In this way, his achievement parallels Soyinka's, without the latter's resolute aestheticization of the metaphysical and the numinous.

THE MOTIVE FOR READING

The involuted finesse of *No Longer to Ease* permits Achebe to foreground a protagonist who shares his social location, even as this character's plans for authorship in the novel turn out to be Achebe's own discursive achievement. In this, we see a dynamic closely reminiscent of Soyinka's relationship to Olunde of *Horseman*. Obi and Olunde define themselves in pointed contrast to their fathers. What we encounter in the texts we've been discussing, then, are relationships of men with their own images, sons with fathers. It is this blindspot that Achebe addresses in *Anthills of the Savannah,* where he uses the character of Beatrice Okoh to criticize the sexism of the educated elite and the state apparatuses they manage. *Anthills of the Savannah* recognizes, at the least, a resounding silence in the canonical postindependence writers' discursive struggle, namely, woman as locus of action and social agency in all its ramifications (Cobham, "Misgendering"; Ogunyemi; Stratton, *Politics*). Educated and self-assured, Beatrice is made to narrate her own story and warn the three male protagonists not to mistake their stories—stories of sons and fathers, so to speak—for the story of the Nigerian nation in particular, and black Africa's modernity in general.

Like Soyinka and other African writers, Achebe judges his generation of educated "sons" to have failed in resolving the contradictions confronting postcolonial Africa. That Obi's relationship with Clara breaks down soon after Isaac's atavism suggests that his attempt to move his father toward the abstract norm of secularism does not carry much conviction. Obi's own resolve as moral and civic agent is subjected to criticism, his agency rendered suspect. For by the end of the novel, he has succumbed to the materialism and general lack of direction of the growing elite in modern Nigeria. This elite comes fully to center stage in *A Man of the People* and *Anthills of the Savannah*. Between the publication of *A Man of the People* in 1966 and *Anthills of the Savannah* in 1987, a lot had happened in the political history of Nigeria. There had been a brutal civil war (1967–70), three "successful" military coup d'etats, a brief spell of civilian rule between 1979–1983, the return of a military government in 1983, and yet one more military coup in 1985. In the continent more generally, there had arisen a number of murderous dictators who used a self-serving appeal to indigenous culture to legitimize their hold on power. In this sense, the critique of postcolonial society offered in African writers' works does not change the path of history: it only offers us a source of hindsight and contingent knowledge.

A similar thought is applicable to Soyinka and his evocation of Olunde, and it is on this point that we will conclude this chapter. History goes on despite Olunde's class-bound gesture, even as Africa's political and economic failures proceed despite Soyinka's work of discursive self-retrieval. But this does not negate the meaningfulness of Olunde's act of will, or Soyinka's act of language. Perhaps, then, the overarching lesson that Soyinka's passion teaches us is that acts of language are no more than acts of language, that literary structures cannot be conflated with social structures. As it were, the fine deconstruction of imperialism achieved in *Death and the King's Horseman* cannot in itself reorder the phenomenal reality of imperialism. This merely tells us something we all know, but often repress in the inner logic of contemporary theory. Wherever postcolonial theory and criticism, by conflating the linguistic text with the social text, is able to bracket this basic proposition, the value of the texts we have been exploring is that they witness to the conceptual error in such a conflation.

Epilogue

We ended the last chapter by insisting that literary structures not be conflated with social structures, and that wherever such a conflation is in force, the challenges of the concrete world, as well as the unpredictable vagaries of human agents, are most likely to be inadequately posed. The burden of that chapter and also the fourth was to demonstrate that two "arch-canonical" texts by D. O. Fagunwa and Wole Soyinka direct readers' attention to the "real world" in two ways. First, they both thematize, in the intrinsic story they tell, their overarching condition as allegorical explorations of, as well as discursive participants in, an extrinsic reality. Second, where at one level both texts present heroes whose achievements are rendered as positive and necessary acts of will, they also curtail at a reflexive level the reach of those achievements.

Fagunwa's protagonist finally ratifies his formidable powers through a self-naming that paradoxically implies limited agency. If as Akara-ogun, compound of spells, he actualizes a dream of epic mastery, he is also *baba òmúlèmófo*—patriarch of those who reach out only to grasp a void. In turn, Soyinka's Olunde—literally "my lord arrives"—acts on behalf of the community, but the act is neither an unqualified redirection of communal trauma nor a meaningless self-immolation. By contesting their protagonists' cognitive awareness within the internal logic of the texts, and by inscribing a metafictional layer over the passions explored in the forest of a thousand daemons or the Oyo community, the texts by Fagunwa and Soyinka dramatize a perspective on agency that needs to be put on the table of current literary theory and cultural criticism.

I have also suggested that these texts exist in an intertextual relationship to specifiable discursive contexts and history. The thinking and writing of these writers takes shape in dialogue (conscious or otherwise) with previous or contemporaneous texts and figures. We thus appreciate Fagunwa's struggle if we place him in the context of the ferment of Christianization and Yoruba literacy that preceded him, as well as the emergence of a Tutuola or a Soyinka, hot on his heels. By the same token, we appreciate Soyinka's contributions and disavowals if we locate him against a background of a Fagunwa, as well as a Chinua Achebe: what he inherits, as well as what surrounds him.

My argument in relation to these specific writers is not designed to introduce or even recommend a "new," all-encompassing theory of African literature, or a new way of interpreting the ongoing literary productions of black Africa. This book is a caution against all-encompassing theories. It develops the suggestion that we venture beyond a priori prescriptions, and listen closely to storytellers who happen to be African, telling stories designed to get a handle on our shared insecurities in modernity. I do not assume or claim any measure of coverage with regard to the emerging "canon" of African literature. Rather, I am interested in the heuristic value of both writers for the theoretical issue of agency. Since part of my argument has to do with points of intersection as well as divergence among successive generations in African letters, Fagunwa and Soyinka constitute an instructive pair to use in exploring such issues. I should hope that the theses I have offered stimulate, at the least, a discussion of their applicability to other writers from Nigeria, as well as from other parts of Africa. If my reading elicits further work that specifically contradicts or modifies the theses I have offered, it would have stimulated the sort of discussion that genuinely tracks agency-in-motion, the sort of perspective I defend in the foregoing pages.

It has been the burden of this book to develop this perspective of agency for two reasons. The first is to tease out a dimension of poststructuralist postcolonial theory that not only stands in the way of productive dialogue with a discursive tradition like African letters but is also—on the logic of poststructuralist theory itself—self-contradictory. Second, I have tried to formulate the logic of African letters at a level of metacritical abstraction so as to contribute to the ongoing adventure of African letters, while also saying something of value to Anglo-American critical theory. In this epilogue, I should like to outline other ways in which the concerns and perspectives developed in this book, as well as the mode of argumentation instanced in it, can be useful.

On the analysis conducted in chapters 4 and 5, a conceptual demarcation of the symbolic-linguistic from the concrete-phenomenal realm is not only necessary for a full appreciation of the predicaments of postcoloniality staged in texts like Fagunwa's or Soyinka's, it is also useful for a thoroughgoing deconstruction of one of the most resilient tendencies in modern attitudes to literary representations of external reality. This tendency can broadly be characterized as the reflectionist tendency. By this I mean a tendency to slip into modes of talking about

literature (or textual representation in general) in a way that assumes
that a representation of reality in language can (or should) strive to
approximate that reality without "inaccuracies" or "distortions." The
presupposition underwriting a reflectionist grasp of the literary is that
adequate (read: free of distortions) representation of a community and
its constellation of values is possible and progressive. Related to this is
the assumption that literature encodes, or at any rate can be made to
encode and identify cultures, nations, or races in their full dimensions as
phenomenal realities. From a hastily politicized perspective, the assumption is commonsensical and harmless; indeed, it is to be embraced as an
ideal worth defending or striving after. To suggest otherwise will be,
from this perspective, to seek to escape from the real world to the cosy
realm of language. Yet, this book is in part an argument for the precise
reversal of this piece of common sense. My argument has been that it is
exactly when we do not conflate the linguistic with the social, representation with what it purports to represent; when, that is, we insist on a
fundamental conceptual demarcation of these two realms, that we are
most incisively placed to appreciate the challenge of the real world. The
African writers we discussed have dramatized the plausibility of this idea
for us. After the readings set out in chapters 1 through 3 of this book, it
should be easy to specify, in the terms of contemporary theory and criticism, why this turns out to be the case, and what we stand to gain by
stressing it as the case.

The Beninoise philosopher Paulin Hountondji has drawn attention to
what he calls *theoretical extraversion,* a condition that for him marks scientific practice in black Africa.[1] He uses "science," of course, in its broad-
est sense, taking in both the hard and the human sciences. The story he
tells is in itself a familiar one, but the conclusion he draws therefrom is
germane. According to him, the economic relation established since the
colonial era—and still very much in place as we begin a new century—
poses the colony as a repository of raw materials. These raw materials are
tapped and transported to the metropolis, there to be processed, transformed into luxury and consumer goods which are thereafter circulated
back to the periphery. Knowledge production proceeds along a similar
line. The colony serves as the uninscribed soil of raw data: oral histories,
native customs, medicines, expressive practices, etc. The researcher ventures to "the field" primarily to collect data, but the actual labor of theo-
rization is located in the metropolis. Just as raw materials leave the colony
to be processed, so too do data leave the colony to be transformed—theorized—into "knowledge" in the metropolis. Consequently, the economic
and epistemological relation established between the metropolitan centers

and their colonial peripheries remains intact, surviving the achievement of formal independence. Formal independence is from this perspective little more than a juridical evocation: it is historically necessary and existentially affective, but at a different level of abstraction, it serves ultimately to confirm Western claims of incremental knowledge, instrumental reason, and the free market of goods, ideas, and texts.

This account carries a minimal thesis that is relevant to contemporary literary theory and cultural criticism. To get at this relevance, it is useful to distinguish between modernity as (i) a socioeconomic organization, and (ii) an epistemological order—both in a relation of mutual overdetermination. At the least, what Hountondji presses to our attention is the reality that modernity, understood in the first sense—i. e., as an actually existing socioeconomic order—embraces within its operative logic the West and the non-West. Put crudely, the minimal thesis will be that, to the extent that current economic relations require a particular structural positioning for the third world economies in the organization of production, we are all Eurocentric. Similarly, to the extent that the cultural realm itself operates on a model of commodity fetishism, the same operative logic welcomes (as consumable product) an image of third world alterity. In this scenario, the notion of decolonization readily gets cast in terms of stepping up to modernity (in the first sense) by having a discourse of one's own (i.e., modernity in the second sense). Discursive agency assumes in this way an analogical relationship to a wishful agency in the concrete-political sphere, a yearning for change in the real world. As a consequence of this, there flourishes a model of cultural understanding wherein the postcolonial object is thought, when it is, ultimately as a repository of otherness. Whether this otherness is in fact celebrated or bemoaned is immaterial since, in either case, the predicative conceptual topography remains intact. In essence, what plays itself out could be called an acquiescent resistance. In its oxymoronic tension, the phrase "acquiescent resistance" captures the oblique dynamic I am struggling to articulate: the other swells in its culturalist antagonism, all the more to submit to the call of the market.

We came upon this dynamic in our discussion of African literary criticism in chapter 3. As we saw in that chapter, even as the nativists sought to "correct" the distortions of colonialist representations and the Marxists sought from literature an authentic and sympathetic representation of the working class, the terms "Africa" and "literary tradition" remained unproblematized as object of knowledge and purveyor of cultural *and* political emancipation. As we all know, however, repressions leave a trace even as they enable the business of living. In the case of Africanist literary criticism, the repressed returns in the shape of the brutal economic and political failure of nominally independent sub-Saharan nations. This reality should disorient the formalist versus non-formalist divide. It should also reveal their shared inattention to the complex historicity and material underpinning of both the literature being contemplated, *and* the criticism engaged in the contemplation. And it should point up the limitation of the conceptual tendency to frame decolonization simply in terms of catching up with modernity: that is, modernity understood in social theory as the progressive extension of instrumental reason toward universal enlightenment and emancipation, and in literary criticism as a reflectionist understanding of literature, where literature is taken to mirror and superintend social processes.

My contention, then, is that the real world has stepped up, so to speak, to impress itself on our business of living, and it is worth our while to allow it to impact our protocols of reading. To do so is to make it possible to supply a comprehensive genealogy and context for such visceral narrative events as the images of war and starvation that I evoked at the beginning of this book. Without such comprehensive genealogies and specifications of context, theory and criticism can only denounce (or celebrate) this or that representation; it cannot richly enhance our understanding of social or discursive determinations. In this sense, a productive commitment to the real world turns out to require us to reject, at the level of conceptualization, any elision of that world with "good" or "bad"—accurate or inaccurate—representations of it.

There is yet another immediate benefit to be gained from the sort of antireflectionism advocated in this book. In current Anglo-American criticism, what some have called the "culture wars" is in its broad strokes rooted in a certain apprehension of what literature does or should do. On the one hand, you have those who claim to be defending the Western heritage from leftist, feminist, third world, or "minority" scholars because the latter are out to "deconstruct" Western civilization by "deconstructing" Western letters. On the other, you have those who insist that the reason to read non-Western literature is because it subverts the distortions of Western writers and thinkers regarding non-Western societies and peoples. At the heart of the canon debates in the United States, then, is the salutary impulse to redress a history of exclusions. However, to argue that reading some set of texts can lead, by some unelaborated logic of causality, to some form of actual political-cultural redemption or, as the case may be, contamination, is to enact an ancient theory of literature—and that theory is the reflectionist view of the literary object. Of course, contemporary canon-busters as well as canon-preservers cannot really demonstrate how literature can in fact do the massive work they claim for it: more often than not, they simply assume it.

It is this powerful area of intersection between canon-busters and canon-preservers, and the epistemological leap that sustains it, that motivates Henry Louis Gates Jr. to write, with a charming sense of irony and understatement: "Ours was the generation [i.e., the American civil rights generation] that took over buildings in the late 1960s and demanded the creation of black and women's studies programs, and now, like the return of the repressed, we have come back to challenge the traditional curriculum. And some of us are even attempting to redefine the canon by editing anthologies. Yet it sometimes seems that blacks are doing better in the college curriculum than they are in the streets" ("The Masters Pieces," 19). Like other non-Western writing, modern African literature in the European languages enters this discursive field ripe for a reflectionist deployment. Particularly because its very emergence was with the independence struggle and triumph in Africa, the understandable tendency is to expect in it, and celebrate through it, the truth of the "other" in political struggle, the undistorted truth at last, of black African humanity and reality.

As I argued in chapter 2, theories of postcoloniality are no less vulnerable to this tendency. With the influence of a poststructuralist register, we would seem to have moved beyond the illusion of a direct relation between language and reality, or representation and the object represented. However, what has become equally evident in current theory and criticism, more resoundingly so in postcolonial theory, is the systematic elevation of the purchase of theoretical intervention in and of itself. This elevation of the purchase of theory is accompanied by an inadequate attention to the history of the criticism of, as well as the stresses intrinsic to, postcolonial literatures themselves. If we for now limit ourselves to literary theory in general, it has often been remarked that poststructuralism's value for cultural analysis is significantly weakened wherever its signal categories (paradox, contradiction, etc.) are consigned to their linguistic valence. For then, moments of linguistic self-contradiction—by definition endemic to the process of thought and the scene of writing—become all that we can uncover. This reduces the reading process to a tautological maneuver: texts begin to unveil contradictions for the predictable reason that textuality defeats mastery and totalization.

If this problem applies to poststructuralist literary theory in general, its manifestation in the area of postcolonial studies raises the problem to a higher level. Here, at the very moment that theory urges us to accept contradiction as a fact of culture, the framing and analysis of non-Western literatures tend to be predicated on celebration. The destination of interpretation tends to be to show that non-Western writing subverts so-called Eurocentric modes of seeing. We thus have a situation where theoretical claims about postcolonial societies seem to diverge from specific interpretive evidence drawn from the cultural products of those same societies. If at the level of theory, we are urged to accept that contradiction and paradox are inevitable coordinates of society and culture, at the level of literary analysis, we are given non-Western literatures that somehow subvert Eurocentric ideology without contradiction.

These observations do not constitute an argument against poststructuralist or deconstructive theory in general; this much should be clear from the first to the third chapters of this book. What I am pointing to, rather, is the very specific way in which poststructuralist critical theory—Derridian, Foucaultian, or Lacanian—has been and is being brought to bear on the terrain of postcolonial literary and cultural criticism. Consequently, although there are heterogeneous conceptual schools within postcolonial theory—some of them mutually antagonistic—it remains the case that even as poststructuralist premises have by and large the single most visible influence in our conceptual vocabulary, the interaction of that vocabulary with non-Western literatures is marked by a certain easy understanding of what theory can do. As we saw in our discussion of postcolonial theory, the idea of agency is argued about in ways that conflate (i) the constative content of a theoretical elaboration, with (ii) the concrete direction of the external reality to which theory refers.

This confusion is so commonplace and naturalized that both poststructuralists and their interlocutors fall prey to it. The result is that current postcolonial theory is locked into a silent logic whereby it assumes that historical agency (resistance, subversion, and so on) can be specified in the abstract—that is to say, independently of the constraints of particular contexts. Thanks to this logic, it becomes possible to talk of a singular "Eurocentrism" or a singular "resistance," without the need for careful distinctions between classroom reading lists and the tangible social meaning of the American dollar in the contemporary world system. In its own way, then, this tendency in postcolonial theory can only collapse representation with what it purports to represent. If reflectionist criticism aestheticizes politics, this understanding of the purchase of theory collapses politics into a game of expository form, a game of what books say to each other.

This last point leads up to yet another problematic tendency in current postcolonial theory. To the extent that it emerges at all in contemporary literary theory and cultural criticism, the conceptual space accorded to economics as an instance in the totality of modern society is rather fuzzy. For example, as a description of the contemporary global order, the idea of "arrested decolonization" that came up toward the end of chapter 3 presupposes that decolonization was at some point in time in motion. But, following Hountondji, it is useful to distinguish between different realms of the social totality. With specific reference to sub-Sahara Africa, we might say that decolonization had been taking place if by that term we refer to the artistic and cultural sphere; that is to say, if by that term we refer to (i) the establishment of institutional infrastructure to enable and encourage the expressive arts in the former colonies, and (ii) the cultural productions—creative and critical—thus stimulated. On the other hand, decolonization had never left the ground if by that term we mean a reorganization of economic relations between the peripheral states and the postindustrial centers. If this much is granted, it becomes possible to entertain the suggestion that the understanding of decolonization which often informs Africanist literary criticism as well as postcolonial theory tends to be restricted to the cultural realm. The faith which drives the project is that critical explication of literary texts, or theoretical critique of culture and society, would facilitate material decolonization.

We are thus brought back to an aspect of Althusser's theory that we set aside in chapter 1. If the economic failure of African nation-states now exerts its force-field on such a scale that even the cultural decolonization, in motion from about the 1960s, is "arrested," it seems to me that we are now in a position to rearticulate Althusser and say that at the present conjuncture, and insofar as Africanist criticism (or African postcoloniality as a sociopolitical moment) is concerned, the "relatively autonomous" cultural sphere is being shown to be in the last instance mediated by economic determination. My sense is that even after admitting the critiques of economism that have been leveled at the Althusserian dictum of a last instance, it is legitimate for our present purposes to qualify its meaning, such that it becomes applicable to the experience of postindependence African societies in the global arena of knowledge production. That is to say, the claim of a last instance offers a way of accounting for the institutional underpinnings of knowledge production at the present conjuncture. We may therefore accept Laclau's and Mouffe's claim that social processes are not solely determined by and within the topographic instance of the economic, and still insist on the usefulness—insofar as the specificity of African letters is concerned—of the notion of a last instance. If this recasting of the Althusserian dictum is persuasive, it points to an important determining realm of the social totality, one that can only be repressed, not escaped, so long as the literary text is elided with the social text—either in theory or in criticism.

What all of this adds up to is as follows. If the antireflectionist view adumbrated on these pages is identified as broadly poststructuralist, it should be with the qualification that poststructuralist postcolonial theory in its present state is often not consistent with its own premises. As we saw in chapter 3, the reflectionist critical models offered by Eliot or Leavis (or even a version of Lukács) should indeed be contested, but for the contestation to be thoroughgoing, it has also to accent the cultural work an Eliot or a Lukács performed in constituting European letters into a specific way of recognizing the world in language. To the extent that this "recognition" is oblivious to the reality of the non-West, and to the extent that this reality needs to be represented, Africanist literary criticism performs a specific cultural work that should not be easily dismissed as reverse-discourse. By appropriating Eliot or whomever in the service of the representation of Africa in discourse, even the most nativist versions of Africanist literary criticism may be read as instances of discursive agency, limited though they have to be. This is why this book argues for a kind of analysis that moves beyond simple rejection of reflectionist African criticism by historicizing its specificity, thereby foregrounding its datable cultural work.

Properly pursued, the logic of poststructuralist theory lies in tracing the genealogy and effects of discourses, as against simply declaring their "constructed-ness." This is as it should be, since a theoretical deconstruction of, say, nationalism does not actually wipe nationalist feelings off the pages of books and minds, still less the streets of practical labor. Consequently, if it stops at the negative moment of the deconstructive procedure, a poststructuralist approach to postcoloniality merely short-circuits its own rigor. To follow the path I have argued for is to follow Walter Benjamin's vision of historical reconstruction, expressed in the following passage:

> Where thinking suddenly stops in a configuration pregnant with tensions, it gives that configuration a shock, by which it crystallizes into a monad. A historical materialist approaches a historical subject only where he [sic] encounters it as a monad. In this structure he recognizes the sign of a Messianic cessation of happening, or, put differently, a revolutionary chance in the fight for the oppressed past. He takes cognizance of it in order to blast a specific era out of the homogenous course of history—blasting a specific life out of the era or a specific work out of the lifework. As a result of this method the lifework is preserved in this work and at the same time canceled. (262–63)

Such a mode of analysis takes Benjamin's suggestion all the way: it zeroes in on a historical phenomenon and, by means of immanent critique, preserves this specificity without inflating its purchase. What I have done in the foregoing pages is to take Anglo-American postcolonial theory, alongside a specific moment in African letters, as discursive formations—language about language—that allude to historical phenomena. Language about language can enrich our minds, sharpen our thinking, and generally make the world clearer and more livable, but it remains, in the last instance, more language.

We may use 1958, the year of the publication of *Things Fall Apart,* as the moment of the inauguration of African literature as it has come to be known in the world of formal education. We may go back a further ten years, and use instead the collection *Anthologie de la nouvelle poésie nègre et malgache de langue française* (1948). Either way, the institutional category we have come to know as "modern African literature" did not exist some fifty years ago. What this implies is that five decades or so ago, this book could not have been written—principally because its object was not a category available to theoretical attention. And yet, in this book we have been examining selected discursive engagements with reality, where Euro-America is the (largely unthematized) occasion and referent, in coeval time with similar engagements, where black Africa is the (loudly proclaimed) referent. That, at the beginning of the twenty-first century, it is possible to call a field of writings "African letters" is therefore, in itself, a testament to the view of agency this book has been defending. By confronting Anglo-American theory with the evidence of African letters and vice-versa, this book has attempted to draw attention to the gains and limitations inherent to both. I have also been concerned to show how we might proceed, as well as what we might gain, from fully theorizing the limitations, as well as the contingent benefits. In this way, the agency of African letters may ultimately be located in the fact that, alongside Anglo-American critical theory, it has made possible the book you hold in your hands.

NOTES

CHAPTER 1
ISSUES AND CONTEXT: ON KNOWLEDGE AS LIMIT

1. I borrow the phrase "body in pain" from Elaine Scarry in *The Body in Pain: The Making and Unmaking of the World.*

2. Here and in the rest of this book I use terms like "third world" or "non-Western," so it is useful to justify my use from the outset. With regard to the first, various critics have noted that, implicitly, the three-world model sets up a norm, thereby activating a hierarchical differential. In this sense, the "first world" presides as the norm in relation to which the other worlds take their place, or, in Gayatri Spivak's term, are "worlded." I agree with this observation, and part of my project is to expose the discursive logic that underwrites the three-world formula—that is, the logic of modernity and progressive modernization—thereby making visible its historicity and problematic grounding. A similar logic governs the designation "Western," posed as a homogenous category that makes sense primarily in its epistemological distance from the non-West. I shall therefore be using the oppositions "first world" and "third world," or Western/non-Western, mainly as shorthand designations.

3. Homi Bhabha, "Interrogating Identity," and Terry Eagleton, "The Politics of Subjectivity," *ICA Documents* 6 (1987): 5–11; 47–48. Portions of Bhabha's contribution appear in revised form as sections of chapter 2 of his book *The Location of Culture* (40–65). My quotations are drawn from the version that appears in *ICA Documents,* in part because Bhabha's central claims remain consistent in the book as in the earlier piece. More crucially, quoting from the original site of the dialogue enables us to encounter the substance and rhetoric of the issues as they were set out on the pages of *ICA Documents.* In other words, it is the implication of the dialogue as it was conducted on that occasion that I am interested in illustrating.

4. For a discussion of the debate around the so-called death of the subject and an account of agency along the lines I have sketched, see Kwame Anthony Appiah, "Tolerable Falsehoods: Agency and the Interests of Theory."

5. On this point, see Appiah, "Tolerable Falsehoods." According to Appiah, "Theories are, like all our products, imperfect things—we are, after all,

fallen creatures. Since we do not have perfect theories we might want to proceed with the best theories we can muster; and it may be that the best theory at some level, for some purposes, is better—for *those* purposes—than the best theory that meets this methodological demand" (78–79).

6. I have tried to use words that make our prescientific peoples overtly abstract, and my reference to their beliefs and actions as qualified as the English language allows. This is because my access to "them" as far as human sacrifice goes is based on what books say about them—books they are not likely to read and therefore cannot refute. We shall have occasion to take up the topic of human sacrifice (or ritual murder) in chapter 5.

7. See Michael Sprinker, *Imaginary Relations: Aesthetics and Ideology in the Theory of Historical Materialism.* The classic recuperation of Althusserian theory from the onslaught of poststructuralism remains Fredric Jameson's *The Political Unconscious: Narrative as a Socially Symbolic Act.* I am indebted to Jameson's reading of Althusser, as I am to his interpretive approach to literary texts. However, Jameson does not push the epistemological skepticism initiated in Althusser's famous ISAs essay, towards a critique of European imperialism in its specific epistemic (as against grandly economic, world-historical) valence. It is this direction that I am pursuing here.

8. The most famous of this kind of indictment is of course E. P. Thompson's fierce attack on Althusserianism in *The Poverty of Theory.*

9. See Louis Althusser, "Ideology and Ideological State Apparatuses (Notes Towards an Investigation)," *Lenin and Philosophy and Other Essays,* 127–86. For critical assessments of Althusserian theory framed specifically by the challenge of postmodernism, see Warren Montag, "Beyond Force and Consent: Althusser, Spinoza, Hobbes" in *Postmodern Materialism and the Future of Marxist Theory: Essays in the Althusserian Tradition,* 91–106; Stuart Hall, "Signification, Representation, and the Post-Structuralist Debates," 91–117; Alex Callinicos, "What is Living and What Is Dead in the Philosophy of Althusser," *The Althusserian Legacy,* 39–49.

10. It is worth stating that the ISA essay may in fact represent an attempt by Althusser to reformulate the dogmatic claims about "scientificity" made in the earlier texts (see Sprinker, 270–71, esp. note 5). See also Joseph Fracchia, "Dialectical Itineraries"; and Warren Montag, "Beyond Force and Consent: Althusser, Spinoza, Hobbes."

11. See Antonio Gramsci, *Selections from the Prison Notebooks,* 210–76, 323–77.

12. See Alan Sheridan's "Translator's note" to Jacques Lacan, *Écrits. A Selection.* ix–x. See also Fredric Jameson, "The Imaginary and the Symbolic in Lacan."

13. According to Jane Gallop, "the imaginary is made up of *imagoes.* An imago is an unconscious image or cliché 'which preferentially orients the way in which the subject apprehends other people.' In the imaginary mode, one's under-

standing of other people is shaped by one's own imagoes. The perceived other is actually, at least in part, a projection" (60–61). See Gallop, *Reading Lacan.*

14. Patrick Brantlinger, *Crusoe's Footprints: Cultural Studies in Britain and America,* 92.

15. By stressing Althusser's turn to Lacan, my aim is to underline the conceptual struggle it dramatizes, not to suggest that Lacanian psychoanalysis is compatible with dialectical materialism. Spivak insists that the turn to Lacan only gets Althusser into trouble partly because the Lacanian apparatus derives from a gendered frame. In "Althusser's Marx, Althusser's Lacan," Michèle Barrett concludes that "although he used some Lacanian ideas in thinking about ideology and 'the subject,' Althusser remained completely unaffected by them in going about his usual theoretical business as a Marxist" (172). This, then, is a case of what we might call strong misreading. Althusser misreads the full dimension of the Lacanian "Real," and thereby achieves what I am here claiming for it: a simultaneous negation and affirmation of critical knowledge, a redirected elaboration of the story of human agency in the production of knowledge and the creation of culture.

16. Ernesto Laclau elaborates the theory of radical democracy further in *New Reflections on the Revolution of our Time,* 3–85.

17. In Gramsci's thinking, according to Laclau and Mouffe, "even though the social elements have a merely relational identity—achieved through articulatory practices—there must always be a single unifying principle in every hegemonic formation, and this can only be a fundamental class. Thus two principles of the social order—the unicity of the unifying principle and its necessary class character—are not the contingent result of hegemonic struggle, but the necessary structural framework within which every struggle occurs" (69).

18. This is the second level, the level of practice or materialization. On the implications of this claim for gendered and sexed identity, see Judith Butler, *Bodies That Matter.*

19. It is on this point that I have to differ slightly from Neil Lazarus in his timely and rich book, *Nationalism and Cultural Practice in the Postcolonial World.* Lazarus contends that "it has today become possible *for the first time since the field was instituted in the early 1980s,* for Marxist scholars to engage postcolonial studies on its own ground. It has today become possible, that is, for Marxist scholars to *oblige* the field to tilt in the direction they favor" (15, emphases in original). I agree with this sentiment, although I am not sure that the label "Marxist scholars" clarifies much. Gayatri Spivak identifies herself as a Marxist theorist, and yet she is one of the objects of Lazarus's critique (obviously because of the heavy Derridian filter with which she approaches Marxist insights). Even the work of Ernesto Laclau and Chantal Mouffe, who explicitly claim a post-Marxist orientation, is unthinkable outside the tradition of Western Marxism. It may well be that not everyone who claims to be a "Marxist scholar" actually thinks like one, in which case the label as used by Lazarus does

indeed clarify more than I am able to see or grant. But this is ultimately a minor issue. The substantive point on which I differ from Lazarus involves the relative weight he gives to poststructuralist postcolonial theory vis-à-vis, say, Habermas. He takes issue with poststructuralist antirealism, arguing that this component of postcolonial theory leads it to reject nationalism too hastily. Lazarus is persuasive in arguing that postcolonial theory should be less doctrinaire in the way it treats nationalist discourses. As I have argued so far, a blanket rejection of nationalist discourse cannot enable adequate appreciation of African letters. However, I believe that the problem is not to be found in "antirealism" or "relativism" as epistemological positions; the problem is in how both positions are deployed. My view is that the logic of antirealism, of *méconnaissance*, can actually serve a proper appreciation of "cultural practice in the postcolonial world." For a cogent and altogether inspiring discussion of current debates in postcolonial theory, nationalism, and Marxism, see Stuart Hall, "When was 'the Postcolonial'? Thinking at the Limit."

20. See Kofi Agawu, *African Rhythm: A Northern Ewe Perspective*, 5.

CHAPTER 2
CONTEMPORARY THEORY AND THE DEMAND FOR AGENCY

1. Max Weber, *The Protestant Ethic and the Spirit of Capitalism*, trans. Talcott Parsons (New York: Charles Scribner's Sons, 1958).

2. Habermas, "Modernity's Consciousness of Time and Its Need for Self-Reassurance," *The Philosophical Discourse of Modernity*, 1–22.

3. From the extensive accumulation of accounts of the postmodern debate and the yet ongoing contest between defenders and opponents of the poststructuralist critique of modernity as discourse (or, under a different label, realist and antirealist positions in current theory), see the following, in addition to the critics and theorists discussed in the previous chapter: Appiah, *In My Father's House* 137–57; Jonathan Arac; Stephen Best; Peter Uwe Hohendahl, 131–55; Martin Jay, "Performative Contradiction."

4. Foucault, *Power/Knowledge*, ed. Colin Gordon, 112.

5. Habermas, *The Philosophical Discourse of Modernity*, 294–326.

6. Habermas, "The Entwinement of Myth and Enlightenment: Max Horkheimer and Theodor Adorno," *The Philosophical Discourse of Modernity*, 121.

7. Satya P. Mohanty's book, which was discussed in the previous chapter, also takes up the question of the Azande and their belief in unverifiable notions of causality. See Mohanty, and also Appiah, 107–36.

8. For Mohanty, the relativist position is strongest when posed in the way Winch poses it. For him as for Winch, practices are often not simply dif-

ferent but incommensurable. Where he parts ways with Winch is in his insistence that acknowledging this incommensurability should not be the culmination of our investigation; it should rather be the starting point. In other words, confronted with historical situations where two practices or systems of belief are in competition, cultural criticism should seek the conceptual equipment by means of which it is possible to evaluate them and decide which is more rational, more consistent.

9. See Hountondji, *African Philosophy: Myth and Reality.*

10. In Fabian's words, "[a] discourse employing terms such as primitive, savage (but also tribal, traditional, Third World, or whatever euphemism is current) does not think, or observe, or critically study, the "primitive"; it thinks, observes, studies *in terms* of the primitive. *Primitive* being essentially a temporal concept, is a category, not an object, of Western thought" (17–18). Fabian is of course writing of anthropological discourse about the non-West, but his observation accurately captures the underlying logic of Habermas's deployment of the Azande as textualized in Pritchard's ethnography.

11. For examples, see Appiah, *In My Father's House,* 137–57; Lazarus, *Postcolonial;* Miller, *Nomads,* esp. 171–209.

12. Lyotard, "Universal History and Cultural Differences," *The Lyotard Reader,* 314–23. See also, Immanuel Kant, "Idea for a Universal History with a Cosmopolitan Purpose," *Kant: Political Writings,* 41–53.

13. Along a similar line, see Christopher Miller's discussion of Deleuze's and Guattari's *A Thousand Plateaus,* which finds in the pair's nomadology a familiar recourse to the imperial archive. I agree with Miller that what he calls the "persistence of representation and ethnographic authority" (208) in *A Thousand Plateaus* [or, in our example, *The Postmodern Condition*] need not invalidate the insights these works otherwise provide. However, "It should . . . serve as a caution to those who would turn to nomadology [or poststructuralism in general] as a wholly 'free' and new perspective on cultural construction, as a prescription for moving 'beyond identity' (Miller 208).

14. See Robert Young, *White Mythologies: Writing History and the West.* See also Bart Moore-Gilbert; and Asha Varadharajan.

15. Jacques Derrida succinctly marks this conjuncture in "The Ends of Man," a lecture delivered in New York, in October 1968, at a colloquium on "Philosophy and Anthropology." Derrida opens the lecture by reflecting on the circumstances of the writing of the text itself, which he dates, "precisely from the month of April 1968" (114). He continues: "it will be recalled that these were the weeks of the opening of the Vietnam peace talks and of the assassination of Martin Luther King [Jr.]. A bit later, when I was typing this text, the universities of Paris were invaded by the forces of order—and for the first time at the demand of a rector—and then reoccupied by the students in the upheaval you are familiar with. . . . These circumstances appear to me to belong, by all rights, to the field and the problematic of our colloquium."

16. This inadequately contextualized rejection of talk of identity based on notions of cultural nationalism is shared by the foundational work of Edward Said. In his civic life and political commitments, Said has been an exemplary activist, and has argued for the agency of individuals and collectives to change their situation in uniquely compelling ways. But in his critical writings, he consistently argues against, and often dismisses, nativism and cultural nationalism. Instead, he favors a version of hybridity and nomadism understood here as indexes of a cosmopolitan standpoint (see for example *Culture and Imperialism,* 239–81). This is in part why his work is severely (and unconvincingly, in my opinion) attacked by Aijaz Ahmad in *In Theory.* At this level, then, the conceptual logic of Said's criticism is more poststructuralist than not, and this puts him closer to Spivak and Bhabha than, say, Aijaz Ahmad or Ngugi wa Thiong'o. As already indicated, I do not discuss Said in this chapter because he has been extensively discussed by others, and because I am primarily interested in the postcolonial theory his work generated. For detailed considerations of Said, see Young; Moore-Gilbert; and Varadharajan.

17. See Slemon et al., *After Europe;* Ashcroft et al., *The Empire Writes Back: Theory and Practice in Post-colonial Literatures;* and Adam et al., *Past The Last Post. Theorizing Post-Colonialism and Post-Modernism.* For a useful appraisal of *The Empire Writes Back,* coedited by Ashcroft, Griffiths, and Tiffin, see Vijay Mishra and Bob Hodge, "What is Post(-)colonialism?".

18. My reading of Bhabha and Spivak has benefited from Robert Young's pioneering study of their contribution to the theoretical critique of Western metaphysics. See *White Mythologies.*

19. On this point, see Young, esp. 148–49.

20. See Bhabha's foreword to the 1986 edition of Fanon's *Black Skin, White Masks:* "Remembering Fanon: Self, Psyche, and the Colonial Condition." *Black Skin, White Masks,* vii–xxvi. Revised and incorporated into the second chapter of *The Location of Culture,* 40–65.

21. In this, I agree with Gates that Fanon himself acts out a problematic, that he is "a battlefield in himself" (470). What this means, as Gates adequately puts it, is that we read Fanon "with an acknowledgement of his own historical particularity, as an actor whose own search for self-transcendence scarcely exempts him from the heterogeneous and conflictual structures that we have taken to be characteristic of colonial discourse" ("Fanonism," 470).

22. Spivak, "The Politics of Interpretations." *In Other Worlds. Essays in Cultural Politics* 118–33. She writes: "Ideology in action is what a group takes to be natural and self-evident, that of which the group, as a group, must deny any historical sedimentation. It is both the condition and the effect of the constitution of the subject (of ideology) as freely willing and consciously choosing in a world that is seen as background" (118).

23. This essay appears in revised and expanded form in her *A Critique of Postcolonial Reason: Towards a History of the Vanishing Present,* 246–311.

24. See R. Radhakrishnan, "Postcoloniality and the Boundaries of Identity" in his *Diasporic Mediations*, 155–84. In Radhakrishnan's words: "Postcoloniality at best is a problematic field where heated debates and contestations are bound to take place for quite a while to come. My point . . . is that whoever joins the polemical dialogue should do so with a critical-sensitive awareness of the legitimacies of several other perspectives on the issue. In other words, it would be quite futile and divisive in the long run for any one perspective, such as the diasporic, the indigenous, or the orthodox Marxist, to begin with the brazen assumption that it alone has the ethicopolitical right to speak representatively on 'postcoloniality.' Such an assumption can only take the form of a pedagogical arrogance that is interested more in correcting other points of view than in engaging with them in a spirit of reciprocity" (171). In a similar vein, see Stuart Hall, "When Was 'the Post-colonial'? Thinking at the Limit."

Chapter 3
The Logic of Agency in African Literary Criticism

1. The "Glossary" to *For Marx* defines the concept of a "problematic" *(problématique)* in the following way: "A word or concept cannot be considered in isolation; it only exists in the theoretical or ideological framework in which it is used: its problematic. . . . It should be stressed that the problematic is *not* a world-view. It is not the essence of the thought of an individual or epoch which can be deduced from a body of texts by an empirical, generalizing reading; it is centered on the absence of problems and concepts within the problematic as much as their presence; it can therefore be reached by a symptomatic reading . . . on the model of the Freudian analyst's reading of his patient's utterances" (253–54). Under a poststructuralist protocol of reading, of course, the notion of symptomatic reading rests on a presumption of mastery, while being blind to the power relation thus set up between the reader as analyst and the text as analysand. But an absolute rejection of symptomatic reading on the basis that it rests on an illusion of mastery is unconvincing because every act of reading is an act of attempted mastery. In this sense, Gayatri Spivak offers a plausible alternative. In an interview with Harold Veeser, she says of symptomatic readings: "the stance of the diagnostician is one in which, if it is consciously taken almost into the first step into the text, it is suspicious of love, of one's own bound place. . . . I would rather think of the text as my accomplice than my patient or my analysand (*Post-colonial Critic*, 164). See Spivak, "The New Historicism: Political Commitment and the Postmodern Critic." My discussion in this chapter begins and ends with just such a notion of "love, of one's own bound place," in relation to the continuing adventure of African letters.

2. See Abiola Irele, "African Letters: The Making of a Tradition"; Robert W. July, *An African Voice: The Role of the Humanities in African Independence*; V. Y. Mudimbe, *The Invention of Africa*.

3. It is worth noting that Isaka Seme later became the founding president of the South African Native National Congress (later the African National Congress) when the Congress was formed in 1912. For a short but informative account of Isaka Seme's biography and his stint in the United States, see Richard Rive and Tim Couzens eds., *Seme: The Founder of the ANC.*

4. On Foucault's concept of the "author function," see "What is an Author?" *The Foucault Reader,* 101–20.

5. For retrospective engagements, from various disciplinary perspectives, with the conditions of possibility, achievements, and consequences of *Présence Africaine* forty years after its founding, see the essays collected in V. Y. Mudimbe's edited collection, *The Surreptitious Speech.* Présence Africaine *and the Politics of Otherness 1947–1987.*

6. For discussions of the critique of ethnophilosophy, see Appiah, *In My Father's House,* 85–106; Denis Ekpo, "Towards a post-Africanism: Contemporary African Thought and Postmodernism"; Abiola Irele, "Introduction," *African Philosophy: Myth and Reality,* 7–30; D. A. Masolo, *African Philosophy In Search of Identity,* 194–212.

7. On the complex social and epistemological underpinnings of Leavisite criticism in Britain and the New Criticism in the United States, see Francis Mulhern, John Guillory 134–75, and Mary Poovey. Both Guillory and Poovey show that the significant transformations that current theory has brought onto literary studies should not blind us to the fact that the teaching of literature in the United States as we begin a new century remains indebted to the New Criticism in many ways. After the advent of theory, cultural studies, and now postcolonial theory, the new-critical regime of ordering knowledge in matters of literature remains hard to throw out the window. Perhaps this is because one cannot (except in theory) "throw" cultural formations "out the window": one can only reorganize and reorient them in preferable directions. In our terms, this would be agency in motion.

8. Peter Benson's Black Orpheus, Transition, *and Modern Cultural Awakening in Africa* (1986) provides an account of the temper of the ferment I am indicating by tracing the history of *Black Orpheus* and *Transition,* two other magazines that, as he puts it, "were at the center of much that happened intellectually and culturally in anglophone black Africa during the period from the late fifties to the late seventies" (ix).

9. Appiah, *In My Father's House,* 47–72. For a sampling of the debate that the nativism of *Toward the Decolonization of African Literature* generated, see Wole Soyinka, "Aesthetic Illusions: Prescriptions for the Suicide of Poetry" and "Neo-Tarzanism: The Poetics of Pseudo-Tradition," *Art, Dialogue, and Outrage;* and E. Palmer, "Chinweizu et. al. and the Evaluation of African Literature."

10. Peter Uwe Hohendahl provides a lucid assessment of the debate between Lukács and the Frankfurt School on the subject of realism in "Art Work

and Modernity: The Legacy of Georg Lukács," *Reappraisals. Shifting Alignments in Postwar Critical Theory,* 53–74.

11. Homi Bhabha's critique of what he calls image-analysis—a category into which Onoge's and Ngugi's prescription easily fits—is therefore appropriate: "The demand that one image should circulate rather than another is made on the basis that the stereotype is distorted in relation to a given norm or model. It results in a mode of prescriptive criticism . . . because it privileges an ideal 'dream image' in relation to which the text is judged. The only knowledge such a procedure can give is one of negative difference because the only demand it can make is that the text be other than itself" ("Representation," 105).

12. For a nuanced elaboration of, and critical engagement with, Ngugi's position on language, see Simon Gikandi, "Ngugi's Conversion: Writing and the Politics of Language"; see also Alamin Mazrui, "Relativism, Universalism, and the Language of African Literature."

13. See Philips, *The Enigma of Colonialism,* and Mamdani, *Citizen and Subject: Contemporary Africa and the Legacy of Late Colonialism.*

14. Adorno, "The Essay as Form," *Notes To Literature Vol. One,* 10.

Chapter 4
D. O. Fagunwa as Compound of Spells

1. On this view, modernity is understood in its tripartite Kantian sense, that is, as a problematic that encompasses domains of the aesthetic, the practical, and the theoretical. See our discussion of Habermas in chapter 2.

2. The specific edition I shall be quoting from here is the American edition, published by Random House in 1982. The Yoruba edition of *Ògbójú Ọdẹ Nínú Igbó Irúnmalè* is the revised one, published in 1983.

3. See *Igbó Olódùmarè; Ìrèké Oníbùdó; Ìrìnkèrindò Nínú Igbó Elégbèje; Àdììtú Olódùmarè; Àsànyàn Ìtàn* (1959); *Ìrìnàjò Apá Kiní* (1949), and *Ìrìnàjò Apá Kejì. London Ìlú Ọba* (1951). I have supplied tonal accents where the original publication does not have them. The issue of orthography and diacritical marks in written Yoruba is an ongoing one that scholars of the language are still tackling. Thus, for instance, the revised edition of *Ògbójú Ọdẹ Nínú Igbó Irúnmalè* published in 1983 modifies and extends the range of diacritical marks that Fagunwa himself adopted in the original. The back cover of the revised edition acknowledges this supplementation of the original text, explaining that the revision is meant to make the prose smoother and more readable than the author could have achieved, given the specific problems of written Yoruba language when Fagunwa was writing. Fagunwa himself reflects upon the problem of inadequate diacritical marking and the challenge this poses for authors of written Yoruba in his preface *(Òrò Ìsíwájú)* to the short story collection *Àsànyàn Ìtàn.* He uses the preface to issue a challenge for future work: "There is one thing that

nobody will accept with regard to written Yoruba: it is that the diacritical marks
on words be inadequate, as this makes the prose unreadable. The word 'come'
[wá] has about eight or ten meanings depending on whether it is pronounced
with a high tone or a low one. And yet these diacritical marks are often inadequately understood by many who write in the language. This is a limitation that
needs to be looked into. Our people should intensify their efforts [E múra si,
ẹnyin ènìa wa]." To my knowledge, this book has not been translated. That
Fagunwa's texts do not simply *reflect* the state of written Yoruba in the first half
the twentieth century, but also *participate* in codifying and extending the language, is borne out by the fact that his texts are cited by R. C. Abraham as
sources for his limited but important *Dictionary of Modern Yoruba* (See Abraham, viii). What all of this indicates is that the reduction of the Yoruba language
to print is still an ongoing project.

4. See Wale Ogunyemi, *Langbodo*.

5. MS 326709, School of Oriental and African Studies Library, London.
Based on a letter, dated February 1, 1979, in the file containing this manuscript,
it appears that Fagunwa's family members are aware of its existence. For more
on this manuscript, see Bernth Lindfors, *Long Drums and Canons*, 153.

6. See Wolfgang Iser, *The Implied Reader: Patterns of Communication in
Prose Fiction from Bunyan to Beckett*, 274–94.

7. For discussions of Fagunwa's negotiation of orality in a context where
literacy and print culture hold political as well as epistemological hegemony, see
Adeleke Adeeko; Pamela J. Smith, "Fabulation"; Irele, 174–97, Molara
Ogundipe-Leslie; and Wilkinson.

8. Quoted in Abiola Irele, *Ideology*, 181. The translation is Irele's.

9. For examples, see E. A. Ayandele, *The Missionary Impact on Modern
Nigeria 1842–1914;* and Philip S. Zachernuk, *Colonial Subjects: An African
Intelligentsia and Atlantic Ideas.*

10. For a recent treatment of Johnson's representational milieu, see the
essays collected in *Pioneer, Patriot and Patriarch: Samuel Johnson and the
Yoruba People*, edited by Toyin Falola. For a literary-critical study of the generation that immediately precedes and includes Johnson, see Michael J. C.
Echeruo, *Victorian Lagos: Aspects of Nineteenth Century Lagos Life*. For a discussion of Johnson's book as an instance of cultural production and invention
(rather than unmediated historical chronicle) see Ato Quayson, *Strategic Transformations in Nigerian Writing*, 20–43.

11. See W. E. B. Du Bois, "The Talented Tenth," *Writings*, 842–61.

12. See Homi Bhabha, "Signs Taken for Wonders: Questions of Ambivalence and Authority Under a Tree Outside Delhi, May 1817." *The Location of
Culture*, 102–22.

13. There is of course a lot of truth to Murby's claim. The scholar of
Yoruba language and literature, Ayo Bamgbose, has traced in detail the influ-

ences discernible in Fagunwa's work, finding in it resonances of Homer, Spenser, Bunyan, and Milton—specifically, *Paradise Lost*. Nonetheless, as Bamgbose's findings also show, there is more to Fagunwa than the trace of his Western influences—biblical or literary. It is this "more" that I am attempting to think through. See Bamgbose, The *Novels of D. O. Fagunwa*. See also Fagunwa's articles in Nigerian newspapers, reproduced and analyzed by Bernth Lindfors in *Long Drums and Canons*, 89–99.

14. Even a cursory look at the plot of *The Palm-wine Drinkard* makes this clear. The plot involves an unnamed first-person narrator who, when we first meet him, prides himself on his extreme self-indulgence and addiction to alcohol. The hero's drinking was such that his wealthy father employed a special palm-wine tapper to procure the beverage for the narrator on a daily basis. The novel begins with the death of the protagonist's father and the tapper. Faced with the death of both, the protagonist decides to go to the "dead's town" in search of his palm-wine tapper. His adventures in the course of his search are presented in an episodic progression. When he finally locates the tapper, the hero is unable to return with him. Instead, the tapper gives the hero a magical egg that makes it possible for him to conjure up whatever he desires. This precious gift thereafter enables the hero to become very rich and, ultimately, to save his community from famine. The fantastic adventures recounted in the novel, then, conform to a basic generic scheme associated with the quest motif as deployed by Fagunwa: the protagonist successfully undergoes an epic journey, but his success is of a dimension altogether different from his original intentions.

15. See Parrinder's foreword to *My Life in the Bush of Ghosts*, 9–15. For samples of the critical reception of Amos Tutuola, see *Critical Perspectives on Amos Tutuola*, edited by Bernth Lindfors. For a discussion of the debate that surrounded Tutuola's novels in the 1950s, see Oyekan Owomoyela, *Amos Tutuola Revisited*.

16. It is this aspect of the novel that Chinua Achebe has in mind when, in a famous reading of *The Palm-wine Drinkard,* he writes: "The reader may, of course, be so taken with Tutuola's vigorous and unusual prose or beguiled by that felicitous coinage 'drinkard,' that he misses the social and ethical question being proposed: What happens when a man immerses himself in pleasure to the exclusion of all work; when he raises pleasure to the status of work and occupation and says in effect 'Pleasure be thou my work!'? *The Palm-wine Drinkard* is a rich and spectacular exploration of this gross perversion, its expiation through appropriate punishment and the offender's final restoration" (*Hopes,* 102).

17. On this point, see Echeruo; and Zachernuk.

18. See Mahmood Mamdani, *Citizen and Subject: Contemporary Africa and the Legacy of Late Colonialism,* on the divide between the rural and the urban in modern African societies.

19. As Molara Ogundipe-Leslie has argued, it is this figure that is incarnated in the fictional narrator to whom Akara-ogun relates his adventures in

Forest. See Ogundipe-Leslie. The awe of writing is famously dramatized by Ezeulu in Achebe's *Arrow of God,* when he urges his son Oduche to master the magic of writing so thoroughly that "if you are suddenly woken up from sleep and asked what it is you will reply. You must learn it until you can write it with your left hand" (*Arrow of God,* 189). I discuss the dynamic of fathers instructing their sons and urging their accession to modernity in the next chapter.

20. See Dan Izevbaye, "Elesin's Homecoming: The Translation of *The King's Horseman.*"

Chapter 5
Wole Soyinka and the Challenge of Transition

1. See for example Ketu H. Katrak, *Wole Soyinka and Modern Tragedy,* and Ato Quayson, *Strategic Transformations in Nigerian Writing,* 65–100.

2. For example, see Soyinka's debates with the authors of *Toward the Decolonization of African Literature,* in *Art, Dialogue, and Outrage,* 86–109, 315–29. For a sampling of the criticism that Soyinka's mythopoeisis has generated, see the following: James Booth, "Self-Sacrifice and Human Sacrifice in Soyinka's *Death and the King's Horseman*"; Geoffrey Hunt, "Two African Aesthetics: Wole Soyinka vs. Amilcar Cabral," *Marxism and African Literature,* 64–93. For Soyinka's response to his critics, see *Art, Dialogue, and Outrage,* 110–31, 146–78, 279–314. For a review of the debate, see Gareth Griffiths and David Moody, "Of Marx and Missionaries: Soyinka and the Survival of Universalism in Post-Colonial Theory," *After Europe,* 74–85; and Tejumola Olaniyan, *Scars of Conquest/Masks of Resistance,* 43–66.

3. See *Myth, Literature, and the African World,* 1–60, 140–60. "The Fourth Stage" is reprinted in *Art, Dialogue, and Outrage,* 21–34. For an account of the myth of Orisa-nla that is similar to Soyinka's, see Bolaji Idowu, *Olodumare: God in Yoruba Belief,* 55–57, 70–74. Idowu's interest is primarily ethnographic and theological; as such, he does not draw the philosophical and artistic implications that Soyinka draws from the myth.

4. See Soyinka, "Author's Note," *Horseman.*

5. "Author's Note." For an account of the "real story" on which the play is based, see James Gibbs, *Wole Soyinka,* 117–18. According to Gibbs, the incident happened in January, 1945, not 1946 as Soyinka's preface suggests.

6. See Dan Izevbaye, "Mediation in Soyinka: The Case of the King's Horseman."

7. Henry Louis Gates Jr. provides a formalist/Aristotelean reading of the play and of Soyinka's art in general in "Being, the Will, and the Semantics of Death," *Harvard Educational Review.* See also Izevbaye, "Mediation."

8. Chinua Achebe's *Things Fall Apart* provides what is perhaps the most well-known literary use of the mask motif in the figure of "Evil Forest." See

chapters 10 and 22 of the novel. I discuss Achebe's use of the mask motif in some detail in a later section of this chapter.

9. I borrow the phrase "mask-in-motion" from H. L. Gates Jr. See *Figures in Black. Words, Signs, and the "Racial" Self*, 167–95. Here is the relevant passage: "The Western concept of mask is meaningless to, say, the Yoruba, precisely because the doll in wood cannot of itself signify. Once in motion, once the signification is effected, the misnomer 'mask' becomes 'mask-in-motion,' or what 'mask' itself implies to theYoruba. Mask becomes functional—indeed, becomes—only in motion" (168).

10. On the *egungun* tradition among the Yoruba, see Bolaji Idowu, 204–9.

11. For Pinnock's own account of this incident, see *The Romance of Missions in Nigeria* (1917), 81–84. I refer to this incident simply to buttress the suggestion that the institution of royalty was, at the time dramatized in Soyinka's play, no longer "pristine," if this is understood to mean utterly alienated from or opposed to British colonial presence. For a contemporary reaction to King Ladigbolu's political and cultural legacy, one that is in line with Atanda's analysis, see the article written by Obafemi Awolowo in response to Ladigbolu's passing, "Siyanbola, Alafin of Oyo: The King and the Man." For a discussion of Awolowo's article as evidence of the power jockeying that was taking place between the traditional aristocratic system and the educated elite composed of politicians and nationalists like Awolowo, see Atanda, especially chapters 6 and 7. See also, Dan Izevbaye, "Elesin's Homecoming."

12. The incident itself inspired a historical play, entitled *Kurunmi*, by another Nigerian playwright, Ola Rotimi.

13. See Soyinka, "Director's Notes." Production file of *Death and King's Horseman*, The Goodman Theater, Chicago.

14. Appiah is correct that talk of "an African world" is a discursive invention, subsisting finally only on the strength of desire. His critique of an essentialized "African world" joins those of Paulin Hountondji and V. Y. Mudimbe that we touched on in chapter 3. My point is specifically that although Appiah's critique of Soyinka's essentialism is valid, his reading of *Death and the King's Horseman* does not draw out as comprehensive a theoretical lesson as the play makes available. As I have argued at various points so far, a complex text cannot simply bear out the writer's sentiments without irruptions. Thus, a play like *Horseman* says many things that Soyinka the theorist of culture wants it to say, but it also says more that the playwright may not have intended—in this way, as our reading has shown, the play's intrinsic contents offer a critique of an essentialized and unitary African identity.

15. The phrase comes from Bill Ashcroft et al.'s *The Empire Writes Back: Theory and Practice in Post-colonial Literatures*.

16. Legitimately, some commentators have drawn attention to the gendered undercurrent of Soyinka's positing of the lone figure as custodian of the cosmic fate of an entire community. Florence Stratton, for instance, has shown

that not only the esteemed protagonists of Soyinka's mythology but also the notion of social redemptiveness he presents as specifically African, rest on a masculinist gender system. Another illustration of this tendency is the sexualization of cultural change that lies at the heart of *The Lion and the Jewel*. Lakunle's and Baroka's competition for Sidi is posed as metaphor for the relative promise of two different attitudes to change. Soyinka thus relies on an ancient motif, wherein womanhood symbolizes culture because it is posed as the site of a contest between two suitors (who represent rival cultural alternatives). In this sense, Sidi is not the active initiator of dramatic action, but the ground around which the action proceeds. See Stratton, "Wole Soyinka: A Writer's Social Vision." See also Carole Boyce Davies, "Maidens, Mistresses and Matrons," 75–88.

17. The editions I will be quoting from are the following: *Things Fall Apart* (New York: Doubleday, 1976); *Arrow of God* (New York: Doubleday, 1969); *No Longer at Ease* (New York: Doubleday, 1994).

18. For examples, see the following: Michael Valdez Moses, *The Novel and the Globalization of Culture*, 107–47; Simon Gikandi, *Reading Chinua Achebe: Language and Ideology in Fiction*; C. L. Innes, *Chinua Achebe*; Robert M. Wren, *Achebe's World: The Historical and Cultural Context of the Novels*.

19. Mahmood Mamdani, *Citizen and Subject. Contemporary Africa and the Legacy of Late colonialism*.

20. See Wren, *Achebe's World: The Historical and Cultural Context of the Novels*. Achebe confirms this in the preface he wrote to *The African Trilogy* (London: Picador, 1988), a collection of *Things Fall Apart, No Longer at Ease,* and *Arrow of God* in a single compact volume.

21. See Gikandi, *Reading Chinua Achebe*; Rhonda Cobham, "Making Men and History: Achebe and the Politics of Revisionism," *Approaches to Teaching Achebe's* Things Fall Apart, 91–100.

22. Fredric Jameson, "Third-World Literature in the Era of Multinational Capitalism," 68.

23. See Appiah, "The Postcolonial and the Postmodern." *In My Father's House,* 145.

24. On this point, see Cobham n. 21. See also her essay on Nuruddin Farah, "Misgendering the Nation: African Nationalist Fictions and Nuruddin Farah's *Maps*," 42–59.

EPILOGUE

1. See Paulin Hountondji, "Recapturing," and "Scientific Dependence in Africa Today."

WORKS CITED

Abraham, R. C. *Dictionary of Modern Yoruba*. London: U. of London Press, 1958.

Achebe, Chinua. *Anthills of the Savannah*. New York: Doubleday, 1987.

———. *Arrow of God*. New York: Doubleday, 1989.

———. *No Longer at Ease*. New York: Doubleday, 1994.

———. *The African Trilogy*. London: Picador, 1988.

———. *Hopes and Impediments: Selected Essays*. New York: Doubleday, 1989.

———. *Things Fall Apart*. New York: Doubleday, 1994.

Adam, Ian, and Helen Tiffin eds. *Past the Last Post: Theorizing Post-Colonialism and Post-Modernism*. Calgary: U. of Calgary Press, 1990.

Adeeko, Adeleke. "Rethinking Orality and Literacy in African Literary History: The Fiction of D. O. Fagunwa." *Pretexts: Studies in Writing and Culture* 6.1 (July 1997): 35–51.

Adorno, Theodor W. *Negative Dialectics*. Trans. E. B. Ashton. New York: Continuum, 1987.

———. "The Essay as Form." *Notes to Literature Volume One*. Trans. Shierry Weber Nicholsen. New York: Columbia UP, 1991.

African Literature Today 1 (1968): 1–2.

Agawu, Kofi. *African Rhythm: A Northern Ewe Perspective*. Cambridge UP, 1995.

Ahmad, Aijaz. *In Theory: Classes, Nations, Literatures*. London and New York: Verso, 1992.

Ajayi, J. F. A. "Bishop Crowther: An Assessment." *Odu* 4 (October 1970): 3–17.

Althusser, Louis. *For Marx*. Trans. Ben Brewster. London and New York, 1990.

———. *Lenin and Philosophy and Other Essays*. Trans. Ben Brewster. New York: Monthly Review Press, 1971.

Andrade, Susan Z. "The Joys of Daughterhood: Gender, Nationalism, and the Making of Literary Tradition(s)." *Cultural Institutions of the Novel.* Eds. Deidre Lynch and William B. Warner. Durham and London: Duke UP, 1996. 249–75.

Appiah, Kwame Anthony. *In My Father's House: Essays in the Philosophy of Culture.* Oxford: Oxford UP, 1992.

———. "Tolerable Falsehoods: Agency and the Interests of Theory." *Consequences of Theory.* Eds. Jonathan Arac and Barbara Johnson. Baltimore and London: Johns Hopkins UP, 1991. 63–90.

Arac, Jonathan. "Introduction." *Postmodernism and Politics.* Ed. Jonathan Arac. Minneapolis: U. of Minnesota Press, 1986. ix–xliii.

Ashcroft, Bill, Gareth Griffiths, and Helen Tiffin eds. *The Empire Writes Back: Theory and Practice in Post-colonial Literatures.* London and New York: Routledge, 1989.

Atanda, J. A. *The New Oyo Empire: Indirect Rule and Change in Western Nigeria, 1894–1934.* London: Longman Group Ltd., 1973.

Awolowo, Obafemi. "Siyanbola, Alafin of Oyo: The King and the Man." *West Africa* 3 March 1945: 183.

Ayandele, E. A. *The Missionary Impact on Modern Nigeria 1842–1914.* New York: Humanities Press, 1967.

Bamgbose, Ayo. *The Novels of D. O. Fagunwa.* Benin City, Nigeria: Ethiope, 1974.

———. "Yoruba Studies Today." *Odu* 1 (April 1969): 85–100.

Barrett, Michèle. "Althusser's Marx, Althusser's Lacan." *The Althusserian Legacy.* Eds. E. Ann Kaplan and Michael Sprinker. London and New York: Verso, 1993. 169–82.

Behler, Ernst. *Irony and the Discourse of Modernity.* Seattle and London: U. of Washington Press, 1990.

Benjamin, Walter. "Theses on the Philosophy of History." *Illuminations.* Ed. Hannah Arendt, Trans. Harry Zohn. New York: Schocken Books, 1969. 253–64.

Benson, Peter. *Black Orpheus, Transition, and Modern Cultural Awakening in Africa.* Berkeley: U. of California Press, 1986.

Best, Steven. *The Politics of Historical Vision: Marx, Foucault, Habermas.* New York and London: The Guilford Press, 1995.

Bhabha, Homi K. "Foreword: Remembering Fanon. Self, Psyche, and the Colonial Condition." *Black Skin, White Masks.* By Frantz Fanon. Trans. Charles Lam Markmann. London and Sydney: Pluto Press, 1986. vii–xxvi.

———. "Interrogating Identity." *ICA Documents* 6 (1987): 5–11.

————. "Representation and the Colonial Text: A Critical Exploration of Some Forms of Mimeticism." *The Theory of Reading*. Ed. Frank Gloversmith. New Jersey: Barnes & Noble Books, 1984. 93–122.

————. *The Location of Culture*. London: Routledge, 1994.

Booth, James. "Self-Sacrifice and Human Sacrifice in Soyinka's *Death and the King's Horseman*." *Research in African Literatures* 19.4 (Winter 1988): 529–50.

Brantlinger, Patrick. *Crusoe's Footprints: Cultural Studies in Britain and America*. London and New York: Routledge, 1990.

Callinicos, Alex. "What is Living and What is Dead in the Philosophy of Althusser." *The Althusserian Legacy*. Eds. E. Ann Kaplan and Michael Sprinker. London and New York: Verso, 1993. 39–49.

Chinweizu. "Towards a Liberated African Culture." *Contemporary African Literature*. Eds. Edris Makward and Leslie Lacy. New York: Random House, 1972. 403–17.

Chinweizu et al. *Toward the Decolonization of African Literature*. Washington D. C.: Howard UP, 1983.

Cobham, Rhonda. "Making Men and History: Achebe and the Politics of Revisionism." *Approaches to Teaching Achebe's Things Fall Apart*. Ed. Bernth Lindfors. New York: MLA, 1991. 91–100.

————. "Misgendering the Nation: African Nationalist Fictions and Nuruddin Farah's *Maps*." *Nationalisms and Sexualities*. Eds. Andrew Parker et al. New York and London: Routledge, 1992. 42–59.

Conrad, Joseph. *Heart of Darkness*. Ed. Robert Kimbrough. New York and London: W. W. Norton, 1988.

Curtin, Philip D. *The Image of Africa Volume 2: British Ideas and Action, 1780–1850*. Madison: U. of Wisconsin Press, 1964.

Davies, Carole Boyce. "Maidens, Mistresses and Matrons: Feminine Images in Selected Soyinka Works." *Ngambika: Studies of Women in African Literature*. Eds. Carole Boyce Davies and Anne Adams Graves. Trenton, NJ: Africa World Press, 1986. 75–88.

Derrida, Jacques. "The Ends of Man." *Margins of Philosophy*. Trans. Alan Bass. Chicago: U. of Chicago Press, 1982. 109–36.

Diop, Alioune. "The Spirit of 'Présence Africaine.'" *The Proceedings of the First International Congress of Africanists*. Eds. Lalage Bown and Michael Crowther. Evanston: Northwestern UP, 1964. 46–51.

Du Bois, W. E. B. "The Talented Tenth." *Writings*. Ed. Nathan Huggins. New York: The Library of America, 1996. 842–61.

duCille, Ann. "Discourse and Dat Course: Postcoloniality and Afrocentricity." *Skin Trade*. Cambridge, MA: Harvard UP, 1996. 120–35.

Eagleton, Terry. "The Politics of Subjectivity." *ICA Documents* 6 (1987): 47–48.

Echeruo, M. J. C. *Victorian Lagos: Aspects of Nineteenth-Century Lagos Life.* London: Macmillan, 1977.

Ekpo, Denis. "Towards a Post-Africanism: Contemporary African Thought and Postmodernism." *Textual Practice* 9.1 (1995): 121–35.

Eliot, T. S. "The Metaphysical Poets." *English Critical Texts: 16th Century to 20th Century.* Eds. D. J. Enright and Ernst De Chickera. London: Oxford UP, 1962. 293–301.

———. "Tradition and the Individual Talent." *English Critical Texts: 16th Century to 20th Century.* 302–11.

Fabian, Johannes. *Time and the Other: How Anthropology Makes Its Object.* New York: Columbia UP, 1983.

Fagunwa, D. O. *Àdììtú Olódùmarè.* Apapa, Lagos: Nelson (Nigeria) Ltd., 1961.

———, ed. *Àṣàyàn Ìtàn.* London: Nelson, 1959.

———. *Expedition to the Mount of Thought.* Trans. Dapo Adeniyi. Ile-Ife, Nigeria: Obafemi Awolowo UP, 1994.

———. *The Forest of a Thousand Daemons.* Trans. Wole Soyinka. New York: Random House, 1982.

———. *Ìrìnàjò Apá Kejì. London Ìlú Ọba.* London: Oxford UP, 1951

———. *Ìrìnàjò Apá Kiní.* London: Oxford UP, 1949.

———. *Igbó Olódùmarè* rev. ed. Walton-on-Thames, Surrey: Nelson, 1982.

———. *Ìrèké-Oníbùdó* rev. ed. Walton-on-Thames, Surrey: Nelson, 1982.

———. *Ìrìnkèrindò Nínú Igbó Elégbèje.* London: Nelson, 1954.

———. "The Mysterious Plan of the Almighty." Typescript. MS 326709. School of Oriental and African Studies, London.

———. *Ògbójú Ọdẹ Nínú Igbó Irúnmalè* rev. ed. Walton-on-Thames, Surrey: Nelson, 1983.

Falola, Toyin, ed. *Pioneer, Patriot and Patriarch: Samuel Johnson and the Yoruba People.* African Studies Program, U of Wisconsin-Madison, 1993.

Foucault, Michel. *The Order of Things: An Archaeology of the Human Sciences.* New York: Vintage, 1973.

———. "Truth and Power." *Power/Knowledge.* Ed. Colin Gordon. New York: Pantheon Books, 1980. 109–33.

———. "What is an Author?" *The Foucault Reader.* Ed. Paul Rabinow. New York: Pantheon Books, 1984. 101–20.

Fracchia, Joseph. "Dialectical Itineraries." *History and Theory* 38.2(1999): 169–97.

Gallop, Jane. *Reading Lacan.* Ithaca, London: Cornell UP, 1985.

Gandhi, Leela. *Postcolonial Theory: A Critical Introduction*. New York: Columbia UP, 1998.

Gates, Henry Louis Jr. "Being, the Will, and the Semantics of Death." *Harvard Educational Review* 51.1(1981): 163–73.

———. "Critical Fanonism." *Critical Inquiry* 17 (Spring 1991): 457–70.

———. *Figures in Black: Words, Signs, and the "Racial" Self*. New York: Oxford UP, 1987.

———. "The Masters Pieces: On Canon Formation and the African-American Tradition." *The Bounds of Race*. Ed. Dominic LaCapra. Ithaca and London: Cornell UP, 1991. 17–38.

Gérard, Albert, ed. *European-Language Writing in Sub-Saharan Africa*. (2 vols.) Budapest: Akadémiai Kiadó, 1986.

Gibbs, James. *Wole Soyinka*. London: Macmillan, 1986.

Gikandi, Simon. *Reading Chinua Achebe: Language and Ideology in Fiction*. London: James Currey, 1991.

———. "Ngugi's Conversion: Writing and the Politics of Language." *Research in African Literatures* 23.1 (Spring 1992): 131–44.

Gramsci, Antonio. *Selections from the Prison Notebooks*. Ed. & Trans. Quintin Hoare and Geoffrey Nowell Smith. New York: International Publishers, 1971.

Griffiths, Gareth and David Moody. "Of Marx and Missionaries: Soyinka and the Survival of Universalism in Post-Colonial Literary Theory." *After Europe: Critical Theory and Post-colonial Writing*. Eds. Bill Ashcroft and Helen Tiffin. Sydney: Dangaroo Press, 1989. 74–85.

Guillory, John. *Cultural Capital: The Problem of Literary Canon Formation*. Chicago and London: U. of Chicago Press, 1993.

Habermas, Jürgen. "Modernity—An Incomplete Project." *The Anti-Aesthetic: Essays on Postmodern Culture*. Ed. Hal Foster. Port Townsend, WA: Bay Press, 1983. 3–15.

———. *The Philosophical Discourse of Modernity: Twelve Lectures*. Trans. Frederick Lawrence. Cambridge, MA: MIT Press, 1987.

———. *The Theory of Communicative Action. Volume 1: Reason and the Rationalization of Society*. Trans. Thomas McCarthy. Boston: Beacon Press, 1984.

Hall, Stuart. "Signification, Representation, Ideology: Althusser and the Post-Structuralist Debates." *Critical Studies in Mass Communication* 2.2 (June 1985): 91–114.

———. "When Was the 'Post-colonial'? Thinking at the Limit." *The Post-Colonial Question: Common Skies, Divided Horizons*. Eds. Iain Chambers and Lidia Curti. London and New York: Routledge, 1996. 242–60.

Hohendahl, Peter Uwe. *Reappraisals: Shifting Alignments in Postwar Critical Theory*. Ithaca and London: Cornell UP, 1991.

Hountondji, Paulin J. *African Philosophy: Myth and Reality*. Trans. Henri Evans and John Rée. Bloomington and Indianapolis: Indiana UP, 1983.

——. "Recapturing." *The Surreptitious Speech: Présence Africaine and the Politics of Otherness 1947–1987*. Ed. V. Y. Mudimbe. Chicago: U. of Chicago Press, 1992. 238–48.

——. "Scientific Dependence in Africa Today." *Research in African Literatures* 21.3 (Fall 1990): 5–15.

Hunt, Geoffrey. "Two African Aesthetics: Wole Soyinka vs. Amilcar Cabral." *Marxism and African Literature*. Ed. Georg M. Gugelberger. Trenton, NJ: Africa World Press, 1985. 64–93.

Idowu, Bolaji. *Olodumare. God in Yoruba Belief*. 2nd ed. New York: Original Publications, 1994.

Innes, C. L. *Chinua Achebe*. Cambridge, England and New York: Cambridge UP, 1990.

Irele, Abiola. "African Letters: The Making of a Tradition." *The Yale Journal of Criticism* 5.1 (Fall 1991): 69–100.

——. "Introduction." *African Philosophy: Myth and Reality*. 7–30.

——. *The African Experience in Literature and Ideology*. 1981. Bloomington, Indianapolis: Indiana UP, 1990.

Iser, Wolfgang. *The Implied Reader*. Baltimore and London: John Hopkins UP, 1974.

Izevbaye, Dan. "Elesin's Homecoming: The Translation of the King's Horseman." *Research in African Literatures* 28.2 (Summer 1997): 154–70.

——. "Mediation in Soyinka: The Case of the King's Horseman." *Critical Perspectives on Wole Soyinka*. Ed. James Gibbs. Washington, D.C.: Three Continents Press, 1980. 116–25.

Jameson, Fredric. "Imaginary and Symbolic in Lacan." *The Ideologies of Theory: Volume 1*. Minneapolis: U. of Minnesota Press, 1988. 75–115.

——. *The Political Unconscious: Narrative as a Socially Symbolic Act*. Ithaca: Cornell UP, 1981.

——. "Third-World Literature in the Era of Multinational Capitalism." *Social Text* (Fall 1986): 65–88.

Jay, Martin. "The Debate over Performative Contradiction: Habermas versus the Poststructuralists." *Philosophical Interventions in the Unfinished Project of Enlightenment*. Eds. Axel Honneth et al. Cambridge, MA: MIT Press, 1992. 261–79.

Jeyifo, Biodun. "The Nature of Things: Arrested Decolonization and Critical Theory." *Research in African Literatures* 21.1 (Spring 1990): 33–48.

Johnson, Samuel. *The History of the Yorubas*. 1921. Lagos: C.M.S. Bookshop, 1957.

July, Robert W. *An African Voice: The Role of the Humanities in African Independence*. Durham: Duke UP, 1987.

Kant, Immanuel. "Idea for a Universal History with a Cosmopolitan Purpose." Trans. H. B. Nisbet. *Kant: Political Writings*. Ed. Hans Reiss. Cambridge: Cambridge UP, 1991. 41–53.

Katrak, Ketu H. *Wole Soyinka and Modern Tragedy: A Study of Dramatic Theory and Practice*. New York: Greenwood Press, 1986.

Lacan, Jacques. *Écrits: A Selection*. Trans. Alan Sheridan. New York and London: W. W. Norton, 1977.

Laclau, Ernesto. "New Reflections on the Revolution of Our Time." Trans. Jon Barnes. *New Reflections on the Revolution of Our Time*. London and New York: Verso, 1990. 3–85.

——, and Chantal Mouffe. *Hegemony and Socialist Strategy*. London and New York: Verso, 1985.

Lazarus, Neil. *Nationalism and Cultural Practice in the Postcolonial World*. Cambridge: Cambridge UP, 1999.

Lea, Kenneth. "'In the Most Highly Developed Societies': Lyotard and Postmodernism." *Oxford Literary Review* 9.1–2 (1987): 86–104.

Lindfors, Bernth. *Critical Perspectives on Amos Tutuola*. Washington, D. C.: Three Continents Press, 1975.

——. *Long Drums and Canons: Teaching and Researching African Literatures*. Trenton, NJ: Africa World Press, 1995.

Lyotard, Jean-François. "Adorno as The Devil." *Telos* 19 (Spring 1974): 127–37.

——. *The Postmodern Condition: A Report on Knowledge*. Trans. Geoff Bennington and Brian Massumi. Minneapolis: U. of Minnesota Press, 1984.

——. "Universal History and Cultural Differences." Trans. David Macey. *The Lyotard Reader*. Ed. Andrew Benjamin. Oxford and Cambridge, MA: Basil Blackwell, 1989. 314–23.

Maduka, Chidi T. "Formalism and the Criticism of African Literature: The Case of Anglo-American New Criticism." *The Literary Criterion* 23. 1–2 (1988): 185–200.

Mamdani, Mahmood. *Citizen and Subject. Contemporary Africa and the Legacy of Late Colonialism*. Princeton: Princeton UP, 1996.

Masolo, D. A. *African Philosophy in Search of Identity*. Bloomington, Indianapolis: Indiana UP, 1994.

Mazrui, Alamin. "Relativism, Universalism, and the Language of African Literature." *Research in African Literatures* 23.1 (1992): 65–72.

Miller, Christopher L. *Nationalists and Nomads: Essays on Francophone African Literature and Culture*. Chicago and London: U. of Chicago Press, 1998.

Mishra, Vijay, and Bob Hodge. "What is Post(-)colonialism?" *Textual Practice*. 5.3 (Winter 1991): 399–414.

Mohanty, Satya P. *Literary Theory and the Claims of History: Postmodernism, Objectivity, Multicultural Politics*. Ithaca and London: Cornell UP, 1997.

Montag, Warren. "Beyond Force and Consent: Althusser, Spinoza, Hobbes." *Postmodern Materialism and the Future of Marxist Theory*. Eds. Antonio Callari and David F. Ruccio. Hanover and London: Wesleyan UP, 1996. 91–106.

Moore-Gilbert, Bart. *Postcolonial Theory: Contexts, Practices, Politics*. London and New York: Verso, 1997.

Morrison, Toni. *Beloved*. New York: Plume, 1987.

Moses, Michael Valdez. *The Novel and the Globalization of Culture*. New York: Oxford UP, 1995.

Mudimbe, V. Y. *The Invention of Africa: Gnosis, Philosophy, and the Order of Knowledge*. Bloomington, Indianapolis: Indiana UP, 1988.

——, ed. "Finale." *The Surreptitious Speech: Présence Africaine and the Politics of Otherness 1947–1987*. 435–45.

Mulhern, Francis. "English Reading." *Nation and Narration*. Ed. Homi K. Bhabha. London and New York: Routledge, 1990. 250–64.

Nkrumah, Osagyefo Kwame. "Address Delivered to Mark the Opening of the First International Congress of Africanists." *The Proceedings of the First International Congress of Africanists*. Eds. Lalage Bown and Michael Crowther. Evanston: Northwestern UP, 1964. 6–15.

Ogundipe-Leslie, Omolara. "The Poetics of Fiction by Yoruba Writers: The Case of *Ogboju Ode Ninu Igbo Irunmale* by D. O. Fagunwa." *Odu* 16 (July 1977): 85–96.

Ogunyemi, Wale. *Langbodo*. Ikeja: Thomas Nelson Nig. Ltd., 1979.

Ogunyemi, Chikwenye Okonjo. *Africa Wo/Man Palava: The Nigerian Novel by Women*. Chicago and London: U. of Chicago Press, 1996.

Olabimtan, Afolabi. "Religion as a Theme in Fagunwa's Novels." *Odu* 11 (January 1975): 101–14.

Olaniyan, Tejumola. *Scars of Conquest/Masks of Resistance: The Invention of Cultural Identities in African, African-American, and Caribbean Drama*. New York: Oxford UP, 1995.

Ologunde, Agboola. "The Yoruba Language in Education." *Yoruba Language and Literature*. Ed. Adebisi Afolayan. Ife: Univ. Press Ltd. & U. of Ife Press, 1982.

Onoge, Omafume F. "Towards a Marxist Sociology of African Literature." *Marxism and African Literature*. Ed. Georg M. Gugelberger. Trenton, NJ: Africa World Press, 1986. 50–63.

Owomoyela, Oyekan. *Amos Tutuola Revisited*. New York: Twayne Publishers, 1999.

Palmer, Eustace. "Chinweizu et. al. and the Evaluation of African Literature." *International Fiction Review* 15. 1(1988): 54–57.

———. *The Growth of the African Novel*. London: Hienemann, 1979.

Parry, Benita. "Problems in Current Theories of Colonial Discourse." *Oxford Literary Review*. 9.1–2 (1987): 27–58.

———. "Resistance Theory/Theorizing Resistance, or Two Cheers for Nativism." *Contemporary Postcolonial Theory: A Reader*. Ed. Padmini Mongia. London and New York: Arnold, 1996. 84–109.

Peel, J. D. Y. "Olaju: A Yoruba Concept of Development." *The Journal of Development Studies*. 14.2 (January 1978): 139–65.

Philips, Anne. *The Enigma of Colonialism: British Policy in West Africa*. London: James Currey, 1989.

Pinnock, S. G. *The Romance of Missions in Nigeria*. Richmond, VA: Foreign Mission Board, 1917.

Poovey, Mary. "The Model System of Contemporary Literary Criticism." *Critical Inquiry*. 27 (Spring 2001): 408–38.

Quayson, Ato. *Strategic Transformations in Nigerian Writing: Orality and History in the Work of Rev. Samuel Johnson, Amos Tutuola, Wole Soyinka, and Ben Okri*. Oxford: James Currey, 1997.

Radhakrishnan, R. "Postcoloniality and the Boundaries of Identity." *Diasporic Mediations: Between Home and Location*. Minneapolis: U of Minnesota Press, 1996. 155–84.

Rive, Richard and Tim Couzens eds. *Seme: The Founder of the ANC*. Johannesburg, South Africa: Skotaville Publishers, 1991.

Rotimi, Ola. *Kurunmi: An Historical Tragedy*. Ibadan, Nigeria: Oxford UP, 1971.

Said, Edward W. *Culture and Imperialism*. New York: Knopf, 1993.

———. *Orientalism*. New York: Pantheon Books, 1978.

Scarry, Elaine. *The Body in Pain. The Making and Unmaking of the World*. New York and Oxford: Oxford UP, 1985.

Seme, Isaka Pixley, "The Regeneration of Africa." *Two Centuries of African English*. Ed. Lalage Bown. London: Heinemann, 1973. 52–56.

Slemon, Stephen and Helen Tiffin. "Introduction." *After Europe: Critical Theory and Post-colonial Writing*. Eds. Bill Ashcroft et al. Sydney, Australia: Dangaroo Press, 1989. ix–xxiii.

Slemon, Stephen. "The Scramble for Post-Colonialism." *De-Scribing Empire. Post-colonialism and Textuality.* Eds. Chris Tiffin and Alan Lawson. London and New York: Routledge, 1994. 15–32.

Smith, Pamela J. "D. O. Fagunwa: The Art of Fabulation and Writing Orality." *The Literary Griot* 3.2 (Fall 1991): 1–16.

Soyinka, Wole. *Art, Dialogue, and Outrage.* Ibadan: New Horn Press, 1988.

———. *Collected Plays 2.* Oxford and New York: Oxford UP, 1974.

———. *Death and the King's Horseman.* New York: Hill & Wang, 1987.

———. "Director's Notes." Production file of *Death and King's Horseman.* The Goodman Theater, Chicago, Illinois.

———. *Idanre and Other Poems.* London: Eyre Methuem, 1967.

———. *Myth, Literature, and the African World.* Cambridge: Cambridge UP, 1976.

Spivak, Gayatri Chakravorty. *A Critique of Postcolonial Reason: Towards a History of the Vanishing Present.* Cambridge, MA: Harvard UP, 1999.

———. "Can the Subaltern Speak?" *Marxism and the Interpretation of Culture.* Eds. Cary Nelson and Lawrence Grossberg. Urbana, Chicago: U. of Illinois Press, 1988. 271–313.

———. *In Other Worlds: Essays in Cultural Politics.* New York and London: Routledge, 1988.

———. *Outside in the Teaching Machine.* New York and London: Routledge, 1993.

———. *The Post-Colonial Critic: Interviews, Strategies, Dialogues.* Ed. Sarah Harasym. New York and London: Routledge, 1990.

Sprinker, Michael. *Imaginary Relations: Aesthetics and Ideology in the Theory of Historical Materialism.* London and New York: Verso, 1987.

Stratton, Florence. *Contemporary African Literature and the Politics of Gender.* London and New York: Routledge, 1994.

———. "Wole Soyinka: A Writer's Social Vision." *Black American Literature Forum* 22.3 (Fall 1988): 531–53.

Thiong'o, Ngugi wa. "Wole Soyinka, T. M. Aluko and the Satiric Voice." *Homecoming: Essays on African and Caribbean Literature, Culture, and Politics.* Westport: Lawrence Hill, 1972. 55–66.

———. *Decolonising the Mind: The Politics of Language in African Literature.* London: James Currey, 1986.

Thompson, E. P. *The Poverty of Theory and Other Essays.* New York: Monthly Review Press, 1978.

Tutuola, Amos. *My Life in the Bush of Ghosts.* New York: Grove Press, 1954.

———. *The Palm-wine Drinkard*. New York: Grove Press, 1953.

Varadharajan, Asha. *Exotic Parodies: Subjectivity in Adorno, Said, and Spivak*. Minneapolis, London: U. of Minnesota Press, 1995.

Weber, Max. *The Protestant Ethic and the Spirit of Capitalism*. Trans. Talcott Parsons. New York: Charles Scribner, 1958.

Wilkinson, Jane. "Between Orality and Writing: The Forest of a Thousand Daemons as a Self-Reflexive Text." *Commonwealth: Essays and Studies* 9.2 (1987): 41–51.

White, Landeg. "Literature and History in Africa." *Journal of African History* 21 (1980): 537–46.

Wren, Robert M. *Achebe's World: The Historical and Cultural Context of the Novels*. Boulder, CO: Lynne Rienner Publishers, 1980.

Young, Robert. *White Mythologies: Writing History and the West*. London and New York: Routledge, 1990.

Zachernuk, Philip S. *Colonial Subjects: An African Intelligentsia and Atlantic Ideas*. Charlottesville and London: Virginia UP, 2000.

Žižek, Slavoj. "Beyond Discourse-Analysis." *New Reflections on the Revolution of Our Time*. 249–60.

INDEX

Abraham, R. C.: (*Dictionary of Modern Yoruba*), 205–06n. 3
Achebe, Chinua: historicity of novels, 174, 210n. 20; on Tutuola, 207n. 16; on utility and Literature, 85–86; *Anthills of the Savannah*, 185–86; *Arrow of God*: 183–85; agency in, 184; reading of, by Soyinka, 173–74; *No Longer at Ease*: agency in, 181–82; Christianity in, 180–82; class interpellation in, 182–83; patriarchy in, 176; involution of, 182; *Things Fall Apart*: 174–82; agency in, 175; patriarchy in, 176; secularization in, 177–80
Adeeko, Adeleke, 206n. 7
Adeniyi, Dapo, 111
Adorno, Theodor W., 48, 102, 205n. 14; (and Max Horkheimer), *Dialectic of Enlightenment*, 34–38. See also Habermas, Jürgen
Africa, media images of, 1–4, 191
African Literature Today, 91
Africanists, 1962 Congress of, 77, 78
Afrocentricity, 69
Agawu, Kofi, 28, 200n. 20
Agency in motion, in African letters, 27–28, 71–72, 101–04, 195–96
Ahmad, Aijaz, x, xi, 202n. 16
Ajayi, J. F. A., 130
Ajiboye, Gabriel O., 111
Althusser, Louis, 5–11, 14–28, 66, 73; contrasted to postmodernism, 15–16; on reproduction of structure, 17; on ideology, 18–19; use of Lacan, 20–22; on subjectivity and agency, 25–26; applied to African letters, 84–85, 102; determination in the last instance, 194
Andrade, Susan, 106
Appiah, Anthony Kwame, 52, 76, 91, 107, 146, 167, 168, 180, 197nn. 4, 5, 200n. 3, 209n. 14, 210n. 23
Arac, Jonathan, 200n. 3
Ashcroft, Bill, 53
Atanda, J. A., 166, 209n. 11
Awolowo, Obafemi, 209n. 11
Ayandele, E. A., 206n. 9
Azande, the, 38, 39, 46, 149, 198n. 6, 201n. 10

Bamgbose, Ayo, 109, 123, 129, 130, 206–07n. 13
Barrett, Michèle, 199n. 15
Behler, Ernst, 31
Beloved (Toni Morrison), contingency in, 13, 14
Benjamin, Walter, 195
Benson, Peter, *Black Orpheus, Transition, and Modern Cultural Awakening in Africa*, 204n. 8
Best, Steven, 200n. 3
Bhabha, Homi K.: 5, 9–11, 30, 48, 49–53, 56–62, 69–72, 197n. 3; on hybridization of Christianity, 131–32; on "image analysis," 205n. 11; on mimicry, 56–61;

AEH-8097